Contents

Part 3 Buildings

CONTENTS

Part 4 The building in use

Appendices

How to use *Building for Everyone*

Part one: Context, chapters 1–3, introduces the concept of universal access to buildings and the external environment and outlines the principles on which *Building for Everyone* is based. It shows the consequences for design and management of considering the broad range of ability and outlines the role and contribution of the various professions and agencies which are involved in shaping the built environment.

Part two: The external environment, chapters 4–5, offers advice on all aspects of the external environment, from mountain paths to letterboxes, dealing with access and general design issues in chapter 4 and detail design in chapter 5. **Part three: Buildings**, chapters 6–9, follows the same plan, dealing with general design issues in chapter 6 and detail design in chapter 7. Chapter 8 provides advice on appropriate furniture and fittings. Chapter 9 considers specific issues raised by particular building types, including public offices, hotels and housing. All dimensions on drawings are in millimeters unless otherwise indicated.

Part four: The building in use, chapters 10–11, deals with day-to-day issues in the management and maintenance of buildings and includes sample maintenance and access audits to assist in assessing the accessibility of newly commissioned and existing buildings. Strategies for retro-fitting are suggested. Appendices provide assistance in locating particular components and suggest sources of more detailed information.

In keeping with the theme of the book, *Building for Everyone* uses several tools to aid the reader to navigate the text.

- The four parts of the book are colour-coded: magenta for **Part one**, green for **Part two**, blue for **Part three** and brown for **Part four**.
- Key words are highlighted in red.
- References to relevant information located elsewhere in the book are indicated in the text by ●, while related drawings are indicated by ■.
- A comprehensive index begins on page 235.

Building for Everyone
Inclusion, Access and Use

NATIONAL   DISABILITY   AUTHORITY
ÚDARÁS NÁISIÚNTA MÍCHUMAIS

The text of this book is drawn from the text of *Buildings for Everyone* published by the National Rehabilitation Board in 1998, with additional text by Feargus McGarvey, Mitchell and Associates, and Maureen Gilbert. The material was prepared under the direction of the National Disability Authority and was edited for the NDA by Maureen Gilbert.

Technical illustrations and photography, except where noted, are by ARC Digital ©.

Design and type-setting by Lyn Davies.

The information in this book is offered in good faith as advice to people concerned with providing a better environment for everyone. The National Disability Authority cannot be responsible for the use to which advice in this book is put in any particular circumstance. In preparing material for this book the National Disability Authority had regard to current legislation, regulations and standards, but the book does not purport to give advice on these matters, and compliance with advice given in this book may not be relied upon as satisfying any or all of the requirements of legislation, regulations or standards.

British Library Cataloguing in Publication Data
A catalogue record of this book is available from the British Library.

ISBN   1 870499 03 4

Part one

Context

Building for everyone

1

This book is about how to achieve equality and inclusiveness for everybody in buildings and the external environment. It is also about how to ensure that everyone can make full use of the buildings and environments they live in, work in and visit. This means more than just an interpretation of laws or regulations. Fundamentally, the book is about how to implement the following set of principles.

Access

Everyone should be able to get into buildings and environments. They should be able to approach and enter unaided, with ease and without embarrassment.

Use

Everyone should be able to use buildings and external spaces with equal facility. The design and management of buildings and external spaces must not make them more difficult to use for one person than another.

Enjoyment

Everyone deserves the right to enjoy their surroundings.

Safety

Everyone has the right to live, work and relax in safe surroundings. The design and management of buildings and external environments must make them safe for every person.

Consideration

Everyone deserves equal consideration from those who commission, design, construct and manage buildings and environments. Consideration costs nothing.

If we believe in building for everyone, then it is unacceptable that a woman should suffer disadvantage because she is pregnant, a child because of being small or older people simply because they are elderly. It is equally unacceptable that people should be disadvantaged because of their impaired sight, hearing or mobility. It is particularly unacceptable when the disadvantage suffered is the result of carelessness or thought-lessness, and is entirely avoidable.

If the needs of a group of people are not considered in the design of a building or environment, then that group is denied equality with the those whom the building or environment is designed to suit. There is no principle that would defend the denial of rights simply because the owner, designer, contractor or manager of a building simply hasn't con-sidered them or mistakenly thinks that it is too difficult or expensive to provide for them.

Everyone is different

Many inequalities and injustices of the past were built on the concept of the 'normal' person. To define one group in society as the norm, even a very large group, is to privilege that group and marginalise everybody else. Ireland is full of great charitable institutions, built with Victorian energy and zeal, to house people with disabilities. It was then thought not only proper but also laudable to separate from society any group thought different from the norm. Thankfully we no longer take this view.

In the 21st century we recognise that people are all different. People change. Difference is a part of everyday life. As children we are small, weak and less aware. As we grow old we grow weaker, probably less aware, and sometimes we even grow smaller. Any 'normal' society con-tains within it adult men and women, children, older people and people in all these groups with a wide range of disabilities. Both internationally and in Ireland, through the development of policy and law, we are mov-ing to an ever more inclusive definition of what is normal, and building rights upon it.

There is a significant proportion of the population whose faculties, whether physical, intellectual or emotional, are impaired, temporarily or permanently. Impairment of the body or mind may change, limit or render impossible someone's ability to undertake a particular task. The environ-ment can offer supports or obstacles.

Environments can enable

If the first and last step of a flight is clearly marked, a person with impaired sight will find a stairs easier to use. An induction loop in a busy environment will enable communication with people whose hearing is impaired. An easily accessible seat at a cinema or theatre will facilitate someone using crutches or a wheelchair. A threshold with no step provides access for everyone. None of these provisions is costly.

It is the function of our environments to enable. We make buildings to live, work and play in. We build to enable these activities and many others. A building or environment which does not enable fails in its purpose. Only if a building provides for the full range of potential users can it claim to fulfil its purpose.

Environments can disable

A smooth circular doorknob will be very difficult to use if a person has poor grip. Even a single step can make entry for a person pulling a suitcase on wheels, or a person using a wheelchair, almost impossible. It is the environment which disables, not any impairment.

When an environment is intended to provide for an activity, and yet through its design or management prevents someone from carrying it out, that environment fails in its purpose.

Environments can injure

What should be a pleasant stroll down any street can, for visually impaired people, become an unpredictable journey through a painful obstacle course. For children under 16 statistics indicate that accidents account for more hospital admissions than all other causes put together. Half of these accidents occur in the home, where many could be avoided by better design. Statistics suggest that more people die as a direct or indirect result of stair falls than die from lung cancer. Stairs with landings and short flights greatly reduce the chances of a long fall and serious injury. They are also more comfortable for everybody than long straight flights, and do not take up more space or cost more money.

Special needs versus universal access

Everyone experiences disability. The common assumption that 'a person with a disability' equals 'wheelchair user' is inaccurate. Everyone is disabled by the environment at some stage in their life. An elderly person, or someone who is short of breath, or has a broken ankle or bad back, will find a stairs difficult or impossible. Young children often cannot reach door handles and light switches. With a sprained wrist it is impossible to turn most taps. High kerbs are difficult to negotiate with a child in a buggy. The examples are endless. Disability is part of everyday experience.

Special needs

Historically, access to the built environment for people with any impairment was thought about as a 'special need'. Most people could manage a 'normal' environment. A minority could not. This view held that the 'normal environment' had to be modified to be made usable by people with impairments of one kind or another, but only in so far as was 'reasonable', as defined by people who have no significant impairment.

With this approach, accessibility was treated as an add-on issue. The building was designed for the 'normal' person. Only afterwards were additional features such as lifts, ramps, larger lavatories and tactile warnings on stairways added, so as to improve access and use by people with disabilities.

Universal Right of Access

A more inclusive approach is to think in terms of the Universal Right of Access and to seek to improve accessibility and usability for everyone. This way of thinking benefits everybody, not just those with impairments. Properly working doors, adequately sized passageways, appropriately designed lavatories, easily legible signs and so on are of use to everybody. Accessibility for everyone becomes the norm: Building for Everyone.

This approach is as relevant to the retro-fitting of old buildings as it is to the design and construction of new ones. It is the most practical and sustainable way of creating an environment in which everyone can participate. The user is at the centre of the issue and process, not the building or the designer. In this approach, accessibility, central to the process from the outset, can become invisible, properly integrated into the general building design. In Ireland, the National Development Plan 2000–2006 speaks of:

> the Government's undertaking to promote equality, involving the full integration into Irish society of women, people with disabilities, members of the Traveller Community and persons granted refugee status or permission to remain in Ireland. The National Development Plan contains a range of measures designed to promote social inclusion and the achievement of the Government's objectives in this regard.

Applying the principle of universal access can ensure that people with impaired sight, mobility or hearing can, through their full use of a building or environment, participate fully in society. If applying the principle of universal access gives rise to an initial extra cost, the benefits which accrue through the lifespan of a building can far outweigh the outlay. It is important to remember that the cost of providing facilities when a building is being constructed is usually very much less than that of adding to same facilities after the building is complete.

The principle of universal access also applies to building and environmental management. Staff must be made aware of the reasons for particular design features, so they can ensure that their activities or work practices will not reduce the effectiveness of such features. For example, circulation areas must not be used for storage, even on a temporary basis. Lighting and signage must be kept in proper working order. Good management may also play an important role in overcoming inadequacies in existing buildings.

Universal access is invisible

Like much good design, universal access should be invisible. For buildings the best access is provided by having a flat or gently sloping approach, a level entrance, level floors inside and a lift to move from storey to storey, with audible and tactile indicators along the way. Such access is gentle, smooth, always usable and invisible. On the other hand, a platform lift added beside the stepped entrance of a building is highly visible and requires extra effort, assistance and additional time to use. It can also put an embarrassing spotlight on the person who has to use it, while others wait at the top of the steps.

In the external environment, dished kerbs at road crossings have their origins in the need to facilitate wheelchair users, but they also serve people pushing baby buggies. Tactile indicators on the pavement and audible signals at pedestrian crossings were originally for those with visual impairments, but they make crossing safer for everyone. These features have achieved a different kind of invisibility. They are now so universal that we no longer notice them.

All the senses

We use all our senses to experience our surroundings. We smell the new mown grass, hear the babbling brook, feel the gentle breeze on our cheek and see the dappled sunlight through the trees. We rarely taste our surroundings, but what we do taste always tastes better in surroundings which satisfy our other senses. Environments which appeal to only one sense and impoverish others are themselves impoverished.

Vision is regarded as the principal way most people perceive and interact with their surroundings. However, nobody experiences the environment by vision alone. Hearing is our most three-dimensional sense. We cannot see what is behind us, but we can hear it. Natural building materials can have a distinctive smell, identifying a room and adding to the character and enjoyment of that room. The feel of materials used to make a place can enrich its character. The feel of a material has both a distinctive texture and temperature, an identifiable signature. Polished steel is cold, hard and smooth. Timber is warmer and gentler to the touch, cloth more so. We can sense materials, even if we do not touch them, by the way they absorb or reflect heat or sound.

If one of our senses is impaired or lacking, the others seek to make up for that lack. For example, for people with visual impairments, the audible and tactile environment becomes dominant. Multi-sensory design, which may be crucial to people with impaired hearing, vision or mobility, benefits everybody, and presents both challenge and opportunity to designers and managers of both buildings and environments.

Irish statute law

There is a substantial and ever-changing body of Irish statute law which bears on the commissioning, design, construction and management of the built and made environment. This includes legislation and regulations on planning and development, construction standards, health and safety, equality of status and opportunity, transport, sustainability, conservation and environmental protection. The most immediately relevant to the making of the built environment are the Planning Acts and Regulations and the Building Regulations with their associated Technical Guidance Documents. The Building Regulations have been repeatedly updated to take better account of the needs and rights of people with disabilities.

There is a view that the provision of universal access benefitting children, older people or for people with disabilities can legitimately be curtailed because of cost, and there are elements of Irish statute law that reflect this view. However, the provision of fire precautions is not curtailed because of cost. Fire precautions save lives. We are prepared to bear the financial cost of this, and our laws reflect this fact. Equality makes life worth living, but there are still those who are unwilling to contribute to the cost of making someone else's life worth living. This is a foolish and short-term view. We will all grow old and be grateful for an environment that has been planned to include us.

Against an ever-changing statutory background, how are those commissioning, designing, building or managing our environment to act? This book seeks to promote a commonsense approach. If, when approaching their tasks, those who commission, design, construct or manage any part of the built or made environment truly consider all the people, they are unlikely to fall outside the law.

Operating law and regulation

Those who commission, design, construct or manage any part of the built or made environment have a duty of care to obey the law and to do their best to ensure that what they do does not bring about inequality or result in discrimination against any person. Specific reference to the rights of people with disabilities and the avoidance of discrimination is to be found in Irish equality legislation and in the Building Regulations. But a duty to treat people equally can be taken to exist, even where not specifically covered by legislation.

The Technical Guidance Documents that accompany the Building Regulations are not exhaustive, do not address all building types and, while they offer minimum requirements for meeting the needs of some people, they give no suggestions on how to meet the needs of others. For example, guidance might be given on the design of part of a building so as to make it suitable for wheelchair users, without offering any guidance as to how the needs of visually impaired people might also be met.

Both the Building Regulations and Health and Safety Regulations must be complied with, but simple compliance with these regulations is not always enough. We are required to obey all the law, not just the bits we like or the bits we know. There is a common misapprehension that compliance with one legal requirement can take away the need to comply with another. There is no legal basis for this type of argument. Compliance, for instance, with Health and Safety Regulations, or with requirements for fire protection, do not take away from or supercede the need to comply fully with Part M of the Building Regulations. Solutions must be found that satisfy all legal requirements.

Finding such solutions is not always easy. There are genuine conflicts. Solutions which meet the need to conserve protected structures or monuments and also meet the need for universal access to these buildings can be elusive. We need to develop a design vocabulary which goes far beyond shoving a crude ramp up to the entrance. This book is intended not least to stimulate that development.

When most of our architectural heritage was built, the best way to keep a building dry was to raise its floor off the ground, and an independent life using a wheelchair could not be conceived of. This is not to suggest that older buildings are unsuited to the needs of people with disabilities. They often have a generosity of scale, with gentle stairs and wide doors, that is more comfortable to use than the mean corridors and stairs of many modern buildings, particularly houses. The solutions which may emerge from a consideration of universal access in the context of existing buildings and environments will contribute greatly to the heritage that we leave for future generations to use and enjoy.

Non-statutory provisions

In addition to laws and regulations set down by the State or local authorities, there are other rules and guidelines that apply to the making of buildings and environments. These include Irish, British and International Standards and Codes of Practice, and professional codes of conduct.

A list of relevant Standards and Codes of Practice is given at the back of this book. This list is for guidance only and is not exhaustive. New Standards and Codes of Practice are being drafted and published all the time. Anyone using this book should make themselves aware of the latest developments.

Architects, contractors, engineers, landscape architects, planners, managers, surveyors and sub-contractors, indeed all involved in the making and management of buildings and the environment, are guided by professional codes of conduct and practice. These codes generally seek to enhance the common good, and place a duty on the professions and trades to make environments for the benefit of all. Integrating the concepts and content detailed in this book into their practice will ensure that they do so in the most equitable and inclusive way and that they are indeed building for everyone.

Personal ability

2

2.1 Mobility

Range of ability

Everyone's level of mobility varies widely during their lifetime, from infancy to old age. It can be affected by age, health, sickness or accident, or even by a particular activity. Mobility can be increased, as in the case of the athlete, or reduced, as in the case of a pregnant woman. An impairment to mobility can range from mild to significant and can be temporary or permanent. At its mildest, carrying a heavy load will make movement more difficult for even the fittest person. A sprained ankle, whilst only temporary, will require the use of a crutch for several weeks. Someone using a walking frame or a wheelchair will find use of sanitary fittings, especially in confined areas, very difficult. At its most significant, mobility impairment can mean that somebody is unable to move independently.

Historically, the only people with disabilities considered by designers were wheelchair users. However, at any given time, some 20–25% of people have impaired mobility. Only a portion of this number use wheelchairs but, as their requirements are greater, the provision of space adequate for their needs will generally ensure sufficient space for others.

Space requirements, however, are only the starting point and all other aspects of mobility in building design, including floor finishes, selection of ironmongery, detailing of stairs etc, must also be considered. The range of people whose lives can be improved by careful consideration of all aspects of mobility in building design is far greater than just wheelchair users.

Mobility aids

The space demands of using mobility aids such as crutches, walking frames and wheelchairs vary. The space demands of people using a **crutch** or **walking stick** are not particularly great but such people, more than most, need handrails on steps and ramps and in corridors, and slip-resistant floor finishes. **Walking frames** require a little extra space and are difficult to use on ramps. On an inclined surface, a walking frame either tilts back towards or away from the user, making it less stable.

The **standard manually-propelled wheelchair** is 660mm wide and 1065mm long. The minimum space for operation is 750 x 1200mm, to facilitate hand clearance at the sides and feet extending beyond the wheelchair footplates. The minimum space for a wheelchair user and a person pushing the chair is 750 x 1600mm. An 1800mm diameter turning circle will allow a full 360° turn in a single motion. A 1500mm diameter turning circle necessitates a three point turn.

Many people use chairs which are either larger or smaller than the standard and thus it is unwise to rely on the minimum recommended dimensions when considering whether building access or facilities are adequate in any particular situation. For example, a wide range of **powered wheelchairs** is available for indoor, outdoor or combined use. Most require an 1800mm diameter turning circle. Electric scooters, generally for outdoor use but sometimes used indoors, are bigger.

Specialist chairs are used in a variety of situations, including as a **means of escape in case of fire** or on aircraft.

Consequences for design and management
In the external environment
*   Avoid long travel distances and slopes. A distance or gradient which is easy for most ambulant people can be impossible for a person with a walking frame or using a wheelchair.
*   Some surface finishes, such as loose pebbles or badly maintained footpaths, present hazards and can make wheelchair use impossible.
*   On the footpath, even a small kerb can be hazardous or impossible to climb or descend.

Inside buildings
*   Long horizontal distances can be arduous or hazardous to accomplish.
*   Opening and closing doors is often difficult.
*   A pair of narrow doors can be particularly disabling for people carrying shopping, accompanied by children or using a wheelchair.
*   Space requirements for wheelchair users are greater than for ambulant people. A wheelchair is a rigid item which cannot, for example, squeeze through confined spaces. Be aware of this, especially in traditionally confined areas such as small lobbies and WC cubicles.
*   Steps and staircases can be difficult or impossible to negotiate.
*   Some floor finishes, particularly deep pile carpets, can make wheelchair use impossible.
*   Other floor finishes – slippy tiles or polished linoleum, timber or synthetic flooring – can present a hazard to ambulant people.

Consideration of these issues in the planning of corridors and door opes, the design of pathways, stairs, ramps and lifts, and the detail design and maintenance of floor finishes, will help many people move more easily around the external environment or inside buildings.

Space requirements

The illustration demonstrates the clear space required by people using different mobility aids. As will be seen later in the book, a path or corridor width of 1800mm will allow a wheelchair user comfortably to pass another wheelchair user or someone using crutches.

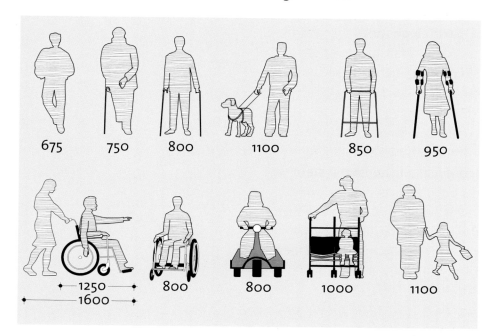

675   750   800   1100   850   950

1250
1600   800   800   1000   1100

figure 1 **Space requirements**

2.2   Hearing

Range of ability

Personal hearing ability ranges from profound deafness, right up to exceptionally acute hearing. In the middle there are people who have some difficulties with normal speech levels or with hearing particular frequencies.

Many people with impaired hearing can lip read. Lip reading is easier when a person is speaking normally and becomes more difficult when a person raises their voice or shouts, as their lip movement becomes distorted. People whose hearing is not actually impaired may still have difficulty in hearing someone speaking in a low voice, someone talking in a noisy environment or someone whose speech is impaired. For someone who is lip reading or using sign language, good visibility and proximity to the speaker are important. The optimum distance between reader and speaker for lip reading is 900–1800mm, while sign language can be read from up to 15.0m by those who have good eyesight.

Aids to hearing

In many public buildings, the general population benefits from the installation and use of clear public address systems. Many people with impaired hearing use personal hearing aids. In a building, an audio induction loop or infra-red system will transmit sound within a certain range, allowing people with hearing aids within that range to receive amplified sound. Induction loops are available at moderate cost and involve no space.

Various types of telephone attachments and services are available. These include inductive couplers fitted into public telephones, loudspeaker devices and, for profoundly deaf people, text telephones which enable typing and transmission in written form. Today, many deaf people are making more and more use of faxes, text messaging on mobile phones and e-mail. Videophone services are planned.

In the many buildings with queueing systems or where announcements are made (eg. banks, supermarkets, transport terminals, health care buildings, municipal offices), a combined visual and audible system facilitates people with impaired hearing. In a building occupied by a deaf person, a video entrance system will allow visual identification of a visitor, prior to opening the door. Deaf visitors will also be facilitated by such systems. Alarms systems should always alert visually and audibly for this reason.

Consequences for design and management

Both personal and environmental factors can contribute to difficulty in hearing. The resolution of conflicting requirements and the selection of suitable acoustic material is a challenging aspect of building design. The use of sound absorbent materials, where consistent with fire safety and hygiene requirements, can improve the acoustic environment considerably. In addition:

- All important information should be delivered both visually and aurally.
- Combined audio/visual alarm systems are most effective in all circumstances. They are essential in all areas to which the public has access and in areas where noise levels can obliterate the audio alarm.
- Fire detection and alarm systems, door bells, intercoms and telephone systems can all be extended by incorporating flashing lights, vibrating pads or other tactile aids.
- In busy public offices and banks, locate discussion cubicles away from noisy areas.

- Audio induction loops should be installed in churches, cinemas, conference centres and auditoria.
- Counter loops should be installed in banks, ticket offices, at information and reception desks etc.
- Portable loops can be used in small meeting rooms or areas where public address systems are not available.

2.3   Vision

Range of ability
Personal vision ranges from very acute to where there is no capacity to distinguish between light and dark. In between, there are people who use spectacles some or all of the time and people whose field of vision is partially blurred or obliterated.

Aids for visually impaired people
Apart from devices availed of by the general population, such as night-time lighting, spectacles and contact lenses, the use of a white cane or guide dog can assist people whose vision is significantly impaired.

A white cane is generally used in a sweeping motion, from side to side, to detect level changes and low-level obstacles ahead of the person. However, this will not locate overhead projections, such as tree branches, low hanging signs, low bulkheads and high-level kitchen presses. Other obstructions, such as doors left ajar and vehicle doors left open, may not be detected until it is too late.

A person with a guide dog requires clear width of 1100mm. Passage through a doorway can be difficult, especially if the door is self-closing. Guide dogs should be afforded access to all areas of buildings, including restaurants, ● section 9.8. Designers should be aware that dogs will not walk on some gridded or serrated surfaces, such as pressed metal with a series of sharp edges. Guide dogs are not pets and should not be distracted from their duty.

Personal help from sighted people is provided by the assistant walking slightly ahead and by the visually impaired person holding the assistant's arm with one hand. Walking side-by-side requires a width of 1200mm. When passing through doorways or other restrictions, the two people generally walk in single file, which helps the visually impaired person to sense the restriction.

Many people with significant visual impairment prefer not to use some facilities, such as escalators, which involve entrapment hazards.

Consequences for design and management
Wayfinding outdoors is aided by the strategic positioning of features such as lamp standards and fountains, by changes in texture and by defining routes within large open areas, ● chapter 5.

A simple, logical internal building layout facilitates everyone and is of particular benefit to people with visual impairments. Logical positioning of furniture or fittings helps them to orientate and locate themselves. Ensure that on entering a building in public use, the reception desk is the first thing encountered, rather than a stairway or a corridor leading to the reception area. Think in detail: hand dryers should be adjacent to wash hand basins, and light switches near to door handles. Consistency of detail design throughout a building is essential, so that the location of common facilities such as light switches and power outlets doesn't have to be rediscovered in each room.

- A good level of ambient light, evenly distributed, facilitates everybody.
- Control of glare benefits all.
- Provide task lighting in particular areas.
- Use tactile clues in floor finishes to differentiate between areas.
- Light switches and door handles should contrast with the surface on which they are mounted so that they can be located easily. Avoid using patterned finishes which may confuse.
- Use raised lettering on building plans, on lift floor indicators and on signs generally to assist both blind and partially sighted people.
- A combination of audible and visual indicators on ticket dispensers, automated teller machines at banks, in shops, queueing areas generally, at pedestrian crossings (where tactiling is crucial) and on domestic appliances such as cookers in self-catering accomodation is readily achieved and facilitates not only people with visual impairments but also children and many others.

2.4   Breathing

Range of ability
Breathing ability is impaired by smoke, by outgassing from synthetic materials such as plastics and synthetic-based paints and by dust from manufacturing processes, as well as by medical conditions. The vast majority of the population spend the bulk of their time indoors and indoor air quality has become an issue of major concern across the European Union. About one in seven people is seriously affected by the everyday levels of dust and gas found in the home, workplace and other areas not commonly perceived as hazardous. Industrial processes have become the focus of safety legislation to regulate air quality.

Consequences for design and management

- Wall, floor and furniture finishes can both generate and harbour dust. Select finishes which are easily cleaned and inhibit dust accumulation.
- Many synthetic-based wall, floor and ceiling finishes, and timber or masonry incorporating toxic preservatives or treatments, contribute to toxic outgassing.
- Avoid details which will gather dust and are difficult to access for cleaning, such as beams and ledges.
- Furniture with recesses or inaccessible corners can be difficult to clean and result in dust build-up.
- The application of alkyd-based paint should be undertaken in controlled conditions.
- Maintenance of relative humidity at levels below 45% causes house dust mites to wither and inhibits mould growth.
- Cleaning should be scheduled at times to minimise adverse impact.

In the external environment, a low allergen garden reduces the incidence of hay fever and asthmatic attacks for those susceptible to them, and can be pleasing for everybody, ● section 4.4.9.

2.5   Grip

Range of ability
Average hand strength allows the ready use of doorknobs, taps, dimmer switches and so on. Grip can be reduced by any number of specific impairments but also by everyday things such as wet hands, which everybody experiences. Similarly, children's hands are smaller and not as strong as adults'.

Consequences for design and management
- Automatic doors require no ability to grip. Elsewhere, lever-operated door handles are easier to use than circular doorknobs.
- Ensure that the profile and dimensions of handrails on stairs, ramps and corridors are correct and easy to hold and grip.
- Lever handle taps are preferred by many people, not only those with reduced grip strength, particularly where dirty hands may otherwise deposit grime.
- Controls of all kinds are easier for everyone to use if generously sized and with adequate space between buttons. This is true for everything from light switches and socket outlets to cookers, washing machines and other appliances.

2.6   Height

Range

Height varies widely. There is no standard height person. Design must take into account the full range of heights from small children to adults, both ambulant and wheelchair users. Careful consideration should be given to the levels of sanitary and other fittings. It is not a question of lowering everything to suit one group and consequently disadvantaging another, but rather of providing fittings at a range of heights which will accommodate everyone. Certain building types, such as primary schools and kindergartens, will require specific provision in relation to heights of sanitary and other fittings.

Clear head height is important, especially for visually impaired people who can collide with low beams or the underside of a stairs. Outdoors, allow for the fact that people may be using umbrellas. Eye level will influence the position of signs, mirrors and window transoms. Shelving should be 700–1300mm above floor level to accommodate a wide range of users. Coat hooks should be 1200–1700mm above floor level. Power points, light switches and controls should be 900–1200mm over floor level. Thigh level and the height of wheelchair armrests require a clear dimension of 700mm to the underside of a table or table frame so that people can get close enough to work or eat.

At all stages of design, the designer should be aware of the potential effect which design decisions may have on the people who are likely to use each space or facility.

Consequences for design and management
- Allow clear head height of 2200mm.
- In public buildings, provide dual-height counters, worktops and reception desks, in order to facilitate people who would prefer to sit, as well as those in wheelchairs.
- In a row of lavatories, 1 in 6 WCs should be of a height to suit children.
- In a row of urinals, 1 in 6 should be sited at a height for boys (380mm).
- Do the same with hand dryers.
- Variable height sinks are available at moderate cost to suit many domestic kitchens and self-catering accommodation.
- Switches and controls to be 900–1200mm over floor level.
- Optimum shelving heights are 700–1300mm.
- Allow clear space of 700mm under counters and tables.

2.7   Other considerations

Simplicity of building layout and operation, along with consistency in design and colour association, improve building legibility for all. People with learning disabilities will find it easier to use a building independently if it is laid out logically. In complex environments, such as department stores, hospitals, shopping centres, entertainment centres, large hotels and banks, an information point and clear signage should be provided. Trained personnel can be reassuring. Measures such as these, while welcomed by all users, may be essential for people who are confused by unfamiliar places and procedures.

Consequences for design and management
*   Strive for simple building layout and straightforward operation.
*   Seek consistency in detail design and in colour association. For example, green signs indicate safety, yellow is for hazards and red for emergencies, ● section 8.2.2.
*   Signs should be clearly visible and as simple as possible, with the emphasis on symbol rather than script.
*   In a building with only one lift and stairway, avoid glass-walled designs, as many people find them frightening to use.

Who's responsible?   3

3.1   The developer

The developer's role and contribution

The developer, whether private or public, is at the centre of the design and procurement process. The developer has the right to the best possible value for money.

Making buildings and environments which facilitate use by all will:
*   result in longer building lifespan through better adaptability for different functions
*   promote a favourable image through the implementation of best practice
*   result in higher market values at time of sale or lease
*   maximise the safety of users and minimise building-related hazards
*   for the commercial developer, improve accessibility and ease of use, and hence trade
*   for the public sector developer, foster the rights of everyone to building access and enjoyment.

How to proceed

*   Become familiar with the accessibility and usability issues discussed in this book.
*   Adopt and promote a policy which seeks to ensure that everything you commission will be accessible to everyone.
*   Liaise with potential users to establish any specific needs.
*   Encourage your design team to use life-cycle costing procedures.
*   Explain to your managers the importance of access for all.
*   Ensure that the consultants you employ to design your buildings are familiar with all aspects of accessibility, not just the minimum standards required by the Building Regulations and other legislation.
*   Carry out an access audit as part of commissioning and handover to tenants, ● section 10.3.

3.2   The designer

The designer's role and contribution
Everyone who makes design decisions has an important role in ensuring that places are usable by all. This responsibility has often been perceived as a threat and a burden, particularly in the context of other responsibilities. This is inaccurate. Many of the measures this book suggests are straightforward to design, simple to implement, cost little and will result in better buildings and environments. There are many readily available sources of support and advice for designers, including this book, other professionals such as occupational therapists and, most importantly, building users themselves.

How to proceed
*   Become familiar with the accessibility and usability issues discussed in this book.
*   For general building types, use the advice in this book.
*   For special building types, eg. kindergartens, primary schools, day activity centres, sheltered accommodation, nursing homes and hospitals, consult the references at the back of this book for more specific advice.
*   Ensure that the safety statement required by health and safety legislation includes the necessary advice on maintenance of colour contrasts, floor and wall finishes, door closers and any special devices installed, ● section 10.1.
*   In detail design, leave nothing up to the discretion of others, including builders and managers. Care in dimensioning is essential. Pay particular attention to setting out dimensions for WCs, including all fittings such as grab rails, hand dryers, mirrors etc. Dimensions must be clear and comprehensive and unobstructed by any other items indicated.
*   Ensure that your staff are fully aware of access issues. Continuous professional development courses should be considered.

3.3   The builder

The builder's role and contribution
The builder is often forced to make decisions on details which are simply not shown on drawings. Such decisions can impact positively or negatively on the lifetime performance of a building. For example, inadequate advice on setting out dimensions means that the builder fitting a grab rail in a WC must decide how far to distance the component from the wall. This lack of direction is not acceptable. Similarly, lack of information on door furniture, bath, toilet and shower fittings can put the builder in the thankless position of having to make on-the-spot decisions which should properly be made by the designer. Where the information is provided, it

is essential to use to the setting out dimensions on the drawing. Where there is any ambiguity, consult the designer for clarification.

During construction, it is important to ensure adequate protection of construction sites to minimise risk to passers-by, especially to people with visual impairments.

How to proceed
- Become familiar with the accessibility and usability issues discussed in this book.
- Prior to commencement of any installation, ensure that the drawings supplied to you contain all necessary setting out dimensions for fittings.
- Adhere to the specification and precise layout of components.
- If information is vague, unclear or incomplete, ask the designer for clarification.
- Protect the site adequately, so that the building process does not constitute a hazard to passers-by, or to building users in the case of renovations, ● section 5.5.2.

3.4　The manager

The manager's role and contribution
When the designer and the builder are long gone, the manager is responsible for the success or failure of the building in use. Good management can overcome many, although not all, design inadequacies, while poor management can render an accessible environment unusable by those it is intended to facilitate. The use that disabled people can make of a building can be greatly facilitated by well-trained staff.

How to proceed
- Become familiar with the accessibility and usability issues discussed in this book.
- Pay particular attention to the advice in Part 4.
- Ask people with disabilities what they want.
- Prior to acceptance of the building project at Practical Completion stage, audit the works in accordance with the advice in section 10.3 .
- Ensure that your staff are aware of the particular needs of people with impairments in your building or area.
- Organise shop and restaurant layouts and displays to ensure maximum accessibility for all, ● chapter 9.
- Ensure that escape plans include specific provisions for assisting people with disabilities.
- Identify staff to assist in emergency evacuation and ensure that everyone knows what to do.
- Ensure that temporary signs or sandwich boards, put on the street to attract business, do not intrude on circulation routes or present a

hazard for visually impaired people.

- Think accessibility when specifying equipment (eg. new telephones) and ensure that all new items are usable by all.
- Pay particular attention to staff training, the provision and maintenance of toilets for wheelchair users, proper and clear signage and prevent casual storage in corridors, ● maintenance audit, section 10.4.

3.5   Central Government

The Government's role and contribution
It is the role of central Government to legislate, to develop and promote agreed standards for the design of the external environment, to set standards for good building design, construction and maintenance, to promote good practice through preparing technical and other guidance and to facilitate public consultation on matters of mutual concern. Legislation to ensure access and use of buildings and environments by people with disabilities is constantly being updated, ● chapter 1.

At the same time, when central Government or its agents act as building developer, designer, builder or manager, the practical advice under the relevant headings in this book should be followed. Legislation and non-statutory regulations require public bodies to take a lead in setting standards of best practice.

3.6   Local Authorities

The Local Authority's role and contribution
The Local Authority has an immensely important role, both as a building control authority and in its development and maintenance of the external environment. In recent years, there have been major improvements in ensuring access for people with impairments. For example, kerb dishing at road crossings is now mandatory and audible pedestrian crossing signals are commonplace.

Local Authorities should ensure that the public and private sector housing needs of disabled people are met, by incorporating relevant provisions in Development Plans and housing programmes.

Aside from this, when a Local Authority or its agents act as building developer, designer, builder or manager, the advice under the relevant headings should be followed. See also advice on public offices, ● section 9.2.

How to proceed

In general

- Become familiar with the accessibility and usability issues discussed in this book.
- Pay particular attention to Parts 2 and 4.
- Integrate action on a barrier-free environment into all strategy planning and County, City and Local Development Plans.
- Undertake detailed access audits of significant streets.
- Reduce footpath clutter by the rational arrangement of street furniture.
- Ensure that all municipal parks include some garden spaces with flowers, plants and shrubs selected so as to be enjoyable by people with visual impairments. Avoid planting which exacerbates asthma and other breathing difficulties, ● section 4.4.9.
- Ensure that car parking, whether provided by the public or private sector, incorporates spaces suitable for people with disabilities in accordance with section 5.4.
- Protect any building or repair works adequately, so that they do not constitute a hazard for passers-by.

As Building Control Authority

- Ensure that building designers and owners understand and comply with Part M of the first schedule to the Building Regulations.

As Housing Authority

- Provide lifetime adaptable housing in accordance with the advice in section 9.11.
- Incorporate provision for housing for disabled people in Local Development Plans and housing programmes.

As Roads Authority

- When granting licences for contractors to occupy footpaths and roads temporarily during construction works, ensure that works are properly protected, ● section 5.5.
- Ensure that repairs to roads, paving and underground services are adequately screened for pedestrian safety.

As employer

- Promote staff training, particularly for those dealing directly with the public and those concerned with the maintenance or control of the external environment, to improve understanding of issues regarding people with disabilities, ● section 10.2.

3.7   The National Disability Authority

The National Disability Authority (NDA) is an independent agency established under the ægis of the Department of Justice, Equality and Law Reform. It is intended to act as a key focal point for disability in the mainstream.

Its functions include:
- acting as a central, national body to assist in the co-ordination and development of disability policy
- undertaking research and developing statistical information for the planning, delivery and monitoring of disability programmes and services
- advising on the development of standards for programmes and services for people with disabilities
- monitoring the implementation of standards and codes of practice in programmes and services for people with disabilities
- liaising with service providers and other bodies to support the development and implementation of appropriate standards for programmes and services for people with disabilities.

The NDA Library is the only source in Ireland for a number of titles on disability issues, including accessible design. It holds over 10,000 books, stocks more than 200 journals and can advise on useful websites. Lists of books and articles available from the NDA Library, and borrowing details, are available by contacting the library. Appointments to visit the library can be made for Monday to Friday, 10.00am–12.30pm and 2.00–4.30pm.

NDA Library
25 Clyde Road
Dublin 4
TELEPHONE (01) 608 0433
FACSIMILE (01) 660 9935
EMAIL library@nda.ie
WEBSITE www.nda.ie

The NDA has issued guidelines on web and other IT accessibility. These can be accessed at www.accessit.nda.ie.

NATIONAL   DISABILITY   AUTHORITY
ÚDARÁS   NÁISIÚNTA   MÍCHUMAIS

Part two

The external environment

Outdoor access for everyone 4

4.1 Universal access in the landscape

People access both urban and natural landscapes in two ways. The most obvious is in order to get from A to B. Less obvious, but just as important, is the need to be able to access landscapes for recreation. In its broadest terms, this means being able to partake physically and mentally in the cultural and natural resources that landscapes offer. This involves people being able to enjoy their own physicality in the outdoors, opportunities for understanding and appreciating our natural heritage, for experiencing the seasons and for feeling the weather. It offers opportunities for understanding cultural heritage as it is expressed in the landscape, for appreciating the diverse beauty of nature and for socialising with different people in different ways and in different places. It offers physical and mental challenges that help everybody who chooses to realise their full potential. The range of experience offered by the external environment allows people to connect with the world and to understand their place in it.

In recent years the concept of the Universal Right of Access has been extended far beyond the notion of regulations and add-on 'solutions',
● chapter 1. Once understood, its application to places beyond buildings becomes a simple and logical process. It is not only the threshold to buildings that should be subject to good accessibility – after all, what is the point of a fully accessible building if someone can't actually get to it? Universal access includes all aspects of external design.

The extension is clear. At one end of the spectrum are wild places – mountains and rivers, beaches and bogs – where the **natural landscape**, among other things, becomes the focus for relaxation, recreation and challenge. Buildings hardly feature, if at all.

Nearer to cities and towns are country parks, historic sites and woodlands for the recreation of everyone. Although these landscapes appear natural, they have been formed and controlled to a great extent by the activities and livelihoods of the people who live there. People have cleared forests for timber and drained land for agriculture. Hedgerows have been planted and walls built to enclose land and corral animals. Woods have been planted to create shelter and microclimates, habitats and visual amenity.

This is the tempered landscape, adapted for industrial endeavour: agriculture, forestry, energy, tourism and recreation. Each action has been a direct result of what was required of the landscape. Consequently it is a living and dynamic expression of our cultural actions. Further interventions in these landscapes, on a more detailed scale, such as rights of way, gates and fences all enable or prevent physical access across the terrain. Viewing points, signage and maps enable people to access interpretation of these landscapes.

These are places that offer the broad amenity of recreation to visitors, where there is not only a collective response to a common experience but also a diversity of individual experience, as diverse as the visitors themselves.

Finally, there are the cities, towns and villages of the tamed landscape. Within this urban form, there are many kinds of amenity – playgrounds, cemeteries, squares, streets – which should all be fully accessible. Legislation, including the Equal Status Act, 2000, increasingly refers specifically to standards of provision in the external environment. Existing legislation is frequently reviewed and updated and, as new legislation is introduced, better standards of accessibility become requirements for the designer and manager of public open spaces.

It is important to understand universal access in the external environment in context. Environmental legislation, such as the Wildlife Act, 1976, has a bearing on protected areas. People have different expectations when accessing different kinds of places and existing services and resources have a bearing on accessibility. The following table summarises the issues involved.

Tamed landscape	Tempered landscape	Natural landscape
Streets, squares, parks and gardens, playgrounds, cemeteries and sportsgrounds.	National monuments, country parks, caravan and camping sites, picnic areas, woodlands and arboreta, waterways, golf courses, interpretive centres.	Mountains, beaches, bogs, remote places.

Context

Natural features highly adapted, mostly manmade environment. Spaces defined by built form. Frequent ornamentation.

Challenge

No risks and challenges other than those created by people.

Population

Many opportunities for meeting and involvement with other people.

Independence, information and services

Most people expect to be able to go alone, although information upfront is useful. Support services frequently available.

Design

Complex and inter-related design considerations. Intense detail and refined, exotic materials.

Management

Structured and controlled. Highly serviced.

Context

Natural landscape form is legible, though there is strong evidence of human intervention and activity. Spatial form dictated by topography and vegetation.

Challenge

Few risks, though basic skills and awareness required.

Population

Some opportunities for meeting other people and for involvement with them.

Independence, information and services

Most people can go alone, though visitors are often in groups. Information required upfront for travel to the place and detailed information required on site. Few support services immediately available, other than those provided by personnel at core areas.

Design

Design is led by existing form, or requires significant resources for large-scale intervention.

Management

Controlled, although sometimes informal and low key. Services and facilities are generally site-specific.

Context

Open country and wild landscapes with little evidence of human intervention other than low intensity agriculture. Topography is dominant factor in defining spatial form.

Challenge

Many risks and challenges. Outdoor skills required.

Population

Few people, if any, evident.

Independence, information and services

Few people, especially visitors, go alone. Information on accessibility in the general area, as well as site-specific information, is important. Support services rarely at hand.

Design

Any design intervention will have a notable impact.

Management

Simple management or none at all. Few services or none at all.

Adapted from *BT Countryside for All,* 1997.

A useful resource for understanding accessibility standards in context is *BT Countryside for All*, 1997, which offers guidance and detailed design ideas for access in the countryside, ● Appendix 2.

The same principles of good design apply to all places, whether urban or rural. They are reinforced by the principles of universal access. Both will assist the designer or manager in achieving or enhancing the *genius loci*, or spirit of a place:

- understand the context, possibilities and limitations of the environs
- be aware of relevant legislation and policies
- identify all possible users
- think broadly and creatively
- allow the function to dictate the form
- use materials appropriate to the location and purpose.

Identifying all possible users and thinking broadly and creatively are germane to ensuring that everybody, regardless of ability or disability, can experience the external environment, whether a city street or a remote beach, in their own unique way. Imagination can sometimes be the only significant factor limiting the provision of design that opens up experience of the external environment to the broadest range of potential users and visitors.

4.2 Natural landscape

4.2.1 General

Many people visit, and others work and live, in some of Ireland's wild places. These include, for example, national parks, natural heritage areas, special areas of conservation and nature reserves, beaches, bogs, mountains and other remote places.

Whilst it may not seem easy or necessary, say, to make a mountain path accessible to someone using a wheelchair, the starting point should be with the accepted principle of making a path at all. That is, a path reduces the difficulty of access for some people; a well-designed path or route will enable access for many.

Considering that most visitors to remote places are unlikely to venture out alone, remote places become much more accessible when assisted. Furthermore, outside support is not expected in remote places and individuals and groups usually prepare to be self-sufficient. This does not mean that facilitation should not be considered. It is important that obstacles such as stiles or gates, even onto a mountain path, are easy to negotiate, without having to make special provision and without affecting the challenge of the pursuit. Cattle grids are often difficult to cross, particularly when wet, and should have a suitable alternative pedestrian gate. After all, it is the terrain that should be the challenge, not the cattle grid.

In some instances, it may seem impossible or inappropriate to provide universal access. This approach underestimates human endeavour. People may employ ingenious methods to access wild landscapes. Any facilities that are provided, such as car parks, gates or seats, should be designed for universal access.

The concept of the Universal Right of Access, therefore, is as applicable to a mountain as to a public building. This does not mean that natural landscapes have to be as accessible as urban landscapes. In the most remote places, after all, people expect to make their own way. What it does mean, however, is that if a new element, such as a route or signage, is to provided, the following should apply:
- good accessibility should be the goal
- new elements (eg. routes, information etc) and/or alterations to existing conditions should be made to be as accessible as possible and not inadvertently to create obstacles to access
- existing obstacles to access should be removed where possible.

4.2.2   Policy and the natural landscape

Access to the natural landscape is governed by two sets of legislation and policy. The first deals with equality and accessibility; the other with the conservation of natural heritage. The former is enshrined in equality legislation, the latter lies with laws such as the Wildlife Act, 1976, and the Planning and Development Act, 2000, as well as other statutory and non-statutory policy and regulations.

The following are agencies related to development and access in the landscape, with their *relevant areas of responsibility in italic*, their mission statements in green, and any additional information in black.

Department of the Environment and Local Government; Dúchas
environment in general
Works to promote sustainable development and improve quality of life through the protection and preservation of the built and natural environment, infrastructure provision, balanced regional development and good local government. Responsible for national environmental and heritage policy, co-ordination of policies and programmes, in particular relating to EU and international measures, promotion of specific programmes and projects, designation of national and regional parks and the protection of natural heritage.

Department of Agriculture and Food
farmland
Responsibilities include developing the agriculture and food sectors in a manner which maximises their contribution to the economy and to sustainable employment, while protecting the environment and advancing food safety and animal health and welfare.

Department of Communications, Marine and Natural Resources
forestry
Responsibilities include promoting and managing the safe and sustainable use and development of Ireland's marine, forestry and natural resources.

Department of Community, Rural and Gaeltacht Affairs
Gaeltacht and the islands
Responsibilities include rural development and the conservation and promotion of culture and heritage, including the sustainable development of inhabited offshore islands.

Department of Arts, Sport and Tourism
tourism and recreation

Responsibilities include contributing to the economic and social progress of Irish society by developing:

- a sustainable tourism sector which champions high standards in marketing, service quality and product development
- an active culture in sport and recreation, including the achievement of excellence.

Department of Transport
transport

Responsibilities include promoting the provision, development and regulation of competitive, safe, secure and high-quality services, as well as optimum asset utilisation in transport.

Local Authorities
local areas

To deliver, in support of Government policies, high-quality services in property, construction and procurement on time and on budget. Responsibilities include the provision of Building Control and Access Officers to ensure compliance of new works with Part M of the Building Regulations.

Office of Public Works
Government-owned land, built heritage

Responsibilities include the design, provision and maintenance of Government buildings and property, and the management and operational aspects of built heritage.

Waterways Ireland
waterways

Waterways Ireland is a North-South body. It upholds the principles of equality, and seeks to comply with the most onerous legislation, where legislation differs in each jurisdiction.

The Heritage Council
heritage

Its role is to propose policies and priorities for the identification, protection, preservation and enhancement of the national heritage. National heritage is defined as including monuments, archaeological objects, heritage objects such as art and industrial works, documents and genealogical records, architectural heritage, flora, fauna, wildlife habitats, landscapes, seascapes, wrecks, geology, heritage gardens, parks and inland waterways.

Environmental Protection Agency
environment in general
To promote and implement the highest practicable standards of environmental protection and management which embrace the principles of sustainable and balanced development.
Monitoring, advice and information on environmental protection.

Coillte Teoranta
forest recreation
To have due regard to the environmental and amenity consequences of its operations. While all of Coillte's forests are open to the general public, Coillte provides wheelchair access at some of its more frequently visited sites and Forest Parks. Coillte will continue to improve universal access on its property.

An Taisce
environmental quality
An Taisce seeks to inform and lead public opinion and official policy on the environment, through partnership where possible.

Bord Failte
tourism
Promotes and develops tourism. Encourages community participation in amenity projects such as the Tidy Towns Competition and National Gardens Scheme.

4.2.3   Accessing the natural landscape

Sympathetic design in the natural landscape does not preclude better access. **Appropriate use of local materials**, eg. stone, earth and vegetation, and a good understanding of the constraints and potential of the local terrain, coupled with an imaginative and creative approach to problem solving will result in a suitable design. An access audit, ● section 11.2, should be carried out in order to develop a brief for a new project. This will identify any problems and assist in finding solutions.

In accessing the natural heritage, the most fundamental requirement is to provide people with **information** about a place before they arrive so that they can assess the challenges and make their own informed choices. This means that information in the form of published guides, the internet and helplines should communicate clearly the available standards of accessibility, ● sections 7.6 and 9.2.

Maps should illustrate difficulties such as steep gradients and other challenges. When preparing this information, think of the user. Clear print and the logical presentation of information is important. The consistent use of colour and symbols will make it easier for everyone, including children, to use, ● sections 8.2 and 9.2.

Ensure that **car parks** prioritise parking spaces for people with disabilities close to the beginning of routes. For design and management of car parks, ● section 5.4. If **signage** is provided, it should indicate clearly accessible paths and the average time it takes to complete a circuit. This information is convenient and helpful for most users, and critical for some.

Some terrain, particularly in mountainous areas, can be difficult to negotiate. A **gradient** of 1:10 or steeper will be extremely difficult and dangerous for most people with disabilities to use. This is the point in the natural landscape where accessibility, particularly for those with mobility impairments, will become an issue for assistance and/or special provision. Where it is appropriate to provide a ramp or steps, they should be designed to accessible gradients, with handrails, firm, non-slip surfaces, landings and resting places, ● section 5.2. Resting places should be sheltered, for instance beside a wall or existing vegetation.

Maintenance of surfaces and other elements is made easier if local skills and materials have been employed in the original project. It will be quicker and cheaper to source local than imported stone, for instance, and local people will have the skill base to be able to implement the repairs.

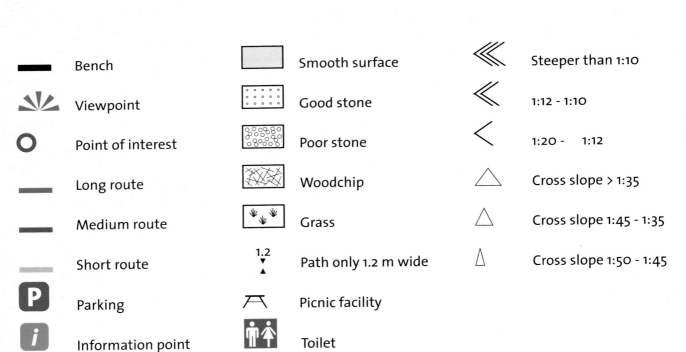

figure 2
Example of information map and key

4.2.4   Mountains

Mountains pose many difficulties for people who wish to access them. Indeed, the challenge is part of the motivating force for them to try. Whether mountaineering, hill walking, pilgrimage or orienteering, reaching the destination and arriving safely back is a satisfying experience. These activities are by no means exclusive to able-bodied people, and many people with disabilities are up for the challenge. Consideration should be given to universal access, even in remote places, to ensure that, for instance, a right of way is not blocked by a cattle grid and that signage offers clear information. These are often issues for land managers, who should ensure that rights of way are maintained.

In some instances, telecommunications masts and wind turbines have tracks leading up to them for service and maintenance vehicles. Where this is the case, and where access is permitted, the provision of even a small car park, ● section 5.4, accessible gates, ● section 5.3.5 and a simple information panel, ● section 8.2, will greatly enhance the potential for people to enjoy the benefits of the great outdoors.

4.2.5   Viewing points

Viewing points are popular places for people to enjoy the natural landscape without having to tackle the challenges of moving through it. Although they are primarily about looking at a landscape, the updraft from a cliff edge or the thundering sound of a waterfall and its refreshing spray can be exhilarating for everybody, including people with visual impairments. Viewing points are frequently located close to car parks, where parking spaces for people with disabilities should be provided, ● section 5.4. If access involves crossing a road, good sightlines, signage and surfacing indicating a crossing point will help make it safe, ● section 5.1. Where the viewing point is some distance from a car park, an information point should indicate the extent of access to allow the visitor to make choices. For example, it would be frustrating for a wheelchair user to get almost to the destination, only to be confronted by a long flight of steps. In the same instance, an adult may choose to carry an infant rather than use a buggy.

Partial access is better than none. Although it may not be possible to climb up to see a waterfall from above, the view from below may still be spectacular. Prior information will enable visitors to make choices.

Safety is of primary importance. A safety barrier, 920mm high, will allow most people, including wheelchair users, to see over it. If it must be higher than this, it may be possible to provide seating or a viewing point away from a barrier that allows people to see over. Gaps in railings should be less than 100mm so that children cannot get their heads stuck.

The safety barrier may also be useful for providing a ledge to lean on when looking through binoculars. A fixed telescope with an adjustable height and legroom beneath will allow more people to use it.

4.2.6   Peatlands

Indiscriminate access to raised bogs, blanket bogs and fens, which constitute Ireland's peatlands, causes erosion and damage to the delicate habitats and the archaeology associated with them. On the other hand, it is only by visiting these bogs that the public can fully understand their ecological importance and sensitivity, and learn about conservation. Networks of paths and boardwalks across sites give some protection because they keep people off the delicate surface and can direct them away from sensitive areas. Where this management is implemented, information panels, car parks and paths should be designed to universally accessible standards.

4.2.7   Beaches

Mobility and orientation difficulties can arise in trying to negotiate a wide expanse of soft or pebbly beach. Flexible and temporary **surfaces** made from timber or recycled plastic boards or mats, can be rolled out to give greater access for wheelchairs and buggies, ● Appendix 1. They will also assist in orientation for people with visual impairments. Other products can bind sand into a hardened surface, although the lack of colour contrast makes the improved area hard to detect. There are also 'beach' wheelchairs available, which are designed to be non-corrosive and waterproof with wide tyres that don't sink into soft sand. Some are also suitable for rough terrain and snow. The availability of these products indicates people's enthusiasm to access the landscape to the greatest extent possible.

The wide expanse of beaches and the noise generated by excited holiday-makers, as well as crashing waves, means that **communication** by signs such as flags is very effective, particularly for people with hearing impairments. However, this will not be effective for people with visual impairments, and is a particular consideration when training lifeguards in dealing with people with disabilities, ● section 10.2.

Sand dunes are frequently under threat from erosion caused by too many visitors. Like peatlands, they are places that people enjoy visiting, and need to visit in order to learn more about them. **Pathways** allow access to take place, whilst minimising erosion. Universal standards of access should apply when designing these path systems, as well as for any signage and interpretive information, ● sections 5.1 and 8.2.

4.2.8   Conservation

Conservation areas, including national parks, natural heritage areas (NHAs) and special areas of conservation, by their nature must have restricted access to protect wildlife, habitats and cultural artefacts. While **paths** facilitate increased access, they also protect sensitive areas by guiding people along designated routes. The paths in themselves should be fully accessible, ● section 5.1.3.

NHAs often include information points and **hides** in order to experience and understand the flora and fauna. Where hides or screens are used, peepholes should accommodate viewing from different heights. Most people would be more comfortable viewing from a seated position and lower heights will also suit children. Where seating is provided, it should be to accessible standards, ● section 5.3.7, and include gaps for wheelchair users. A person with a visual impairment may identify birds by their songs and interpretive information, in alternative formats, should facilitate this, ● section 8.2.2.

Checklist
Natural landscape

- Consider all potential users, employing imaginative and practical solutions to achieve maximum access for people with different levels of ability.
- Carry out an access audit of the existing area to obtain a clear understanding of what is required.
- Partial access is better than none.
- Safety is of primary importance.
- In conservation areas, plan paths which control movement and provide signs to assist in understanding sensitive habitats.
- Maximise use of local materials in order to make interventions sympathetic with the landscape and to facilitate maintenance.
- Prioritise car parking spaces for people with disabilities.
- Maps and signage should include clearly marked routes, highlighting obstacles and gradients and giving average times for completion of routes.
- Allow for resting places and shelter, especially after steep gradients or long sequences.
- Maintain and repair surfaces, overhanging vegetation, manmade changes in level and fittings to gates regularly.

4.3   Tempered landscape

4.3.1   General

Places typical of the tempered landscape include country parks, historic and archaeological sites, woodlands, caravan parks, golf courses etc, involving both permanent and temporary amenities.

Tempered landscapes are typically accessed by coach and car, less frequently by public transport. They often have buildings associated with them, such as public toilets and cafes. These should be designed with maximum accessibility in mind, ● Part 3.

Interventions are easily accommodated aesthetically within these landscapes as they have already experienced human activity. **Materials** employed are usually natural and sourced locally, such as timber, stone and earth. For example, timber boards are frequently used for crossing boggy ground and streams, indicating and enhancing the experience of a local change in the landscape. The logical ordering of materials is both true to form and function and aesthetically pleasing.

Whilst many archaeological sites are in grassy fields, the insertion of sensitively designed **paths** will assist in orientation and access, whilst routing people away from environmentally sensitive areas and minimising trampling of meadow habitats. For longer distances and very sensitive sites it may be desirable to implement bussing from a car park to a monument.

Many of these places are in public ownership (Dúchas, Local Authorities etc). Any development in areas under private ownership may be subject to comment by relevant public bodies, particularly if a site has historical or ecological significance.

When developing a new project, or making alterations to an existing situation, consider the following:
*   where appropriate, study the existing vernacular to understand the context of any design work
*   carry out an access audit on an existing site, or with design plans for a new site, to determine the requirements for universal access
*   plan strategically for the implementation of the work
*   consult with relevant public bodies that have an interest in the project
*   comply with both equality and conservation legislation.

4.3.2   Policy and the tempered landscape

As with the natural landscape, access is governed by two sets of legislation and policy. The first deals with equality and accessibility, the other with the conservation of both natural and cultural heritage. In landscapes where there has been an intense amount of human activity, there will be a greater number of artefacts worthy of conservation. In many cases, the landscape will be a complex physical representation of many layers of activity. Legislation on natural conservation will be relevant for some areas. Legislation and policy relating to cultural conservation, such as the Heritage Act, County Development Plans and requirements by interested or responsible bodies such as Dúchas and Waterways Ireland will also frequently apply, ● section 4.2.2.

4.3.3   Accessing the tempered landscape

Information on sites and their levels of accessibility is important so that people with disabilities can make decisions about visiting. This information should be available from a multiplicity of sources in alternative formats and via web pages designed to best access standards, ● section 9.2. Staff employed at places where the public have access, even if it is only at certain times of year, should receive disability equality **training** in order to provide information and assistance in an appropriate manner. This training should be provided as part of quality customer care programmes, ● sections 9.4 and 10.2 .

For guidelines on signage on site, ● section 8.2, and for other furniture items such as seats, bins, drinking fountains etc, ● section 5.3.

As many of the places described in this book are used for exercising **dogs**, special bins (pooper-scoopers) for dog faeces should be provided and, where necessary, fines imposed for leaving a mess. It is a health hazard to everyone, will not be seen by visually impaired people, and is particularly unpleasant for wheelchair users when it comes up on the wheel of a wheelchair.

4.3.4   Temporary events

Whilst many places considered in this chapter are open all the year round, albeit with peak seasons, temporary events are often held in places which do not have a permanent infrastructure. Ploughing championships, county shows, fun fairs and concerts are just some examples that take place in open fields. Temporary car parking and **amenities** such as cafes and toilets should all be universally accessible and should follow the advice in this book.

Grass **paths** inevitably become muddy and inaccessible with intense use. Duckboarding and wood chippings provide a drier surface but are still not fully accessible. Purpose made non-slip synthetic or timber planking will provide better access for people with mobility impairments, although care should be taken to ensure that the jointing does not become a tripping hazard. **Signage**, even when temporary, should be designed to the standards in this book, ● section 8.2. All elements associated with temporary events should be robust, in order to withstand the weather and being moved around from place to place.

Private gardens are sometimes open to the public on a temporary basis. Whilst the small scale of gardens can inhibit access, with small paths, overhanging vegetation and uneven surfaces, designing for universal access may create a new perspective for the garden. Many gardens have a hierarchy of spaces, with terraces and seating areas which are ideal for people to rest, view the garden and to socialise.

Staff and managers of temporary events and owners of gardens open to the public should be trained in providing service to people with disabilities and be on hand to assist when needed, ● sections 9.4 and 10.2.

4.3.5   Interpretive centres

Some important landscapes have interpretive centres that assist visitors and researchers in understanding a landscape and its artefacts and in controlling the numbers and movement of people across a sensitive site. They are sometimes located at the site of interest, as at the Ailwee Caves or

Ceide Fields, or at a discreet distance, as at the Boyne Valley or the Blasket Islands. Although they are often located in the natural landscape, their intensity of use and intervention is such that they temper the landscape and have the potential for facilitating a high degree of accessibility.

Access is generally by private, rather than public, transport. Drop-off points close to buildings are required, along with accessible car parking spaces with a direct route to the building, ● section 5.4. The buildings themselves should conform to the standards described in this book, from reception through to exhibition, café, shop, toilet facilities, research facilities and lecture rooms. Interpretive centres offer employment opportunities to people living locally and should be accessible, not only to visitors, but also to potential employees and researchers who may be disabled. Staff should be trained to understand issues of universal access and the requirements of people with disabilities as part of comprehensive customer care programmes. Resources should be on hand to assist visitors where necessary.

Interpretive centres often provide models and replicas of outside features as a service to people who do not wish to venture into the landscape itself. These **displays** should be provided in ways that make them accessible to all in the form of written, aural and visual presentation, ● section 9.6. This offers the opportunity to create interesting and imaginative universally accessible information. For instance, audio tapes will allow people with visual impairment to access information. A loop system should be fitted to facilitate people with hearing impairments, ● section 7.6. Clear presentation of all information will be of benefit to those with learning difficulties, as well as children.

While an interpretive centre will usually give a comprehensive understanding of a place, the experience of visiting the landscape and its artefacts should not be underestimated. Interpretive centres are, after all, about helping people to understand the landscape they are visiting and to encourage them to spend more time experiencing the landscape heritage in an informed way. It is therefore still important to give as full access as is possible to the external environment.

4.3.6   Golf

The setting of existing woodlands, dunes and rolling topography is often the basic landscape type altered to accommodate a golf course. The development of car parking, clubhouse and links is simply a manipulation of the existing landscape to create a terrain that is accessible and playable. It is a short step therefore to create a universally accessible golf course.

Golf is a sport that can be played by most people, once the rules of the game have been mastered and mini-golf can be enjoyed by those who are not keen golfers. While at present there may be relatively few disabled golfers in Ireland, experience elsewhere suggests that accessibility for spectators attending tournaments and to courses and clubhouses in general will be met with enthusiasm.

The International Blind Golf Association, www.blindgolf.com, is one of many organisations that promote golf among people with disabilities. The motto of the Scottish Blind Golf Association is 'You don't have to see it to tee it!' People with visual impairments will require assistance with the game. The assistant should not be charged a fee.

© Eastern Amputee Golf Accociation

As with all providers of services to the public, golf course managers should install TDDs that allow deaf people to book sessions, ● section 8.3. Accessible golf buggies should also be provided.

Provide a drop-off point for golf bags close to **parking** spaces for people with disabilities, so that they will only have to make one stop. It should also be possible to bring a golf cart to the car park, so that heavy equipment does not have to be carried.

Teeing grounds, fairways and greens should all be designed to allow **access** for golf carts and wheelchairs. While it may not be considered practical to provide full access to bunkers, some easy access should be considered. The green is of course a precious piece of turf and when it is too soft to mow, it will also be too soft for most wheelchairs, walking sticks or crutches. It may indeed be inappropriate for anyone to play in certain conditions.

A useful guide for golf course managers, offering practical advice and etiquette, is *From Bag Drop to 19th Hole*.

4.3.7 Country parks

Country parks are often associated with historic buildings, arboreta and gardens or picturesque landscapes. Discreetly designed car and coach **parking** to accessible standards, ● section 5.4, should allow disabled visitors to alight close to the point of access. **Signage** may be the only significant element to help visitors to enjoy and understand what is going on, and should be clear and consistent. Poorly designed signage will cause all visitors to become disorientated – they may have to double back, they may not understand the importance of significant elements or may miss them altogether and become frustrated. Follow the guidance on accessible signage, ● section 8.2.

The quality of maintenance required for country parks is such that a **pathway** accessible to vehicles is often required. This means that a circuit path up to 2400mm wide, with a firm surface and cross-fall of maximum

1:50, will be provided, also offering good accessibility for people with mobility impairments, buggies and bicycles. The provision of running tracks also demands a firm, even surface with no trip hazards. The infrastructure of a park will therefore offer circuits, overlapping and alternative routes with different or multiple functions. The use of surfacing of different grades and path widths, signage and tactile warnings will need to be carefully co-ordinated if collisions are to be avoided, ● section 5.1.

The anticipated experience of a country park is that of a safe and comfortable but still 'natural' environment. Careful selection of surfacing is essential therefore to achieve both universal access and to maintain the character of the setting, ● section 5.1.

4.3.8   Woodlands and arboreta

Woodlands can be a source for woodland production, a habitat for wildlife and a place for recreation and amenity. The carrying capacity for different types of recreational activities depends on the size and nature of the woodland. At the simplest level, people find woodlands a pleasant environment to wander through and look at nature. More active recreation can take place in forests, where the presence of suitable tracks allows motor rallying and rambling. The cover provided by trees makes woods a suitable place for military-style games such as paint balling. It also provides a suitable backdrop to stop stray arrows in archery. The terrain and cover of woodlands also encourage orienteering and horse riding. The settings and shelter they provide are ideal for caravan and camping sites.

Woodlands can be diverse in character and whilst some may have difficult terrain, many will be easy to access. As with all places mentioned so far, adequate information provided upfront will enable a person with a disability to make choices about a potential visit.

Where ornamental or exotic trees are planted as an arboretum, people will want not only to admire the trees but also to identify and study them. People are often interested in the botanical and Irish names of trees, not just the common ones. This offers the opportunity to provide raised text as well, ● section 8.2.2. The shapes and texture of leaves, the scent of flowers, leaves and fruit and the feel of bark are all important in enjoying and understanding trees, so it should be possible for everyone to get close to important specimens.

4.3.9   Picnic areas

Picnic areas should be located in sheltered microclimates, with the option of shade for people with sensitive skin. Being easily accessible from the car park does not necessarily mean immediately adjacent.

The **surface** under seats and tables should be solid, with a perimeter extending a minimum of 1500mm around the edge to allow wheelchair users to manoeuvre. The surface should be flat, well drained and flush with the surrounding ground levels. Erosion at the edge of the surface can cause a trip hazard, so this should be made good on a regular basis. For discussion on tables and seats, ● section 5.3.8.

Ensure **litter** is collected regularly to prevent it becoming a tripping hazard. Bins should have a lid so that litter does not get blown around but it should be easy for a child or a person in a wheelchair to use, ● section 5.3.

4.3.10   Camping sites and caravan parks

Logical layouts of plots for tents and caravans will help with orientation around a site. An **orderly layout** will also help minimise the possibility of tripping on the guy wires of tents, by keeping them out of the main routes.

Spaces for campers with disabilities should be provided close to accessible toilets and washing facilities. Plug-in electric points should be on clearly visible posts in order to be accessible and not create a trip hazard. Where path, steps and ramps are provided, make sure they are designed to universal access standards, ● sections 5.1.3 and 5.2. Where no paths exist, for instance on temporary sites, appropriate temporary or semi-permanent surfaces should be used, ● Appendix 1.

Fire rings, barbeques or **cooking stands** should only be provided where there is no risk of fire hazard to nearby vegetation. The surface around them should be solid with a perimeter of minimum 1500mm clear access for wheelchair users. Cooking grills and tray heights should be easily adjusted. A fire point should be accessible, with water or sand and a bucket in order to put out a fire when leaving.

4.3.11   Waterways

Waterways are once more becoming utilised. Having been the main system of transport until the 20th century, they are now being revitalised by tourism. Once people are waterbourne, Ireland's waterways offer an extraordinary alternative view of the landscape.

Towpaths also offer an ideal opportunity for recreation, not just for moving along but also for fishing and even bathing. Whilst towpaths are typically flat for long stretches, they can also pose challenges when they go over, rather than under, bridges or across weirs and locks. In any of these instances, repairs or alterations should be designed to universal access standards. Careful consideration should be given to non-slip surfacing, warning signs and safety handrails, as with any situation which might pose a hazard.

The design of marinas, landing stages and jetties for angling should all take into account the diversity of people who wish to use them. Associated car parking and public toilets should also follow the guidelines in this book, ● sections 5.4 and 6.8. Any fittings, such as waste water disposal, taps for drinking water and electric points should be designed both for safety and accessibility, ● chapter 7. Marinas and harbours are good places to illustrate routes, rules and regulations, hazards and information on wildlife associated with waterways. Where necessary and useful, signs should also be placed along routes. Signage should be designed to universal access standards, ● section 8.2.

Checklist
Tempered landscape

- Design temporary, as well as permanent, sites for universal access.
- Plan logical accessible routes to and from car parks, with clearly signed circulation.
- Provide coherent use of materials, reflecting local changes in the landscape.
- Design associated buildings, fittings and furniture such as toilets, drinking fountains, gate latches and seats for universal access.
- Provide pooper-scoopers in places where people exercise their dogs.
- Locate resting places and picnic areas in sheltered microclimates.
- Service access paths can easily be adapted for universal access.
- Where appropriate, provide a hierarchy of routes.
- Provide a firm, even and free-draining surface on all paths, ● section 5.1.3.
- Provide a firm, even and free-draining surface 1500mm wide around picnic tables and barbeques.
- All provided transport should be universally accessible.
- Provide clear and consistent signage to warn of hazards, for direction and for interpretation.
- Provide staff with disability equality training and ensure they are familiar with accessibility features in the environment.

4.4   Tamed landscape

4.4.1   General

The tamed landscape describes places subjected to a high degree of human intervention, typically urban in character, including sportsgrounds, cemeteries, parks, playgrounds, squares, streets and gardens.

The natural and tempered landscapes are commonly visited by choice and involve a degree of challenge. By contrast, it is necessary for everyone to negotiate the public spaces in villages, towns and cities. In such places, challenge should not be encountered and it should be possible for every-body to use the spaces with the highest level of independence.

For instance, a person with a visual impairment may choose not to visit a beach or walk a mountain path. It is, however, essential for them to be able to walk to the local shop for groceries without stumbling into a badly placed litterbin or stepping inadvertently onto a busy road. It is essential for a person with a mobility impairment to be able to bring her children to the local park and to be able to get into the playground. Indeed, it is essential for a child with a disability to be able to play alongside other children. It is also necessary for people to be able to get to and from work, public offices, schools and hospitals, without it becoming an assault course for them.

The urban environment – the streets, squares and parks that are the matrix of movement and recreation between buildings – is entirely the creation of human activity. We make pavements, steps and ramps, place bollards, signage and lighting standards, lay out car parks and market squares and public parks. We do all this to function in our everyday lives, to create beautiful, ordered places to move through that are expressive of our cultural identity. Universal access requires us to make these places, which we are making anyway, to be inclusive by being more accessible for more people, rather than exclusive through a lack of planning or common sense.

In designing to the principles of the Universal Right of Access in an urban setting, three important objectives will be achieved:

- more people will be able to enjoy what the external environment has to offer
- more people will be able to function independently in the external environment
- more people will be prevented from hurting themselves needlessly because of haphazard or thoughtless design in the external environment.

4.4.2   Policy and the tamed landscape

Environmental legislation is just as pertinent in urban areas as it is in natural landscapes. A natural heritage area in an urban setting needs as much protection as in any other setting. The Equal Status Act, 2000 deals with equality and rights of access and mandates the provision of 'ramps, dished kerbs or other sloped areas at appropriate places at or in the vicinity of any pedestrian crossing ...'. Local authorities have their own policies regarding access, normally outlined in Development Plans, and it is not uncommon for other national bodies to have some responsibility in the planning or development of an area. The Planning and Development Act, 2000 requires the environs of listed buildings, not just the buildings themselves, to be conserved. This should not be used as an excuse to limit alterations to provide better access to existing places but should serve instead to focus attention on carefully considered methods to improve access.

4.4.3   Accessing the tamed landscape

Because places in the tamed landscape must be accessed easily by everybody, and therefore access is assumed, the onus on providing information upfront is lessened. This is not true in all circumstances, however, and good information is still required. **Street maps** should be clear and legible, ● section 4.2.3, not so much for indicating obstacles as for providing information on accessible facilities such as public toilets.

Information at the site itself is vital. Obvious examples include clear lettering and consistent colouring on signposts, pelican crossings and tactile paving indicating a change of surface use, ● chapter 5 and section 8.2. More subtle but equally crucial examples include the use of good planning in location and layout, properly ordered street furniture and the logical use of materials.

The main areas for consideration by the designer in urban spaces are:
- the surfacing of the plane, which is concerned with the appropriate dimensions and materials for the function, including indication of the change in function, ● section 5.1
- the change of levels between planes, which is concerned with ease of movement and safety, ● section 5.2
- the vertical elements on a plane, which are comprised of street furniture, boundaries and trees, ● section 5.3.

4.4.4   Parks

Parks function in towns and cities as places of rest and recreation. Traditionally they have been designed as a 'natural' space within the city or to display horticultural talent. They are for the enjoyment of people of all ages and abilities and are also important for their environmental benefits. Some parks specialise in historical context, ecological habitat or sport as part of a broader network of open spaces, while others offer more comprehensive facilities for recreation, combining open grass areas and trees, floral displays and play equipment.

In parks and gardens that are protected because of their **historical context** access issues are no less relevant. It can be a relatively simple matter to design and incorporate a signage system or provide information that is universally accessible. It takes a little more skill to introduce sympathetic visual and tactile elements that warn of hazards for people with visual impairments. Changes to infrastructure such as the route of a path or the introduction of a ramp can be significant in a historical garden, requiring care and creativity to identify successful solutions. The same applies to built artefacts such as pergolas, glasshouses and pavilions that furnish historic gardens, as well as the houses associated with them. This offers an exciting challenge to the conservationist and designer.

In parks, as with street furniture, seats, bins, lights and signs should all be placed in a **logical formation** so that they are not hazards for people with visual impairments, ● section 5.3. It is often easier to achieve this in a park than in a street, as underground services are less prevalent.

It is traditional in Ireland to close parks between sunset and sunrise. Spaces that do remain open, such as **linear parks**, should have the main paths well lit for ease of access and orientation as well as safety.

4.4.5   Cemeteries

Cemeteries are often used as an amenity for tourism and recreation, as well as by friends and relatives of the deceased. In larger cemeteries, **paths** are normally designed to take small maintenance vehicles and hearses, making them more accessible for people with mobility difficulties. Otherwise paths should be designed to accessible standards, ● section 5.1.3.

Many people who visit cemeteries are elderly and therefore impairments associated with older age should particularly be taken into account. To facilitate people with poor grip or who cannot hold heavy weights, provide water **taps** that are easy to operate, and that incorporate a hook to hold a watering can while it is being filled or a short hose to fill a can or vase sitting on the ground. Provide easily accessible **compost bins** for dead flowers.

4.4.6   Sportsgrounds

Irish interest in and achievement at the Special Olympics and the Paralympic Games have demonstrated the commitment to sports of people with all levels of ability. In other sports, specialised equipment is available to assist people in fishing and skiing. If people can participate in these activities, universal design will allow them access.

Facilities such as changing rooms should all be accessible and adaptable, ● section 9.10. Just as important is the detail design of accessible parking, routes and information, ● sections 5.1, 5.4 and 8.2. Toilets, even if only temporary, should be fully accessible. **Ease of access** is as important for spectators as it is for participants. Even on a small scale, posts and rails for leaning, and a hard standing for wheelchairs and buggies will enhance accessibility. Sports events, even those held on temporary sites, still require full universal access.

4.4.7   Play

Everybody should have the opportunity to play. It is an important way of learning social, physical and emotional skills. Through play we meet challenges in a fun way in a safe environment. Through imagination, many ordinary places become play spaces, eg. walking along a low wall, swinging on a rail or hiding behind a tree. Our environment should stimulate children to play and remind adults how it is done.

Whilst many children in Ireland still grow up with the benefit of large gardens or woods and fields to play in, the majority must use streets and parks. It is important that the general environment is stimulating, however, and because of the lack of opportunities for unmediated safe play, adventure playground and specific play structures are now common.

Playgrounds, play structures and equipment

Acknowledging that play is about challenge, a good play space will present a range of activities for a **wide range of ability**. Making play spaces accessible does not reduce the challenge for children and offers opportunities for greater interaction and for shared experience. Through inclusive play children learn about themselves and to understand their differences and similarities. They can learn about co-operation and compromise and can take pleasure in diversity without prejudice. They build friendships.

The physical challenges presented in **structures** for climbing, swinging and sliding are the most common form of play in playgrounds. These elements can easily be designed to facilitate children with disabilities, where everybody can share the experience of swinging, climbing etc but with different levels of ability. Many designs can be bought 'off the peg' from play equipment companies, whose products have been tested for appropriate health and safety standards, ● Appendix 1.

Rubberised **play surfaces** are easy to clean and are better able to cushion falls than wood chip, gravel or grass, which get worn away and can act as animal litter. Where possible, playgrounds should be fenced in to prevent animals (except guide dogs) from entering. A **self-closing gate** is essential and should be at least 800mm wide to allow wheelchair access. Gate latches should be easy for children to use. **Sand pits** should be covered when not in use to prevent cats from using them as litter. The cover should be made in such a way as to be easy for a child to remove and should be non-slip.

Consideration should be given to the way in which children use the equipment. For instance, if a child leaves a wheelchair behind at the start of a climbing structure, he or she needs a way of getting back to the wheelchair after completing the course. All children, including those with physical disabilities and/or hearing impairments who may have difficulty in balancing, learn to develop balancing skills through play, so appropriate **handrails and supports** should be incorporated.

When selecting **play equipment**, think about how children can explore and stimulate their senses. Children with visual impairments will enjoy strong contrasts in colour, texture and sound as much as other children. This can be explored in different materials, such as the feel or smell or sound of wood in contrast to metal or plastic, the colour of materials and by selecting objects that make sounds or create echoes.

Where possible, provide **supervision** in playgrounds in order to reassure children and to prevent bullying, ● section 10.2. Parents, teachers and supervisors with disabilities will also require access.

4.4.8   Gardens and courtyards

Gardens and courtyards are examples of intimate external spaces that are often provided as places of interest and rest as part of a building complex. For instance, on a industrial, business or education campus, these spaces will be used as a setting for lunch, informal discussions or a rest from the intensity of work. In addition, some private gardens open temporarily to the public, ● section 4.3.4, and gardens can form part of a larger park, ● section 4.4.4.

Being smaller in scale than the surrounding landscape infrastructure, gardens are generally detailed in the use of hard materials and planting. The Universal Right of Access applies. Gardens available to the public should be designed to be accessible for everybody to work in or visit.

In **industrial, business or education campuses**, the designer should consider the work activities that are carried out in order to be able successfully to provide antidotes to work stress. A person who works physically hard will want a comfortable seat; a person who looks at a computer screen all day will want a relaxing and varied view with, for instance, changes in light and shade and distance; a person who is frequently on the telephone or working in a noisy environment will want some quiet space to relax in, or at least a place where the sound of water or birdsong distracts from general background noise.

Water features, especially ponds, should be designed so that they do not present a hazard, causing people to fall into them. Edging should be firm and non-slip and should contrast in colour with the surrounding surface.

Everybody will benefit from a garden that stimulates the **senses**. Being able to touch plants is an intriguing way to create interest for visually impaired and sighted people alike. By the same token, fountains are not the only way to create sound interest in the garden. The breeze rustling through different types of plants (eg beech trees or bamboos), the sound of birds, water running over resonant surfaces, wind chimes and so on can all create a sense of perspective and depth of space as well as being a source of delight.

Garden furniture should be designed so that it is sympathetic to the surroundings and accessible to the broadest range of users, ● section 5.3. Likewise surfacing, ● section 5.1, and changes in level, ● section 5.2, should be designed according to best practice.

Gardens with special provision, such as those associated with hospices or therapeutic units or, indeed, private gardens specifically designed for a person with an impairment, lie outside the scope of this book.

4.4.9   Choosing plants

Trees, shrubs, green and flowering plants soften the visual and acoustic environment and give pleasure through their look, smell, feel and sound. They can be used to provide shelter and can also be placed so as to assist visually impaired people to locate themselves in a space. Whether positioned around buildings or used to create gardens, plants can be used to create features that stimulate the senses and are enjoyable for everyone. Properly used, plants in gardens contribute to a healthier environment and can provide habitats for fauna such as birds and butterflies that are also a source of pleasure and interest for everybody.

There are, of course, many considerations to take into account when planning a **planting scheme**, with soil type and climate being the predominant factors in ensuring healthy growth. **Themed gardens**, focusing on particular species or native origins, colour or season, will always be able to incorporate plants that appeal to the senses. Conversely, **sensory gardens** should not be designed for the senses alone but should also incorporate other ideas, eg of form or origin, that may serve to enhance the enjoyment, interest and education of the user in more subtle and complex ways. **Scent**, for example, even in leaves, is rarely evident except on warm days in the growing season, so fragrant plants, however stimulating, should not be used as the sole 'pathfinding device' in an environment. Traditionally, the **colours** in most planting schemes are complementary, whereas simple, bold colour contrasts are more readily identifiable by people with impaired vision and can be used to exciting effect. In the context of universal access, it is important not to exclude others from, say, a garden designed mainly for enjoyment by people with a visual impairment.

Paths in gardens should have a smooth, regular surface, with tactile warning underfoot of any hazards such as a change in level, ● section 5.1. Context of **materials** in gardens is very important in gardens in order to create the sense of the place. It is a challenge and a creative opportunity therefore for the designer to select and use materials that allow universal access, but do not simply repeat street pavement details, ● section 5.1.2.

Gravel and grass paths are difficult to push on and should be avoided,
● section 5.1.2. Used as a weed inhibiting mulch, however, gravel on beds
is preferable to some organic mulches that harbour moulds which can
aggravate breathing difficulties. A **raised edge**, 75mm high, will help to
keep soil-wash off a path, as well as serving as a tapping rail for a visually
impaired person using a cane and preventing wheelchairs and buggies
from running off the path.

Make sure that creeping plants do not become a tripping hazard beside
paths and ensure that any leaf debris falling from overhanging trees is
regularly cleared to prevent the path becoming slippery. For this reason,
soft fruiting trees should not be planted close to paths. Make sure thorny
plants are kept well back from paths and prune trees to create a clear
walking tunnel free of overhanging branches, maintaining clear headroom
of at least 2200mm even between prunings. Hedges and shrubs should
also be pruned back from paths, particularly on the threshold of private
gardens and public footpaths.

Signs in gardens indicating the names of plants are helpful for those interested in learning about them. As they are usually placed in beds beside the
plants, avoid embossed lettering as they are easily clogged by soil or grit,
● section 8.2.2.

Reducing the discomfort for people with **allergies** in gardens is a challenge
for the designer. Lawns and hedges are repositories of dust pollen and
mould. Consider groundcover and hard landscape instead of lawns, although
these can also contribute to a dusty environment. Water, in pools or fountains, can help to create a moister atmosphere and can therefore help to trap
pollen and dust. In a low allergen garden, avoid plants that produce a lot of
pollen, or those that can cause or aggravate sensitive skin.

Highly **toxic plants** should be avoided in any planting scheme to which the
public has access. Hazardous plants should only be used where they are
inaccessible.

Planting in public places should always be carried out by people with
proper training and knowledge. The following table lists some useful
plants for exploring sensory and low allergen uses.

• colour   • scent   • touch   • other considerations

Trees

Maple
Acer

- many varieties with good autumn leaf colour
- low allergen

Rowan
Sorbus

- many varieties with white flowers, good autumn leaf colour and berries
- low allergen, berries stay on the tree and are eaten by birds

Lime
Tilia

- clear yellow autumn leaves
- flower scent
- some varieties drop sticky residue

Magnolia

- evergreen and deciduous varieties, some with large white flowers
- some varieties have scented flowers
- M. grandiflora has glossy green leaves

Shrubs

Azalea

- many different colours of flower, some evergreen
- some varieties have scented flowers

Butterfly bush †
Buddleia

- flower colours range from purple to blue, some with silver leaves
- low allergen, attracts butterflies

Fuchsia

- typically red and purple flowers contrasting against green leaves
- young flowers can be popped open
- low allergen

St John's wort *
Hypericum

- bright yellow flowers
- low allergen

Cherry laurel
Prunus

- evergreen leaves and white flowers
- glossy leaves
- low allergen

Rose †
Rosa

- many different colours of flower, some with red hips
- many forms with scented flowers
- low allergen, thorny

• colour   • scent   • touch   • other considerations

Periwinkle
Vinca

- evergreen leaves with blue or white flowers
- vigorous creeping groundcover that may need trimming

Wormwood †
Artemesia

- some varieties have silver foliage all year
- some varieties have scented leaves when crushed
- some varieties have a soft feathery texture

Mexican orange
blossom †
Choysia

- evergreen leaves, white flowers
- scented leaves when crushed
- glossy leaves

Juniper
Juniperus

- evergreen conifer
- scented leaves
- fine texture

Lavender †
Lavandula

- blue flowers, silvery leaves, sometimes evergreen
- scented flowers and leaves

Mock orange †
Philadelphus

- white flowers
- scented flowers

Lilac
Syringa

- purple, pink or white flowers
- scented flowers

Hebe

- some evergreen varieties, some with purple flowers
- some varieties have fine soft textured leaves

Thyme †
Thymus

- evergreen
- scented flowers
- fine texture

Grasses

Grasses

- many varieties with green, gold, blue and black forms
- many different textures
- many grasses not suitable for low allergen gardens

• colour	• scent	• touch	• other considerations

Herbaceous and bulbs

Lady's mantle *
Alchemilla

- pale yellow flowers
- fine textured flowers and soft leaves
- seeds freely into cracks in paths

Ice plant ††
Sedum

- pink and white flowers
- fleshy leaves

Lambs' ears
Stachys

- silver foliage most of the year
- soft, hairy leaves

Montbretia †
Crocosmia

- flower colours from pale yellows to strong reds
- soft strap-shaped leaves
- low allergen

Iris †

- many different flower colours
- strap-shaped leaves, some thin, some fleshy
- low allergen

Loosestrife †
Lysimachia

- yellow or white flowers
- low allergen

Narcissus

- yellow or white flowers
- some scented
- low allergen

Scilla

- blue or white flowers
- some scented
- low allergen

*   © *Mitchell Associates*
†   © *Monterey Bay Nursery, Inc.*
††   © *Dorling Kindersley Limited, London*
      "RHS Encyclopedia of Garden Plants"

Checklist
Tamed landscape
- Minimise challenge in streets, squares and other urban spaces,
  ● chapter 5 for detail.
- Provide information in clear and consistent formats.
- In conservation areas, find sympathetic and workable solutions
  for universal access.
- Provide play equipment for different levels of ability.
- Design all gardens open to the public for sensory stimulation.

External detail design

5

5.1   Surfacing the plane

5.1.1   Legibility

Good legibility of surfacing in the natural and tempered landscapes is relatively straightforward to achieve. A footpath will typically be set in grass or groundflora, thereby contrasting with the built surface. In urban situations the layout is more complex, although good legibility can still be achieved. The logical and creative selection of materials will give a clear delineation of the functions of surfaces in a typical street profile of carriageway, kerb and footpath, particularly where the kerb is in a different size or type of material from the footpath. For instance, a typical footpath might be flagged in granite with a typical unit size of 450 x 600mm, laid at right angles to a granite kerb, with a width of 300mm and a length of 750mm, beside a black macadam carriageway. This gives a clear visual signal of footpath (walking), kerb (change in level) and carriageway (vehicles).

The change in level and surface is sometimes further defined by the use of a **granite drainage channel**. The modules of units in the drainage channel are usually smaller because they have to take vehicular traffic. If the channel is too similar to the kerb, it may be difficult for someone with a visual impairment to detect it.

In densely populated urban areas, **shared surfaces** are sometimes used to accommodate large numbers of people. Shared surfaces restrict, but do not altogether eliminate, vehicles and allow pedestrians to move on the same surface across the width of a street. It can become confusing for people unused to this or who have visual impairments that make it difficult to detect where they are safe if a vehicle is passing.

The legibility of a shared surface street is made clearer if the carriageway is defined in a different colour, material or module of the same material. It can be defined further by linear drainage gullies and the arrangement of street furniture, ● section 5.3.

Checklist

Legibility
- Determine selection of materials by function.
- Use surfacing materials along with other elements to define safe areas on shared surfaces.
- Define footpath edges clearly.

5.1.2   Materials

Surfacing materials should be hard and firm with a good grip. Smooth paving surfaces facilitate wheelchair and buggy mobility. Loose surfaces, such as gravel or surfaces with even small irregularities, such as old paving stones or cobbles, are difficult to negotiate in a wheelchair, and can be a tripping hazard for ambulant people. Surfaces should be firm, even, and slip-resistant even when wet (dry friction coefficient should be between 35 and 45).

Natural and tempered landscapes

Gravel, currently a common surfacing material in the natural and tempered landscapes, should be used only if it is of a grade which is well compacted, with no loose stones greater than 5mm. This will ease the passage of buggies and wheelchairs, and reduces the possibility of tripping for people who are unsteady on their feet. Regular maintenance will be required to repair potholes and erosion.

Alternatively, a bound gravel surface, where a top dressing of gravel is applied to a bitumen layer, gives the feel and appearance of gravel on a firm base. This surface will wear with use, requires regular maintenance and is not suitable for intense vehicular movement. New surface dressings should not be so deep to make accessibility difficult. As these surfaces require occasional top dressing, gravel from a local source should be selected, so that it is readily and cheaply available.

Epoxy bound gravel is a more expensive surface that gives the appearance of gravel. Bound in a clear resin, the colour of the gravel comes through but the surface is very firm, non-slip and requires little maintenance. Bitumen macadams will have the effect of 'suburbanising' a landscape but may be necessary where paths are used intensively or where maintenance is sporadic. Different colours are available, made from clear bitumen coloured with a dye and mixed with stone chippings of a similar colour. Buff and red colours are readily available and the source should be local so that repairs are easy to implement. Red is typically used for cycle paths and it may be appropriate to use the same material as a continuation of a wider network of cycle paths in the environs in order to avoid confusion.

Where grass tracks are used, a reinforcing system can be used below the surface to give a firm but free draining layer on which grass can grow. Make sure that the edges do not become a tripping hazard. The disadvantages of grass surfaces are that they inhibit the running of wheelchairs and buggies and that the grass can conceal trip hazards for people who are frail, unsteady on their feet or who have visual impairments. Wide expanses present a further disadvantage to people with visual impairments who will find it difficult to orientate themselves in the space. A mown grass path contrasting in texture and colour with meadow grass, even after the meadow has been mown, may be of some limited assistance with orientation.

Urban environment

The size of materials used in surfacing is indicative of the kinds of functions or loads it is expected to handle. Modular sizes employed in surfacing should reflect use. Large slabs can be employed for light pedestrian use, although the larger the surface area of the slab, the thicker it should be to prevent it from cracking. Large slabs can also be unwieldy, and be difficult to lay evenly, even with a hoist.

The smaller the modular size, the more resistant the paving unit to vehicular loads, although the surface itself may become distorted through use, unless a strong enough bed has been laid. The problem can be rectified easily when the units are bedded in sand but is more difficult when the joints are mortared. However, light traffic on small modular paving bedded on sand can encourage grass and moss to grow in the joints. Such paving requires maintenance to prevent it becoming a hindrance for wheelchair users or people pushing buggies, or from presenting a tripping hazard for ambulant people.

Polished surfaces cause glare and are not suitable in a damp climate, as they remain slippery in a moist atmosphere, even after rain has passed. Likewise, **fine-grained stones** with a high calcium content can erode quickly with use, forming a polished surface, slippery in wet weather. There are numerous mechanical finishes to stone paving, from a simple cleaving or sawing, to pin- and bush-hammering, which produces a non-slip textured finish. Different finishes will also draw out different qualities in the stone.

There are thousands of products readily available for surfacing pedestrian areas, for shared surfaces and for roads. The problem of having too many to choose from is solved by going back to basics, considering factors such as accessibility, cost and importation, the blend and contrast of local materials and the purposes for which the materials are being used.

Checklist
Materials
- Footpaths should be smooth, even, firm, matt and slip-resistant.
- Avoid loose materials such as gravel.
- Determine selection of materials by function.

Surfacing materials

- setting • comments

Natural ground
- Natural landscape: paths made by continuous use.
- Typical of remote areas, allowing limited access because of uneven, sometimes soft ground and risk of slipping. Unsuitable for intensively used areas because of erosion. No cost.

Grass
- Natural and tempered landscapes: paths and swathes.
- Limited access because of uneven, sometimes soft ground and risk of slipping. Usability is increased by the use of reinforcing products. Unsuitable for intensive use over long periods. Low cost, requires regular maintenance.

Gravel
- Natural and tempered landscapes: low key paths from local source.
- Limited access because of uneven soft surface, although if graded and compacted becomes more accessible. Low cost, requires regular maintenance.

Timber
- All landscapes: usually associated with water or wet ground.
- Fully accessible when well detailed and maintained properly. Medium – high cost, requires regular maintenance.

Bitumen bound gravels
- Tempered landscape: surface dressing rolled onto hot blacktop, reduces urban quality of blacktop on its own.
- Limited access because of loose stones on surface but firmer than loose gravel. Low cost, regular maintenance required as surface erodes.

Epoxy bound gravels
- Tempered and tamed landscape: appearance of gravel, but firm.
- Accessible as long as gravel is no greater than 5mm. High cost, low maintenance.

Surfacing materials *cont.*

- setting • comments

Hoggin

- Tempered and tamed landscape: for low intensity of use.
- Can produce a firm, even surface, although access is limited by clay content in surface becoming muddy. Low cost, although has to be imported and requires regular maintenance.

Cobbles and setts

- Tempered and tamed landscape: traditional 19th century paving material for intense use.
- Limited access due to irregular surface, minimised by skilful laying. Can be useful as a implicit tactile warning. Expensive to lay. Low maintenance, unless bedded on sand can become loose with intensive use.

Modular paving

- Tempered and tamed landscape: use can imply urbanisation of a place.
- Fully accessible. Easy to lay due to regularity of units. Medium cost, low maintenance, can become loose with intensive use.

Crazy paving

- Tamed landscape, typically suburban garden paving, although has idiosyncratic urban use.
- Limited access, depending on irregularity of paving material and how skilfully laid. Medium cost, low maintenance.

Bituminous materials

- Tempered and tamed landscape: textures and colours can be used to reduce association with roads.
- Fully accessible, depending on type and when laid correctly. Medium cost, low maintenance.

Stone and concrete flags

- Tempered and tamed landscape: quality varies greatly according to material and how surface is dressed.
- Fully accessible, easy to lay due to regularity of units. Medium to high cost depending on material, low maintenance.

5.1.3   Paths and pavements

Paths

In the natural and tempered landscapes, paths should generally be at least 1800mm wide in order to accommodate wheelchair users and people with visual impairments assisted by a sighted person or guide dog. It will also allow, for instance, an adult and child to walk together. If existing paths are less than 1800mm wide, consider **passing places**, 1800mm wide and 2500mm long, at a reasonable frequency, depending on intensity of use. This will allow groups of people to pass each other, particularly on busy routes.

Where the effective width is constricted by, for example, existing trees or walls, paths may reduce to 1200mm for short distances. A 1200mm wide path is too narrow for people to pass each other, so provide passing places at a greater frequency.

A **change in surface** at the edge, such as a grass or groundflora verge, which often occurs naturally anyway, will help to prevent people from straying off the path. Maintain routes with no low or overhanging vegetation below 2200mm, ● section 4.4.9.

Pavements

An urban pavement should be as wide as necessary to accommodate the amount of people using it. Generally footpaths should be **1800mm wide**. The minimum clearance between a building and a bollard or lamp standard on any footpath should be 1200mm. This will allow two people or a person with a guide dog to walk along without being obstructed. It should also be possible for someone to pass without stepping into the path of a passing vehicle. Doors and windows opening out directly onto a pavement will present a hazard to people with visual impairments unless there is a **tactile indication** or barrier on the pavement, see below.

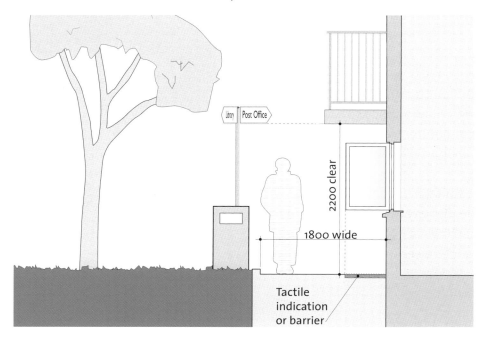

figure 3 **External hazard**

Paving should have an even surface to prevent tripping, and be laid to even falls to allow proper drainage and prevent the formation of puddles. The gap between paving slabs or any vertical deviation between slabs should not exceed 5mm.

Cross falls should be 1:50 maximum. Steeper gradients tend to misdirect buggies and wheelchairs. Where falls are not adequate, silt will accumulate after rain and cause the surface to become slippery. Puddles also cause the pavement to become slippery, lead to glare in bright sunshine after other parts of the pavement have become dry and become a hazard in frosty weather.

Any break in the surface, eg. **drainage channels** or the gaps between boards on a walkway, should not be greater than 12mm and should cross perpendicular to the direction of movement. This will prevent walking sticks and wheels getting caught in the gaps.

Service covers to manhole and inspection chambers should not be positioned on footpaths, particularly at dished crossings. They can be dangerous when opened for inspection, forming a tripping hazard and reducing the clear width.

Checklist
Paths and pavements
- Ensure adequate footpath width for volume of people, minimum 1800mm.
- Minimum clearance between a building and street furniture should be 1200mm.
- Cross falls should be maximum 1:50.
- Avoid changes in vertical deviation greater than 5mm.
- Avoid gaps in surfacing, eg drainage gullies, greater than 12mm.
- Provide a clear walking tunnel of minimum 2200mm in height.

5.1.4   Tactile paving
Use red coloured tactile paving at controlled crossings such as pelican and zebra crossings and traffic lights, and yellow at uncontrolled crossings such as side streets.The **consistent use of different colours** to indicate different crossings assists people who are partially sighted.

Tactile markings can be uncomfortable for some people to walk on and can present a tripping hazard for people using walking sticks or crutches. To minimise these effects, use raised markings of no more than 5mm high. Tactile paving must, however, be maintained to ensure that the profile does not erode away.

The tactile paving used at pedestrian crossings is blistered. It should be laid across the entire footpath where the crossing occurs, and be 600mm wide so that someone can't miss it by stepping over it. Other tactile markings are sometimes used to indicate other hazards, eg ridged or corduroy paving which indicates a hazard that requires caution, such as the top and bottom of a flight of stairs.

Provide a **tactile strip** along the inner edge of a footpath where there is a break in the line of the corridor, eg. at a garage forecourt or a gap in a building façade for an archway. This will allow people with visual impairments to recognise that they are continuing in the right direction, and that they have not reached a junction or missed a turning.

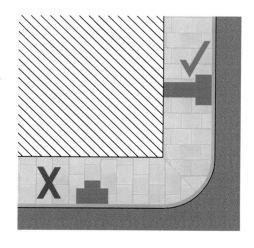

figure 4
Tactiling across entire pavement

Red blistered paving
used for dropped kerbs at controlled crossings
© Tobermore Concrete Products, Ltd

Yellow blistered paving
used for dropped kerbs at non-controlled crossings,
such as side streets
© Tobermore Concrete Products, Ltd

Ridged or corduroy paving
used for top and bottom of a change in level, such as a ramp or steps.
Laid perpendicular to movement

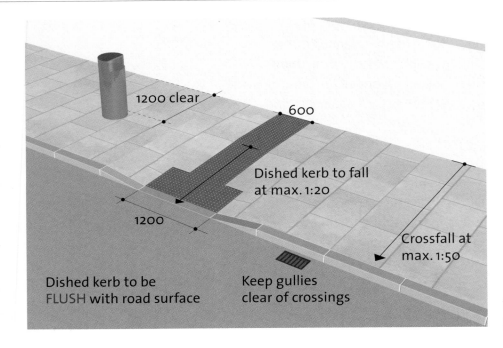

Labels within the figure:
- 1200 clear
- 600
- Dished kerb to fall at max. 1:20
- 1200
- Crossfall at max. 1:50
- Dished kerb to be FLUSH with road surface
- Keep gullies clear of crossings

figure 5
Dished crossings – wide path

5.1.5   Pedestrian crossings

At **main crossing points**, dish the pavement to facilitate people with bug-gies or using wheelchairs. Locate dishing away from corners, on both sides of the street, flush with the road. Kerbs are the best indicators for people with visual impairments to detect the edge of the footpath, so dished kerbs must always have tactile markers. The provision of double yellow line markings to prevent cars parking either side of a dropped kerb will ensure the area remains unobstructed.

Dished pavement ramps should be 1200mm, minimum 900mm, wide. The gradient of the ramp should ideally be **1:20**, and not exceed 1:12. It can be difficult in existing situations to achieve a dropped kerb with a gradient of 1:20 across a pavement and still leave a clear corridor of movement along the footpath. Alternative solutions should be sought by the designer as many people find it difficult to stand on a steeply sloped section of blistered paving while they are waiting to cross the road. For instance, it may be possible to drop the entire surface of the footpath running parallel to the road where the crossing occurs, or to ramp up the road to meet the footpath level at the crossing point. All of these situations can, however, be confusing for people with a visual impairment, so the crossing should still be marked with tactile paving. Different materials should also be used to indicate the change in function between the footpath and carriageway.

Make sure the crossing point is always well drained. Avoid gullies in the immediate area of the crossing, however. The slight kerb lip required to facilitate roadway **drainage** should be maximum 20mm high and cham-fered in section.

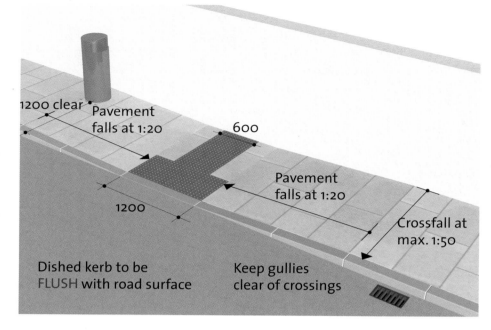

1200 clear
Pavement
falls at 1:20
600
Pavement
falls at 1:20
Crossfall at
max. 1:50
1200
Dished kerb to be
FLUSH with road surface
Keep gullies
clear of crossings

figure 6
Dished crossings – narrow path

In busy streets, provide safe crossing areas with pedestrian operated traffic signals. Audible crossing signals (pelican crossings) help everyone, as well as being essential for people with visual impairments.

Checklist
Pedestrian crossings
- Provide appropriate crossings with dished kerbs marked with tactile paving.
- Dished kerb to be 1200mm wide, minimum 900mm, with maximum gradient of 1:20.
- Maximum height of the edge of a dropped kerb to be 20mm.
- Prevent vehicles from blocking sightlines at crossings.
- Avoid underground services access covers at crossings.

5.1.6   Maintenance

A significant factor in the selection of surfaces is the ease of making **repairs**. An expensive stone from a faraway place, or a peculiar colour of macadam, is less likely to be repaired properly than a local stone or standard colour of macadam that is easily available and replaced. This is not to say that special places should not be celebrated by the use of special materials. They will, however, require a high degree of care when any damage is repaired.

Maintenance should prevent or replace cracked and **uneven paving slabs** and those with loose joints, as they become tripping hazards and are difficult to walk on. They also cause puddles to form and can become slippery.

The selection of paving materials will therefore often be informed by the ability to repair and maintain them.

5.2   Level change

5.2.1   General

Changes in level across a site frequently pose challenges to designers. In **adapting an existing situation**, it is appropriate to consider the impact on the general environs, rather than a piecemeal approach. It may be possible to adjust ground levels more broadly to eliminate the need for a ramp or steps altogether. Arbitrary changes of level should be avoided. For instance, in creating a sense of importance for a **building approach**, a change in the quality of paving or street furniture can have the desired effect, rather than introducing a level change. When a terrace or steps or podium becomes a necessity for a designer, however, the result need not always be an obstruction for people with disabilities if the design is well considered. Changes of level can be interesting, for example for wheelchair users who normally see things from a low angle.

A ramp or series of slopes should be integrated into the level change to facilitate wheelchair users or buggies. Trying to incorporate a ramp after the initial design has been conceived will lead to ungainly solutions.

The steeper the incline, ramp or steps, and the greater the change in level, the more frequent the need for **landings and resting places**. Where resting places are located on landings they should be out of the way of the line of movement. A gradient less than 1:20 does not require handrails and resting places. A gradient of 1:10 or steeper will be extremely difficult and dangerous for most people with disabilities to use. This is the point in the natural landscape where accessibility, particularly for those with mobility impairments, will become an issue for assistance and/or special provision. At these gradients, many people would welcome a place to rest and catch their breath, so consideration should be given to providing suitable places to stop.

Where ramps of a reasonable gradient are not possible, and steps are necessary, steps of appropriate type should be provided, see below.

Checklist
Level change
- Allow for resting places and shelter, for instance, after difficult gradients or long sequences.
- Ramps should be no steeper than 1:20, with landings, handrails etc, see below.
- The top and bottom of changes in level should be clearly marked, see below.
- Regular maintenance of manmade changes in level will ensure continuous accessibility.

5.2.2   Ramps and steps

Ideally, both steps and ramps should be provided. Some people with disabilities find it easier to use steps rather than a ramp, ● section 2.1. However, in the external environment, if there is not room for both, provide a ramp. The route should not be tortuous, nor deliver people out of the way in which they want to go. Keep the route clear of obstacles such as bicycles or bins, and regularly sweep clean of debris.

Where it is not possible to provide a combination of steps and a ramp near building entrances, consider the installation of a platform lift, ● section 6.7.5. When provided in external spaces, such lifts may be difficult to maintain because of tampering or vandalism, but they can be useful in controlled external areas, for example on third level education campuses or hospital grounds.

Checklist
External ramps
- Detail ramps so that water drains away from the ramp surface and from landings.
- Use slip-resistant smooth surfaces such as ribbed or brushed concrete, textured stone or macadam, ● section 5.1.
- Provide top and bottom landings with a textured surface, to give advance tactile warning of the change in gradient, ● section 5.1.4.
- Flights and landings should have a clear unobstructed width of 1200mm, minimum 1000mm.
- On long ramps, provide passing bays, 1800 x 1800mm every 20.0m.
- Landings should be at least as long as the ramp is wide, minimum 1300mm.
- Where a door or gate opens onto a landing, the length of the landing should be at least 1300mm clear of the door swing.

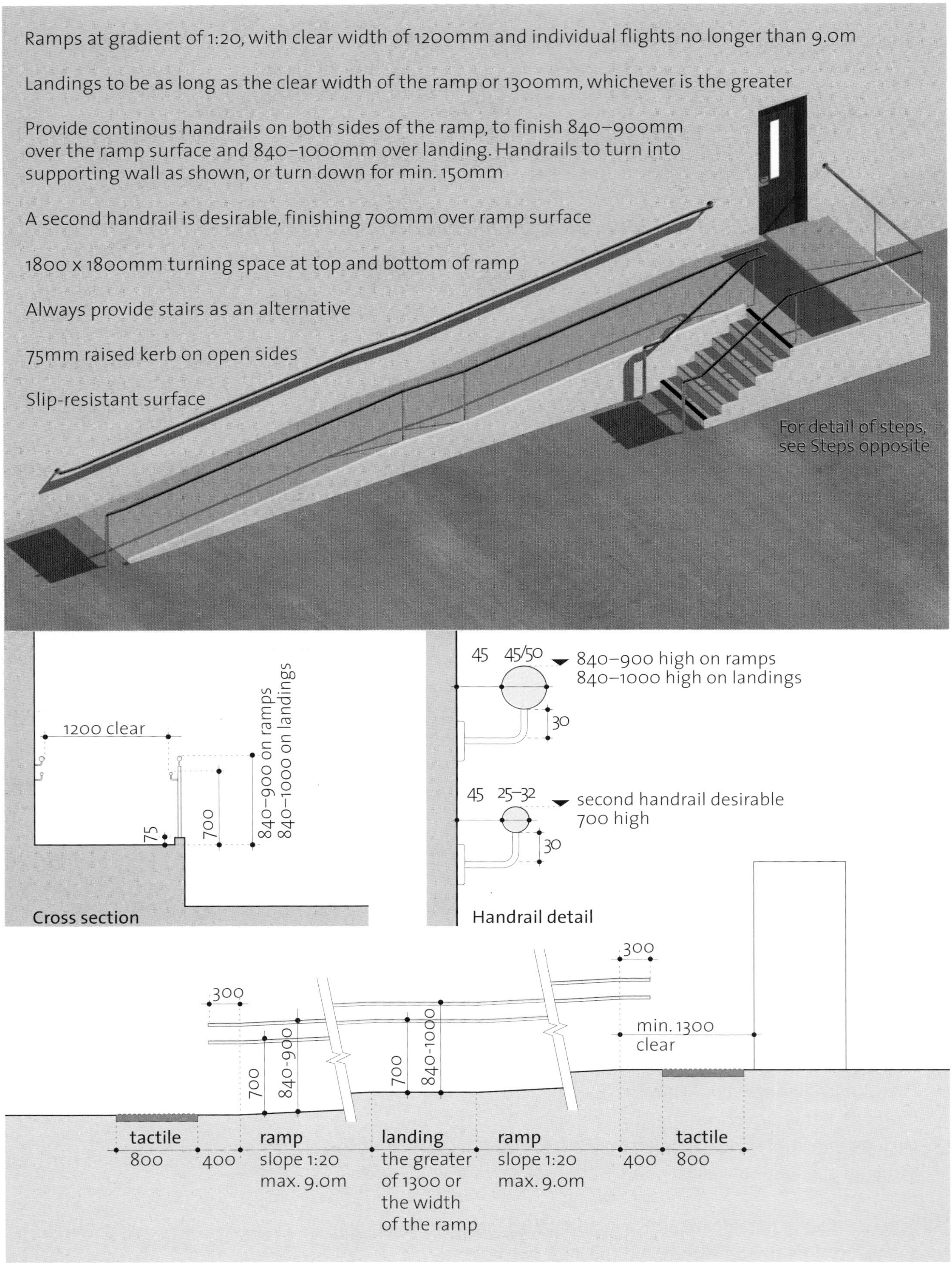

Ramps at gradient of 1:20, with clear width of 1200mm and individual flights no longer than 9.0m

Landings to be as long as the clear width of the ramp or 1300mm, whichever is the greater

Provide continous handrails on both sides of the ramp, to finish 840–900mm over the ramp surface and 840–1000mm over landing. Handrails to turn into supporting wall as shown, or turn down for min. 150mm

A second handrail is desirable, finishing 700mm over ramp surface

1800 x 1800mm turning space at top and bottom of ramp

Always provide stairs as an alternative

75mm raised kerb on open sides

Slip-resistant surface

For detail of steps, see Steps opposite

Cross section

1200 clear

840–900 on ramps
840–1000 on landings

700

75

Handrail detail

45   45/50   ▼ 840–900 high on ramps
840–1000 high on landings

30

45   25–32   ▼ second handrail desirable
700 high

30

300

300

min. 1300 clear

700   840–900

700   840–1000

tactile		ramp	landing	ramp		tactile
800	400	slope 1:20 max. 9.0m	the greater of 1300 or the width of the ramp	slope 1:20 max. 9.0m	400	800

figure 7 **Ramps**

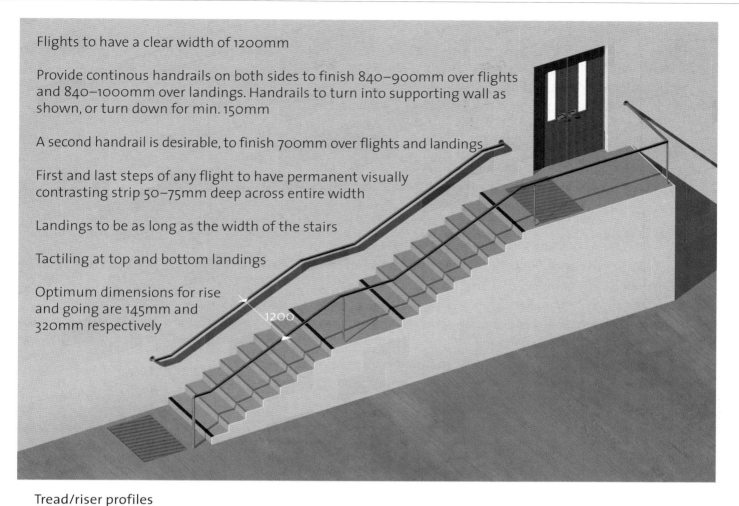

Flights to have a clear width of 1200mm

Provide continous handrails on both sides to finish 840–900mm over flights and 840–1000mm over landings. Handrails to turn into supporting wall as shown, or turn down for min. 150mm

A second handrail is desirable, to finish 700mm over flights and landings

First and last steps of any flight to have permanent visually contrasting strip 50–75mm deep across entire width

Landings to be as long as the width of the stairs

Tactiling at top and bottom landings

Optimum dimensions for rise and going are 145mm and 320mm respectively

1200

Tread/riser profiles

15/25   15/25

Optimum tread and riser dimensions are 145mm and 320mm respectively

For handrail profile,
■ figure 7 opposite

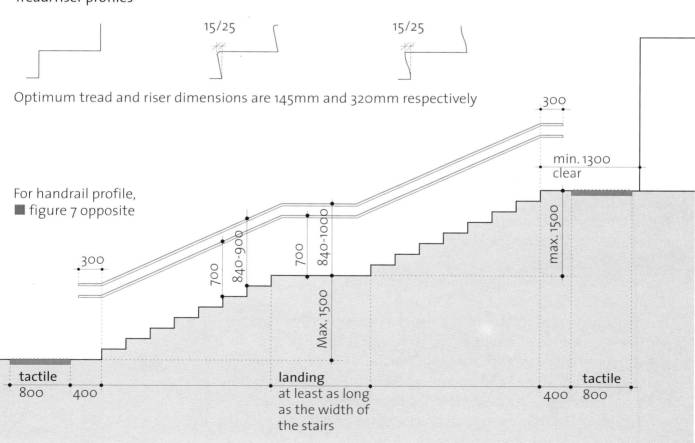

300

min. 1300 clear

max. 1500

300

700

840–900

700

840–1000

Max. 1500

tactile
800   400

landing
at least as long
as the width of
the stairs

400   800
tactile

figure 8 **Steps**

- The gradient should not be steeper than 1:20, and individual flights should be less than 9.0m. Note that BS 8300:2001 limits this to 6.0m. In exceptional circumstances, where site constraints necessitate it, ramps not steeper than 1:12 may be provided if individual flights are not longer than 4.5m (2000mm according to BS 8300:2001).
- A raised kerb at least 75mm high should be provided on any open side.
- Provide a continuous handrail on each side of the flights and landings.
- The handrails should be between 840–900mm above the ramp and landing surfaces. Handrails should extend at least 300mm beyond the ramp at the top and bottom, and terminate in a closed end that does not project into a route of travel. Handrail profile and projection from a wall should be suitable to allow adequate grip, ■ figure 7.
- Provide a second handrail, 700mm above the ramp surface, for children and short people. The diameter of the bar should be 25–32mm for smaller hands.
- Provide guarding at the sides of ramps and landings to prevent people falling through.
- Provide a turning circle of 1800mm diameter at the top and bottom of all ramps.
- Provide grille type gullies across the width of the ramp surface to ensure good drainage.

Checklist

External steps

- Provide top and bottom landings with a textured surface, to give advanced tactile warning of a change in level, ● section 5.1.4.
- The first and last steps should provide a permanent visual contrast with the rest of the steps.
- Flights and landings should have a clear unobstructed width of at least 1000mm.
- The rise between landings should not exceed 1500mm.
- The length of a landing should be at least as great as the smallest width of the flight.
- The optimum dimensions for rise and going are 145mm and 320mm respectively. Heights of risers should be consistent throughout the flight.
- Tapered treads and open risers should not be used.
- Nosings should be avoided.
- There should be a suitable continuous handrail on each side of flights and landings. The handrail tops should be 840–900mm above the pitch line of the flight of steps and above the surface of the landing. Handrails should extend at least 300mm beyond the top and bottom risers and terminate in a closed end that does not project into a route of travel. The handrail profile and its projection from a wall should be suitable to allow adequate grip, ● section 6.7.2.

- Provide a second handrail, 700mm high, for children and short people. The diameter of the bar should be 25–32mm for smaller hands.
- Guarding is required at the sides of ramps and landings to prevent people falling through.
- A single step, other than a kerb, should be avoided, as it is a trip hazard.
- On a stepped path, goings should be long enough to accommodate a wheelchair user and a person pushing them, and should be paced in a way in which an ambulant person is not stepping up or down with the same leg for the whole route. The rise of each step should be no greater than 145mm, consistent throughout the path.
- It is convenient for all users if the numbers of steps in each flight are equal.

5.3 Site furniture

5.3.1 General

Furniture in the external environment consists of a diversity of elements such as light standards, seats, picnic tables, bins, information panels, traffic signs, parking meters and post boxes etc, often placed independently over time and without co-ordination. In urban environments the complexity of the layering of these elements can result in an assault course for most people, particularly for people with visual impairments and those using a wheelchair or pushing a buggy.

5.3.2 Placing

In both rural and urban situations, place furniture out of the line of movement, so that people do not bump into it. Good placing and co-ordination of furniture will result in a tidy, legible pathway or street

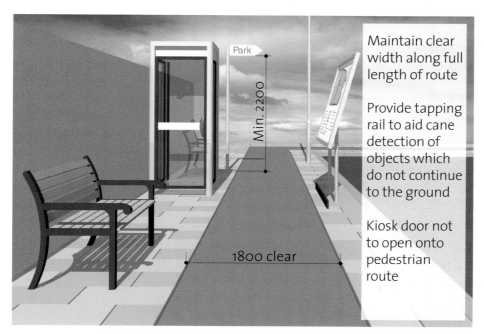

Park

Min. 2200

1800 clear

Maintain clear width along full length of route

Provide tapping rail to aid cane detection of objects which do not continue to the ground

Kiosk door not to open onto pedestrian route

figure 9
Placing: legible pathway and furniture

that is easy to move along. Elements should be placed in **straight lines**. For instance, light standards define the main zone of objects in a street and bollards, traffic signs and post boxes can follow this line. Bulky objects such as parking meters and post boxes should not be placed where they will become a visual obstruction at crossing points. The line of furniture should allow a **clear circulation corridor of 1800mm**, minimum 1200mm, wide, ● section 5.1.3. This dimension allows a wheelchair user and a pedestrian to pass each other without having to give way, ■ figure 9.

5.3.3   Colour and contrast

Furniture should contrast in colour and in tone with the background against which it is seen and should be highlighted by means of a **75–100mm high feature**, such as a crest or band, which contrasts in colour and tone with the furniture itself.

Furniture should be **continuous to ground level**. Avoid pedestal-mounted objects such as litter bins, telephones or letter boxes. Items attached to posts should face in the direction of travel so that they do not interfere with the line of movement. Where eye-level signs, such as maps, are supported on two vertical poles, a **tapping rail** located between the posts at around 250mm above ground level prevents an unsuspecting pedestrian colliding with the sign. The rail and posts should be colour contrasted with their background.

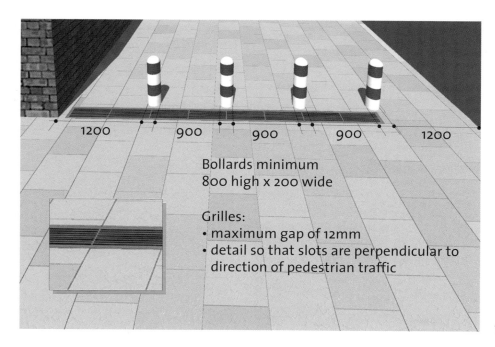

1200   900   900   900   1200

Bollards minimum
800 high x 200 wide

Grilles:
• maximum gap of 12mm
• detail so that slots are perpendicular to
  direction of pedestrian traffic

figure 10   **Bollards and grilles**

5.3.4 Bollards

Bollards are often used to stop vehicles from mounting the footpath and to keep pedestrians away from traffic. Unless positioned carefully they can form a barrier to wheelchair users and are a particular hazard for people with visual impairments. Where they are essential, such as to ensure clear escape routes, bollards should be identifiable by using contrasting colours, and be minimum 800mm high and 200mm wide. Maintain a minimum 1200mm passage width from the kerb edge to the adjacent bollard, in both directions.

5.3.5 Gates

Gates are sometimes hinged or sprung in such a way as to be self-closing. These should be adjusted so as not to slam shut on an unsuspecting pedestrian or to prevent wheelchair or buggy access. The opening mechanism should be robust but easy to grip and manoeuvre. The path should extend 500mm to the side of the gate with the latch to make it easier to approach and open the gate. The approach to the gate should be minimum 2000mm clear.

figure 11 **Gates**

5.3.6 Drinking fountains

Where drinking fountains are provided, make sure they are easy to operate. A drain underneath the tap will prevent the area getting waterlogged and muddy. Consider a shallow tray that can be used to allow a guide dog – or, indeed, any dog – to get a drink of water.

5.3.7 Seating

Seating should be located in sheltered places where people can enjoy a good view, and after a long sequence of paths or changes in level. Seats should be placed **600mm back from the line of movement** so that they do not block the path. The surface should be flush with surrounding levels, as well as firm and stable. A 900mm square of **firm paving** beside a seat will allow a person in a wheelchair to sit with other people. A seat should be no less than **450mm high**, although a perch 500–750mm will be easier to use for some people who have difficulty getting up. A **heel space** at least 100mm deep will also make it easier for people to get off the seat or perch. Seats with **backrests** are useful for additional support, and **arm rests** are also useful to lean against, as well as assisting in getting up out of the seat.

5.3.8 Picnic tables

Although picnic tables placed beside carparks are convenient to use, ensure that they are far enough away from cars to be in a pleasant setting. Picnic tables should be placed on level sheltered sites with accessible paths. The design of the table and seats should be such that they don't topple when unbalanced. A height clearance of **700mm** for the tabletop will allow the arms of a wheelchair to slide underneath. Seating should be as described above. Where table and chairs are joined in the same construction, **avoid beams** that are difficult for people to climb across. A **firm level surface 1500mm wide** around the perimeter of the table and seats will allow someone in a wheelchair to manoeuvre around. It will also be more comfortable for other people to use.

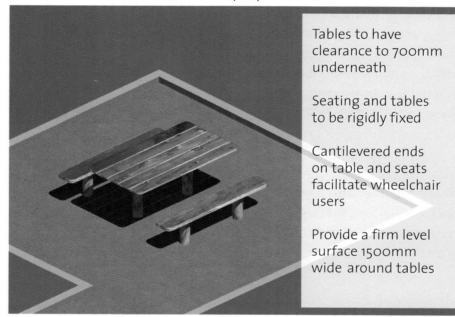

Tables to have clearance to 700mm underneath

Seating and tables to be rigidly fixed

Cantilevered ends on table and seats facilitate wheelchair users

Provide a firm level surface 1500mm wide around tables

figure 12 **Picnic tables**

Checklist
Site furniture

- Outdoor furniture should be placed on stable ground.
- Paths and pavements to be ideally 1800mm wide, minumum 1200mm.
- Do not allow furniture to encroach on the clear width of pathways.
- Street furniture should contrast in colour with the background, and be identified by a 75–100mm marking.
- Avoid pedestal mounted objects if possible. If not possible, fit a tapping rail 250mm above ground, contrasting in colour with the pavement.
- Seating should accommodate wheelchair users and buggies.
- Ensure that bollards do not cause an obstruction or hazard in themselves and maintain minimum 1200mm passage width to get by them.
- Regular maintenance of fittings to gates will continue to ensure good accessibility.

5.4   Parking

5.4.1   Provision and siting

Provide enough parking places to discourage indiscriminate parking, as this can obstruct building access. Where parking is provided, give **priority to people with impaired mobility,** so they may park their cars as convenient to entrances as possible. Parking bays designated for people with disabilities should be clearly marked on the roadway surface and be accompanied by the appropriate sign standing in front of the bay. If such a sign is not visible from the entrance to the car park, provide signage which will lead disabled drivers to the designated spaces.

The number of parking spaces to be designated for people with disabilities depends on the building type. The following guidelines are the recommended provision of reserved parking for people with disabilities.

- *Buildings not normally visited by the public*   Minimum one space of appropriate dimensions in every 25 standard spaces, up to the first 100 spaces; thereafter, one space per every 100 standard spaces or part thereof.
- *Shops and other buildings to which the public has access*   Minimum one space of appropriate dimensions in the first 25 standard spaces; minimum three in 25–50 standard spaces; minimum five in 50–100 standard spaces; and additional three per every 100 standard spaces in excess thereof.

Premises used by a high proportion of people with disabilities require a larger than average number of designated spaces. The parking requirement for such building types should be calculated in relation to the anticipated demand.

Car parks should be laid out in a uniform order, clearly distinguishing between parking and pedestrian areas. Large featureless spaces disorientate people with visual impairments, so design to help orientation, for example, using pathways, tactiling or planting,
● section 5.1.

5.4.2   Designated car parking spaces

Designated car parking spaces may be arranged **perpendicular** or **parallel to the kerb.** Dropped kerbs will facilitate access to the pavement for people using wheelchairs, ● section 5.1.5.

If arranged **perpendicular** to the kerb, provide minimum 900mm clear space beside the designated bay so as to facilitate wheelchair transfer from car to footpath. Cars can be driven forward or reversed into the bay, so that the transfer space is at the right side, ■ figure 13.

Perpendicular parking

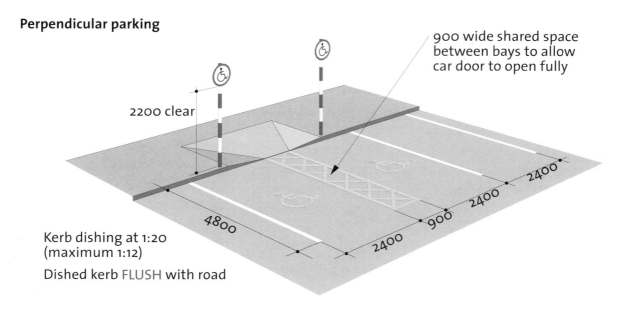

900 wide shared space
between bays to allow
car door to open fully

2200 clear

2400
2400
2400
900
4800
2400

Kerb dishing at 1:20
(maximum 1:12)

Dished kerb FLUSH with road

Parallel parking alternatives

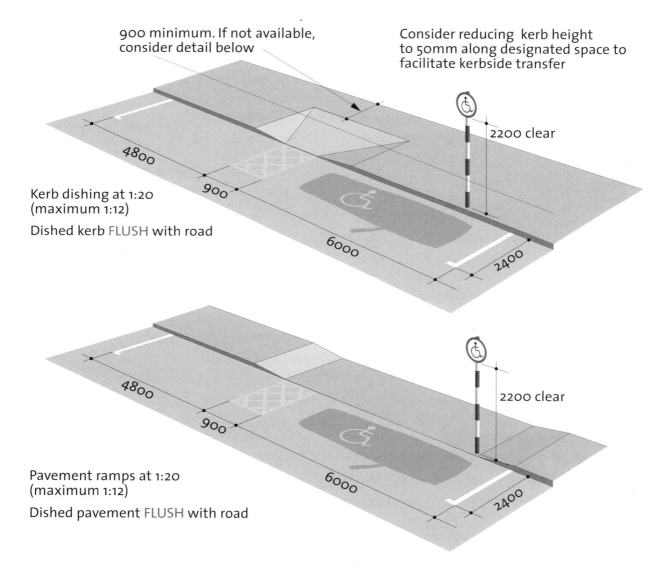

900 minimum. If not available,
consider detail below

Consider reducing kerb height
to 50mm along designated space to
facilitate kerbside transfer

2200 clear

4800
900
6000
2400

Kerb dishing at 1:20
(maximum 1:12)

Dished kerb FLUSH with road

2200 clear

4800
900
6000
2400

Pavement ramps at 1:20
(maximum 1:12)

Dished pavement FLUSH with road

figure 13 **Parking**

Spaces arranged **parallel** to the kerb, ■ figure 13, need to take account of the transfer side. A disabled driver or passenger getting out on the kerb side may transfer directly onto the wheelchair located on the footpath. This can be very difficult if the kerb is high, as it necessitates lifting the wheelchair out of the car up onto the pavement, and then lifting oneself up onto the chair from the car seat. This problem does not present itself if parking perpendicular to the kerb, as transfer will always be onto road level, which may be more convenient, assuming the provision of appropriate dishing providing access to the footpath, ● section 5.1.5. Where parallel parking is the only option, some people prefer to transfer on the road side to avoid the kerb, despite the obvious hazards. If they do so, a clear space must be available at the ends of the car to allow them to gain access to the footpath. In some situations where pavement width is restricted, it may be appropriate to ramp the pavement down to road level for the full length of the parking spaces in question, ■ figure 13.

In car parks of 25 cars or less, the roadway may be used for transfer purposes, provided this area is clearly visible to approaching traffic and the roadway is not a through road.

Alighting from vehicles can be via a side door or an end door. Alighting from wheelchair accessible taxis generally involves using a portable ramp extending maximum 2000mm from the vehicle.

Parking bays should be firm, level and even. A 1:50 maximum gradient is acceptable where essential to remove surface water. An uneven surface or an inclined bay makes transfer from vehicle to wheelchair difficult.

5.4.3   Multi-storey and underground car parks

As in all car parks, provide designated parking bays for cars with disabled drivers and passengers. Designated bays should be on the most convenient level, and at the most convenient position for entrance and exit to the building or car park. Designated spaces should be located close to street or lift exits, so that exposure to exhaust fumes is minimised.

In **underground car parks**, the route from the car park to the building entrance should be accessible for wheelchair users. Where a passenger lift serves car parking above or below the main entrance level, provide direct access to the building at all levels.

Ensure that **controls on ticket machines**, at both entrances and exits as applicable, are easily reachable from inside the car. People with impaired reach or grip often cannot operate conventional ticket machines controlling car park barriers. A **bell or intercom** should be provided so that a user can call for assistance from a member of staff. If payment is made to a member of staff at the exit, ensure that a visual display of amount is provided, and that the counter is reachable. If tickets are to be pre-paid before returning to the car, notices to this effect should be obvious. Pre-paid ticket machines should be simple to operate, and should have clear displays and controls at appropriate heights, ● section 7.8.

5.4.4   Drop-off points

Provide a drop-off point near entrances. Passengers with impaired mobility often move slowly and therefore are vulnerable in bad weather. People with visual impairments also benefit from having direct access to the building entrance. Provide protection from the weather wherever possible. A canopy height of 2500mm facilitates most passenger vehicles.

Drop-off points should be level, with a firm surface. Avoid siting manholes, drainage gullies etc in areas where people get out of cars, in particular at dished kerbs. Such items can impede walking sticks, crutches and wheel-chairs and can become hazardous in cold weather.

Drop-off points should not obstruct circulation areas. Avoid transfer directly onto footpaths or, if this is not possible, ensure that the footpath is at least 2000mm wide at the drop-off point. For advice on dropped kerbs, ● section 5.1.5.

5.4.5   Taxi ranks

Taxi ranks should have adequate space for embarking and disembarking, so that portable ramps do not project into the general circulation area. Shelter at taxi ranks is desirable. Taxi companies should be contactable by means of a TDD (telephone device for the deaf), ● section 8.3.

5.4.6   Parking bicycles

Parking management for both cars and bicycles should control indiscriminate parking, particularly in relation to keeping circulation spaces free. Prohibition notices may help to prevent indiscriminate parking.

Provide adequate bicycle parking to reduce the risk of people locking bicycles to railings and bollards. This can make it impossible for people with disabilities to get by. Even minor injury from bicycle pedals projecting into pedestrian routes can be serious for people with poor circulation.

5.4.7   Escape routes

To ensure free passage from final exits on escape routes to a place of safety (generally located minimum 100m or 10 times the building height from the final exit), the route from the final exit to the place of safety must be clear of obstruction and well lit. Make sure that parking and material storage do not obstruct the route. Place parking bollards to ensure that wheelchair users can move between cars, ● section 5.3.4.

Checklist

Parking

- Provide parking convenient to entrances.
- Provide adequate number of designated parking bays.
- Provide directional signs to designated parking bays.
- Provide signs beside and on the surface of the bay, for clear designation.
- Parking surfaces to be firm and level.
- Route from car park to building entrance to be accessible.
- Control parking spaces to stop unauthorised parking.
- Ensure access and escape routes are not blocked by bicycles or other vehicles.
- Keep routes free of fallen leaves, snow and ice.

5.5   Protection of outdoor works

5.5.1   General

The process of construction work, whether maintenance, repair or new build, can cause significant risk to passers-by unless it is carried out properly. Work to premises on privately-owned land may require the erection of scaffolding or the temporary use of areas of the footpath or roadway for storage purposes. Maintenance and repair work to underground services, such as drains, water mains, gas mains and telephone and electrical cables, involves excavation of public walkways and, frequently, the storage of spoil and construction materials in the vicinity of the works. People with impaired vision are particularly at risk from temporary obstruction.

5.5.2   The perimeter of the construction site

The erection of scaffolding or hoarding on the public pavement can narrow the walking space and can, unless properly protected, increase the risk of collision with protruding objects.

Where scaffolding is positioned over the public pavement, maintain minimum **2200mm clear headroom** and provide an **overhead platform** to protect pedestrians from falling objects. Do not use cross-bracing below 2200mm, unless it is located well away from the typical line of pedestrian travel. Wherever cross-bracing is used, provide a **tapping rail** or board, positioned 250mm above the footway surface, to enable visually impaired people using long canes or guide dogs to detect the presence of the cross-bracing.

Highlight all scaffolding members
below 2200mm in contrasting colour

Highlight hoarding with 150mm high
contrasting colour bands every 700-800mm

No projecting parts below 2200mm
and avoid sharp edges

Provide adequate lighting

Doors not to open onto pavement

Fix notice with name and address of contractor
and local authority

Minimum clear height of 2200mm

Minimum clear width 1500mm

Provide a 250mm high tapping rail or board

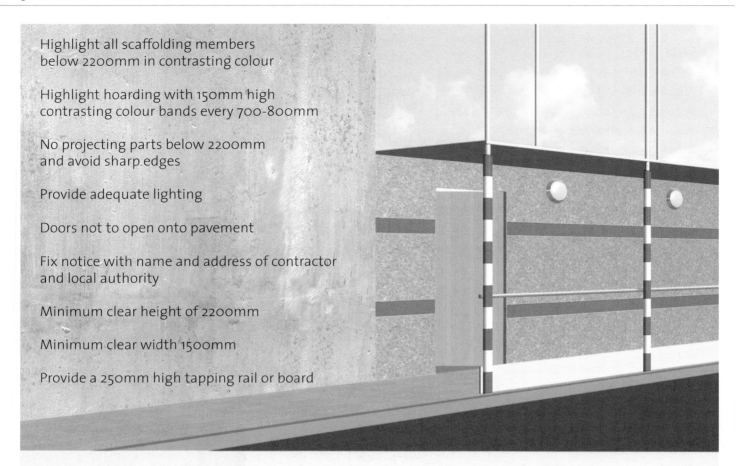

Where hoarding obstructs pavement:

Erect walkway minimum 1500mm wide and
flush with the pavement

Provide continuous 1000mm high handrail
and 250mm high tapping rail as shown

Highlight hoarding with 150mm high
contrasting colour bands every 700-800mm

No projecting parts below 2200mm
and avoid sharp edges

Provide adequate lighting

Doors not to open onto pavement

Fix notice with name and address of
contractor and local authority

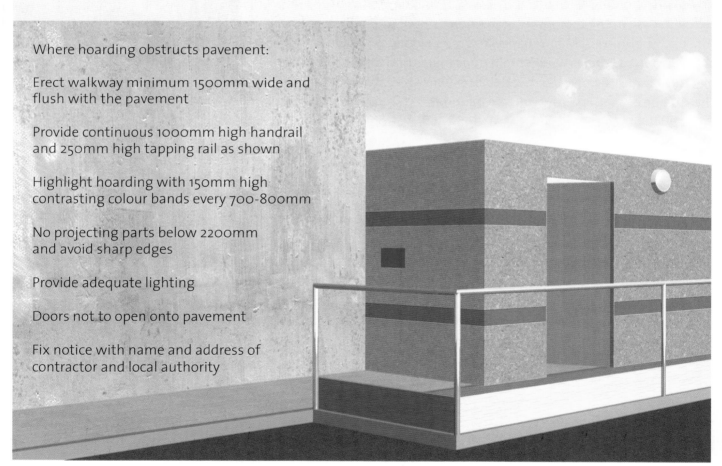

figure 14   **Scaffolding and temporary works**

Highlight all scaffolding below 2200mm in a contrasting colour or tone to aid detection by partially sighted people. Scaffolding should contrast in colour with the background against which it is seen, for example, light against dark or vice versa. Alternatively, use black and yellow tape or red and white pole sleeves. Scaffolding should preferably be enclosed within a hoarding. The hoarding should have no protruding parts, sharp edges or outward opening doors and be well illuminated during darkness.

Where a hoarding is erected on the footpath, and passage is restricted, maintain an **1800mm unobstructed width** in busy pedestrian areas (minimum 1200mm in less populated areas) to enable wheelchair users or people with guide dogs to pass safely. Protruding parts such as poles should be sleeved or boxed in. **Highlight hoardings** with a contrasting colour/tone band, dark on light or vice versa. The band should be at least 150mm deep and positioned 1400–1600mm above ground level and repeated at 700–800mm intervals.

Provide a continuous **handrail** at about 900–1000mm over ground level to enable visually impaired pedestrians to find a safe route through scaffolding and to locate any public entrance. If it is not practical to provide a safe route through the scaffolding, provide an alternative route. If pedestrians are diverted onto the roadway, the pedestrian route should be separated from the traffic and any site vehicles or equipment by a physical barrier on either side.

The name and address of the scaffolding company and of the authority which granted the hoarding licence should be clearly displayed.

Checklist
Construction sites
- If public areas adjoin construction sites, protect them with a hoarding.
- Maintain 2200mm headroom for scaffolding in trafficked areas.
- Hoardings should contrast in colour with their surroundings and be illuminated at night.
- Sleeve scaffolding poles bearing off the ground.
- Maintain 1800mm pathway and provide handrail to guide along any obstruction.
- Provide rigid colour-contrasting barrier at the site of any pavement or services maintenance work.
- Display name and address of contractor and of authority granting roadway repair or hoarding licence.

5.5.3   Maintenance of pavements and roadways

Work on pavements and roadways, such as the renewal of surfaces, of buried cables or pipework etc, can be small in extent and duration, but still present a hazard to passers-by, especially to people with visual impairments or using wheelchairs. Protection must be provided, ideally with a **1100mm high rigid hoarding**, in a colour which contrasts with the surroundings, and which would resist toppling when walked into. Next best is the erection of close mesh, semi-rigid plastic netting, provided that it is properly secured. This can, however, cause difficulties for people with visual impairments, as a long cane can catch in the netting.

Part three

Buildings

Building design 6

6.1   Principles

Circulation throughout a building should be as simple as possible. The journey from pavement or car park, right through to a specific room, should be easy to follow and negotiate. This principle applies to all space en-route, including the car park or pavement, the site itself, the entrance and reception areas, corridors, stairs, lifts, toilets and specific rooms. It must be assumed that not all users of a particular building will be familiar with its layout.

Circulation areas should be spacious and well lit. They should be well defined and differentiated from work spaces or waiting areas. Floor markings, screens, colours and finishes of floors, walls and ceilings, along with different lighting patterns, will assist users in recognising distinct areas and in orientating themselves within the building. Clear and comprehensive signage at appropriate points throughout the building will assist people in locating specific areas or facilities. Similarly, doors and doorways should be of adequate dimension and easily identified, approached and operated.

Each storey of a building should be designed so as to allow independent access and circulation by people with disabilities. Changes of level within a storey should be avoided if at all possible. Where this is not possible in an existing building, necessitating the incorporation of a ramp, passenger lift or platform lift, the new element should be of adequate dimension and detail, and located so as not to discriminate against someone who may be forced to use it.

Buildings should be managed properly, so that circulation areas are not used as storage areas, thereby reducing clear widths.

6.2   Entrances

Every building entrance should be **easy to locate**. The route to the entrance should be free of hazards such as changes in level, poorly located street or garden furniture and branches or balconies overhanging less than 2200mm above the pavement. Doors and windows should not open out onto pavements or circulation routes, ● section 5.1.4.

The entrance should be clearly distinguishable from the rest of the building. The door itself should contrast in colour from the surrounding structure. For people with visual impairments, a change in surface texture in the pavement will signal the entrance. Audio clues, such as a small fountain or rustling plants, will also assist. Artificial lighting can highlight the entrance to a building and make it more obvious at night-time for everyone, but especially for those with impaired vision.

Provide generously-sized doorways, ● sections 6.3 and 6.6, and ensure that doors and their closing mechanisms do not require undue force to operate. Revolving doors are not suitable for use by disabled people. Door furniture should be easy to use, ● section 8.4. Intercom systems should incorporate visual indicators, such as a video monitor or flashing light, in order to facilitate people with hearing difficulties, ● section 7.6. Door furniture and intercoms should be located at an appropriate height,
 ● section 8.4.

Where **underground car parking** is provided, both the lift access and the principal entry to the building from that storey should be accessible from the car park. The principles outlined above should apply to the route from the car to the entrances and lifts, ● section 5.4.3.

In new buildings, the **principal entrance** or entrances must be fully accessible to all. It is not acceptable that people with disabilities should be required to use a secondary entrance. Secondary entrances should, in any case, be fully accessible.

In existing buildings, site constraints may make it difficult to provide independent access for people with physical disabilities to the main entrance. All possibilities, including technical solutions such as platform lifts, ● section 6.7.5, should be considered in these circumstances. It may, however, be necessary to use a secondary entrance as the principal access for people with disabilities. If this is the case, the secondary entrance should be used for general access and not just for wheelchair users.

It is never acceptable that a service entrance be the sole point of access for people with disabilities. Discrimination of this nature would be unacceptable in respect of any group.

Adequate space is required for a wheelchair user to turn outside a door in the event of the entrance being locked. This is particularly important at the top of ramps and at entrances at the end of long passages. An 1800mm diameter circle inscribes the required space. Where an entrance is at the top of a ramp, it is essential that there is adequate landing space so that a wheelchair user does not have to open a door while trying not to roll back down the ramp, ● section 5.2.1.

Every accessible entrance must incorporate a **flush threshold**. This may necessitate a creative approach to weatherproofing. A recessed entrance, or the provision of a canopy, will do much to facilitate weatherproofing and will also provide protection from rain for those waiting outside. The recess or canopy should be a minimum of 1200mm deep and have clear a head height of 2200–2500mm. Plan recessed doorways to allow a wheelchair user 500mm clear space to approach the door handle. Provision of drainage gullies can significantly reduce water penetration while not inhibiting access.

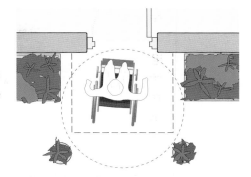

Canopy overhead and
1800mm diameter turning circle

figure 15 **Space outside door**

Checklist
Entrances
- Provide directional signs towards the entrance.
- Make all entrances accessible.
- Where this is not possible in existing buildings, make the principal entrance accessible.
- Avoid making only secondary entrances accessible.
- Provide separate pedestrian and goods entrances.
- Provide adequate lighting.
- Provide a canopy or door recess for people waiting to gain entrance.
- Identify the entrance by structure, colour, sound and/or tactile differentiation of the ground.
- Avoid sharp edges and hazardous projections.
- See guidance on door intercoms, ● section 7.6.

Lobbies with automatic sliding doors

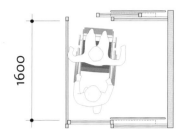
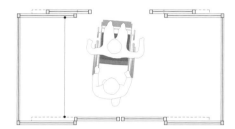

All doors have minimum 800mm clear opening

Lobbies with doors opening in the same direction

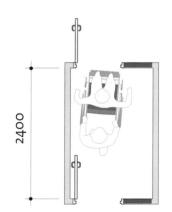
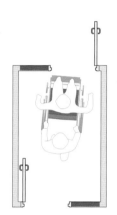
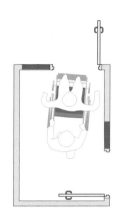
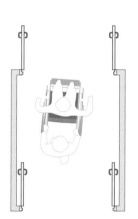

All doors have minimum 800mm clear opening   ▬ 500mm clear space

Lobbies with doors opening in opposite directions

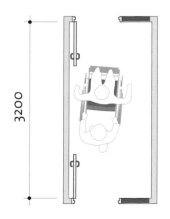
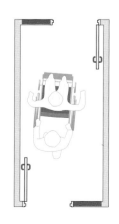
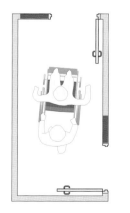
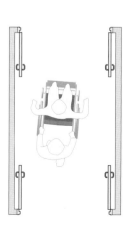

All doors have minimum 800mm clear opening   ▬ 500mm clear space

figure 16 **Lobbies**

6.3   Entrance lobbies

Lobbies should be designed so as to be spacious, with adequate space for wheelchair users to manoeuvre.

Entrance lobbies must be dimensioned in such a way that a wheelchair user and a person assisting them can to move clear of the first door before using the second. This requires a clear dimension between door swings of 1600mm. At the same time, there must be room for another person to pass by in the opposite direction. Matwells should be designed so that the mat is flush with the surrounding floor surface. The mat should not be compressible or have deep pile as this presents a difficulty for people using crutches or wheelchairs. There should be an unobstructed dimension of at least 500mm, minimum 300mm, adjacent to the leading edge of a single door. See opposite for examples of suitable entrance lobbies. For details of doors and doorways, ● section 6.6.

Checklist
Entrance lobbies
- Provide minimum 1600mm long space for wheelchair users to clear one door before approaching the next.
- Where winged doors are used, both sets should open in the same direction.
- Provide 500mm approach to the door handle.
- Avoid matwells projecting over floor level.
- Avoid compressible or deep pile mats or floor finishes.

6.4   Reception areas and waiting rooms

The reception area of a building or floor should be obvious from the point of access. The route to it should be direct and unobstructed. In **public buildings**, facilities for people with disabilities provided in the building should be indicated clearly in the reception area.

The **reception desk** should be placed conspicuously to permit easy location. The desk should be suitable for use from both sides at a height of 1050mm for people standing and 750mm for people sitting down or using a wheelchair.

Floor finishes should be considered in terms of slip resistance and ease of passage for people with impaired mobility. Colour contrast should be used to indicate different areas, ● section 7.2.

Light sources, natural or artificial, should not be sited behind a receptionist. This causes silhouetting, which makes visual communication and lip reading impossible for people with impaired vision or hearing respectively. Ensure that any glazed screens, if required, do not inhibit visual communication.

Lighting generally, whether natural or artificial, should be controllable, in order to provide appropriate levels of light at all times. Light fittings and windows should be located so as to avoid glare and to give uniform spread of light. The provision of blinds, dimmer switches and computer-controlled lighting systems should be considered.

Reception desks should incorporate a counter loop system, ● section 7.6, for communication with hearing aid users. Counter loops should also be used where ambient noise levels or the presence of a security screen makes communication difficult.

Where seating is provided in reception or waiting areas, it should be 450mm high and minimum 455mm wide. Relatively high, stiff-backed chairs are easier to get in and out of. A proportion of chairs should be upright, have armrests and be movable. There should also be adequate free space in the seating layout to accommodate wheelchair users and those with buggies etc.

Queueing systems should have both audio and visual announcements. While a visual signal may be adequate for someone with good vision, it will not inform someone with poor sight. A combined system is preferable.

Wheelchair-accessible toilets should be convenient to the main reception area and other parts of the building frequented by building users.

Adequate signage in reception areas reduces the need for visitors to ask directions. It is particularly important for people with hearing and communication impairments, ● section 8.2.

If public telephones are provided, they should be of a type which facilitates people with impaired hearing, ● section 8.3.

Checklist

Reception areas and waiting rooms

- Reception desk/counter to be placed conspicuously, to permit easy location.
- Desk/counter to be suitable for use from both sides by people both standing and seated.
- Desk to have counter loop fitted for communication with hearing aid users.
- Public telephone to be at height suitable for all users and equipped with inductive coupler, ● section 8.3.
- For external communication, provide a TDD as well a standard telephone, ● section 8.3.
- Select seating for ease of use and comfort.
- Waiting area to have space for wheelchair users.
- Direction signs for people progressing further into the building to be supported by tactile information such as raised print map, Braille information etc, ● section 8.2.2.

6.5   Horizontal circulation

6.5.1   General

Horizontal circulation spaces, whether along corridors or through open plan areas, should be designed for ease of movement. Space requirements vary for different people, depending on their circumstances. The space requirements for a person using a wheelchair are greater than most. As such, they are the most frequently cited and, if adhered to, they will suit everybody else.

While people with disabilities need to have access to all areas of a building, it is nonetheless appropriate, where practicable, to locate the principal spaces in a public building, such as conference or meeting rooms, at the entrance level. This makes things easier for all, both in everyday use and in an emergency, particularly for those with stamina and orientation difficulties.

Circulation routes should be clear of obstacles and have adequate headroom. Where consistent with fire regulations, avoid the use of internal lobbies and minimise the number of door sets along circulation routes.

Windows should not open into circulation areas so as to cause obstruction or to reduce corridor width.

For discussion of finishes to floors and other surfaces, ● sections 7.2 and 7.3.

6.5.2   Internal lobbies

Do not design for lobbies if at all possible. Where essential, internal lobbies should be designed so as to be of optimum size, having particular regard to the requirements of wheelchair users.

Internal lobbies must be of a sufficient dimension to allow a wheelchair user and a person assisting them to move clear of the first door before using the second, minimum 1600mm in length. Another person must also be able to pass in the opposite direction simultaneously. There should be an unobstructed dimension of 500mm, minimum 300mm, adjacent to the leading edge of a single door. For examples of suitable internal lobbies, ■ figure 16. For details on doors and doorways, ● section 6.6.

Checklist

Internal lobbies

- Provide space for wheelchair users to clear one door before approaching the next.
- Both doors should open in the same direction, ● section 6.6.
- Plan to enable a clear 500mm approach to the door handle.
- Door furniture should be easy to use, ● section 8.4.

6.5.3   Corridors

Corridors for general public access should be at least **1800mm wide** to allow two wheelchair users to pass without difficulty. Other corridors must be at least 1200mm wide.

A wheelchair user should never be forced to reverse, as it can be a very difficult manoeuvre, particularly over distance. A turning space is critical at locations such as the top of a ramp, the end of a passageway, in bedrooms, bathrooms and so on.

A corridor must be at least 1500mm wide to permit a wheelchair to make a three point turn. This book, however, recommends turning space of 1800mm as the standard in all but domestic situations. This dimension will facilitate people using all kinds of wheelchair, including powered wheelchairs.

Objects fitted to walls in the range of 700–2200mm over finished floor level must not protrude more than 100mm into circulation spaces, as this will reduce effective circulation space and head clearance and interfere with the requisite dimensions of escape routes. Objects lower than 700mm should not protrude into circulation routes at all, unless they are so low as to start not less than 300mm from the ground.

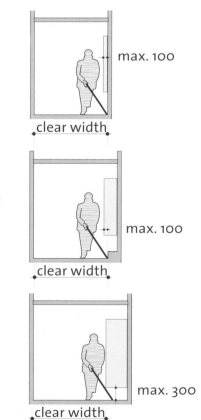

figure 17   **Objects fitted to wall**

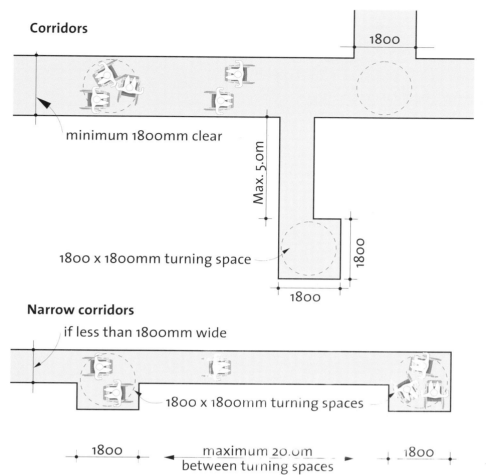

Corridors

1800

minimum 1800mm clear

Max. 5.0m

1800 x 1800mm turning space

1800

1800

Narrow corridors

if less than 1800mm wide

1800 x 1800mm turning spaces

1800

maximum 20.0m
between turning spaces

1800

figure 18 **Corridors**

If a **corridor is over 5.0m long**, and less than 1800mm wide, a **turning bay** 1800 x 1800mm should be provided at each end. On long corridors less than 1800mm wide, a turning bay should be provided every 20.0m. In this situation, the turning bay will also serve as a passing bay.

Handrails assist in support, balance and direction and are essential for people with impaired mobility. Provide handrails on all corridors and seating on corridors over 20.0m long. Where handrails are provided, the clear corridor width should be measured between handrails and not between the walls. Consider the position of radiators in relation to handrails, as some handrails, if they are too close to a radiator, can become too hot to grip.

For details on doors and doorways, ● section 6.6.

Checklist
Corridors
*   Corridors to which the public has access to be at least 1800mm wide.
*   Other corridors to be minimum 1200mm wide, with turning spaces.
*   Provide handrails on all corridors, and seating in those over 20.0m long.
*   Do not allow objects to obtrude more than 100mm into width of corridor.

6.6 Doors

6.6.1 General

It is preferable to have a clear unobstructed space of 500mm at the leading edge of the door, rather than 300mm as has been the practice to date. The extra dimension will allow wheelchair users with limited reach to grasp the door handle far more easily. Vision panels, extending 500–1500mm above floor level, should be provided in all doors where practicable.

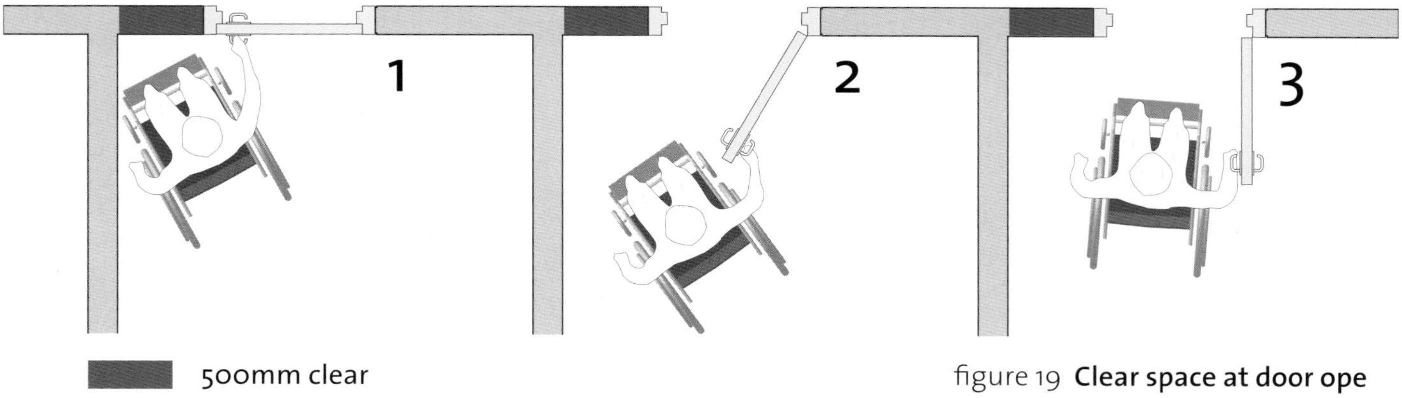
1
2
3
500mm clear

figure 19 **Clear space at door ope**

Many people, particularly those with visual impairments, have difficulty in recognising a see-through door or partition. Where a door or fixed panel is mostly glazed or comprises a single pane of glass, it should be marked permanently within the 1200–1500mm range above floor level, so as to indicate its presence visually. The lower 400mm of such doors or screens should, however, be of a solid material, so as to avoid possible damage from wheelchair footplates. Door furniture and, where fitted, door closers should be suitable for use by people with disabilities, ● section 8.4. Ensure that any surface-mounted door closer or other ironmongery does not inhibit the full opening of the door itself.

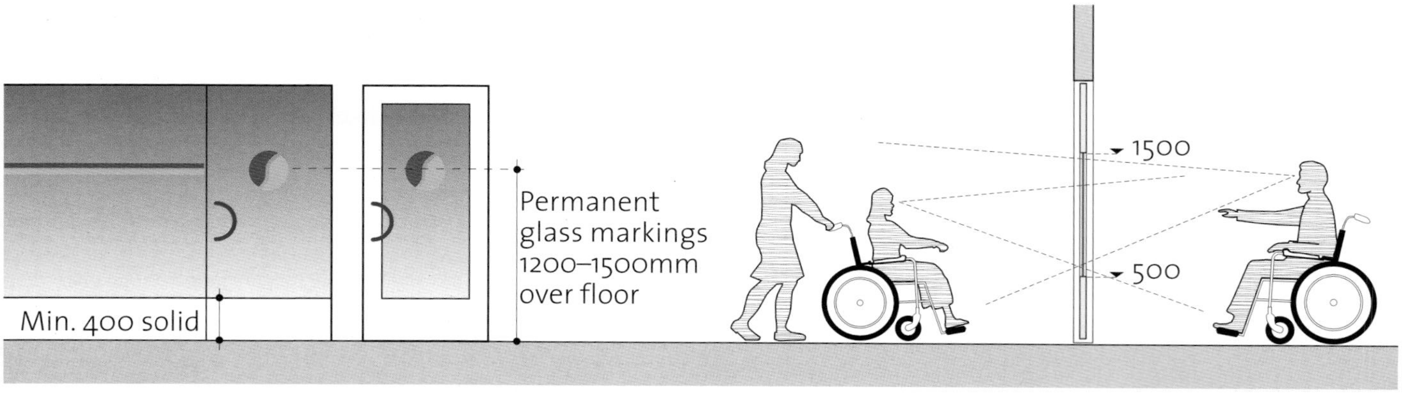
Permanent glass markings 1200–1500mm over floor
Min. 400 solid
1500
500

figure 20 **Marked glazing and vision panels**

6.6.2 Entrance doors

The clear opening width of a door at an entrance to a building must be at least 800mm. Where there are double doors, at least the leading door leaf must have a clear opening width of 800mm.

Revolving doors and turnstiles

Conventional revolving doors present considerable difficulty for many users. They are inaccessible for wheelchair users and can be hazardous to people with visual impairments. Revolving doors should be avoided, in favour of sliding or hinged doors. In existing buildings, revolving doors should be removed.

Turnstiles are not suitable for people with impairments. Accordingly, provide a clearly indicated accessible gate adjacent to the turnstile, ● section 9.9.

Powered doors

Automatic doors make buildings easy to access for everybody, particularly for people with impairments. They are particularly useful where a high force would otherwise be required to open the door, such as a door to a pressurised compartment of a building.

Powered doors can be of sliding or swing type. Sliding doors are preferable to swing doors, as their action is less likely to block users passing through. Such doors should be capable of manual operation in the event of power failure.

Automatic operation: The door opening device should allow adequate time for people who move slowly to pass through. Doors should remain open for more than 3 seconds and require a maximum force of 6.75kg to resist movement. To minimise confusion as people search for opening devices, and to prevent surprise, automatic doors should be indicated as such.

Button control operation: Locate button controls on swing doors at an accessible operation point, clear of the door swing.

Detailing: Powered doors can pose entrapment hazards. Sliding doors can catch a limb or clothing against a stationary surface, while swing doors can have a crushing effect. The danger is lessened by reducing the motive power to the minimum necessary. In addition, sliding doors can be designed to slide into a recess, out of harm's way.

Sensors should be provided to detect people of all shapes and sizes passing through automatic doors to ensure that they do not close onto someone. A continuous beam over the full height of the door will detect all obstructions. Avoid systems which detect obstructions only at specific heights.

6.6.3   Internal doors

While doors and door ironmongery have obvious uses, they can also be obstacles to people with disabilities. Care should be taken not to provide any doors which are surplus to requirements. Doors which are required for reasons of fire safety in circulation areas should, subject to the agreement of the Fire Authority, be fitted with electromagnetic hold-open devices. These will allow the doors to remain open but are linked to the fire alarm system and can be closed automatically in the event of an alarm being raised.

The clear opening of all doors should be at least **800mm**. Ensure that doors open to 90° angle. Where double doors are provided, the leading door should provide this dimension when opened. In thick walls, the door should be located centrally to accommodate the limited reach of wheelchair users.

For advice on circulation areas, ● section 6.5. Except in special circumstances, see below, doors should **open into rooms**. Doors opening outwards into corridors or circulation areas present serious hazards, particularly for visually impaired people. If it is necessary for a door to open outwards for reasons of emergency evacuation, it should be recessed or guarded by a barrier or other device. Doors opening out onto landings should not encroach into an escape route, into a refuge or onto circulation space. Doors opening out onto the landings of ramps should not reduce their effective width, ● section 6.7.3. Doors must not open directly onto ramps.

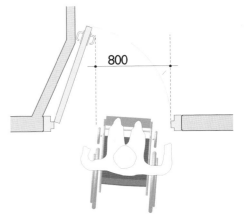

figure 21 **Effective clear width**

Doors opening into a room should be hung so that they open against an **adjoining wall**. In this way, people entering are directed towards the centre of the room rather than to the adjacent wall where, if they are visually impaired, they may collide with obstructions such as furniture, see below. **Door swings** should, if possible, be hinged consistently on the same side throughout a building to facilitate those with impaired vision.

Surface-mounted **door closers** and door handles require sufficient space to facilitate the door leaf to be opened fully, see below.

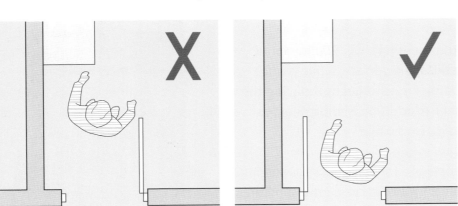

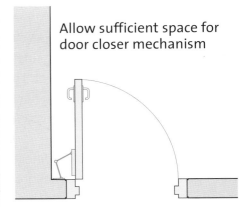

Allow sufficient space for door closer mechanism

figure 22 **Door swing and closer**

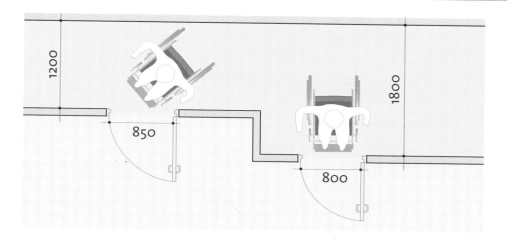

figure 23 **Relationship between clear door ope and corridor width**

It should always be possible for a wheelchair user to approach a door head-on. In existing buildings with corridors less than 1200mm wide, a wheelchair user will have to approach a door obliquely. In this situation, a wider clear door opening will be required. A 1000mm wide door set will provide 850mm clear opening width and, as such, will facilitate wheelchair access from the narrow corridor, see above.

In existing buildings, doors should never be located at the end of a narrow corridor unless the corridor can be made wide enough to allow for the 500mm, minimum 300mm, clear space at the opening side. An 1800 x 1800mm turning space at the end of the corridor will accommodate three accessible doors, see right.

For specific advice on doors to **WC cubicles**, ● section 6.8.

Fire

All **fire-resistant door sets** should, where possible, be kept open using electromagnetic hold-open devices. These are wired in connection with the fire detection and alarm system, and will close automatically in the event of an alarm. Adjust the strength of door closers on escape routes and dividing compartments to the minimum possible consistent with adequate performance.

All doors inaccessible

All doors accessible

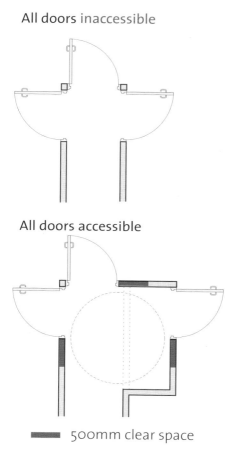

■ 500mm clear space

figure 24 **Turning space**

Checklist

Doorways

Door type selection

- External doors should be readily identifiable, easy to operate and adequate in size (see below).
- Provide glazed panels 900–1500mm over floor/ground in corridor/external doors.

Doorway planning

- Do not install doors unless necessary for functional or safety reasons.
- Provide clear space to door approach where in deep recess.
- Provide 500mm, minimum 300mm, space at leading edge of door for wheelchair user to open door while clear of door swing.
- Hang doors so as to open against an adjacent wall.
- Do not allow doors to open onto ramps or circulation areas.
- Provide alternative unobstructed access beside turnstiles.
- Do not use revolving doors.

Dimensioning

- Minimum clear opening width to be 800mm.
- In double door sets, at least the leading leaf to be 800mm, but preferably both leaves.

Glazed doors

- Mark glazing in doors and screens permanently at 1200–1500mm over floor level.

Powered doors

- Provide powered doors where practicable, particularly where manually-operated doors would be heavy or difficult to open.
- Use presence sensors to detect movement in path of door travel.
- Allow minimum 3 seconds' opening time for automatic doors.
- Provide button controls in accessible location.
- Provide adequate space to accommodate door closing devices to ensure 800mm opening.

6.7   Vertical circulation

6.7.1   General

Vertical circulation is most commonly provided using stairs, escalators, lifts and ramps. Travelators and platform lifts are less common. Equipment such as stair lifts and through floor lifts is sometimes used in adapted housing.

Change of level

Within a storey, avoid changes of level. In existing buildings, where they might be unavoidable, give people the choice of a ramp as well as a stairs. In limited circumstances, a platform lift might be the only solution but this mitigates against independent access.

Difficulty

Most means of vertical circulation are barriers to some degree for most people. Stairs are difficult for people who are pushing buggies, carrying luggage or bulky objects or simply short of breath. Stairs are dangerous for older people who are unsteady on their feet and may have poor grip on the handrail due to arthritis. Even lifts, when they are of inadequate dimensions, can present problems for people carrying large loads, as they may not be able to turn around inside to use the control panel.

Safety

Irrespective of the means of vertical circulation, safety is of paramount importance. Stairs, the most common means, are notorious for causing serious injury, and even death. In many buildings which incorporate lifts, the stairwells might never be used at all in the day-to-day operation of the building. It is essential, however, that the stairs be designed, detailed and maintained in a manner which will ensure their safety for everyone in the event of an emergency.

Provision of lifts

The inclusion of a lift or lifts to all floors within a building, provided in conjunction with flush thresholds, adequate circulation areas and the omission of changes of level within floors, will mean that everyone can access all parts of a building smoothly and independently. While lifts are a requirement under legislation in many cases, it is none the less good practice to provide them even when they are not mandatory. They will make the building more usable for more people, and more adaptable and lettable for different tenants over the lifetime of the building.

6.7.2 Internal stairways

Stairs should be as simple to use and negotiate as possible. They should be as safe as possible for everyone to use. To this end, spiral stairs and stairs with tapered treads should not be used, as they are much more likely to cause tripping, especially for children, older people and people with visual impairments.

Internal stairways should have a clear width between handrails of 1200mm, minimum 1000mm, so as to be suitable for people with disabilities, unless a greater dimension is required by virtue of the number of people using them. The minimum dimension, in any case, should not be reduced by any obstructions. The rise of any one flight must not exceed 1800mm. A half landing should be at least as long as the clear width of the stairs. Maintain a clear headroom of 2200mm in all cases. Visually impaired people who use canes cannot detect obstructions at high level. There is a consequent risk to them and other members of the public hitting their heads against the underside of a stairs. It is essential to provide permanent guarding, detectable by cane, so as to inhibit passage into the space under a stairs where clear head height is reduced below 2200mm. This can be provided by means of railings, planters etc, so long as these in turn do not present a hazard, see opposite.

A tactile warning alerts the building user to the approach to a stairway or change of level. A tactile warning is achieved by providing a readily detectable change of floor covering at the approach to the change of level, e.g corduroy hazard warning, rubberised tiles flush with floor etc. Tactile warnings should be 800mm long in the direction of the flight and should start 400mm from the first step. They should be as wide as the flight itself, see opposite. They are also required on intermediate landings where doorways access the stairway.

A permanent colour contrasting strip should be incorporated into the first and last step of every flight, to assist people with partial sight. The strips should be 50–75mm deep and should extend the full width of the step.

Correct design and detailing of step profile is important. Avoid projecting nosings on steps, as these can cause tripping. Instead, risers can be raked back or simply be square, see opposite. On an existing stairs, a fillet can be fixed to the underside of the nosing to reduce tripping hazard. The ideal tread depth is 280–320mm, which will allow a person to stand and rest with both feet on any step. The optimum riser height is 145mm, maximum 150mm, consistent throughout the flight.

Handrails should be provided on both sides of any stairway and be 45–50mm in diameter, and should contrast in colour with their supporting walls. They should be fixed so as to allow a clear dimension of at least 45mm between the handrail and the supporting wall. The height of the

Tread/riser profiles

15/25   15/25   Add fillets on existing stairs

Optimum tread and riser dimensions are 145mm and 280– 320mm respectively

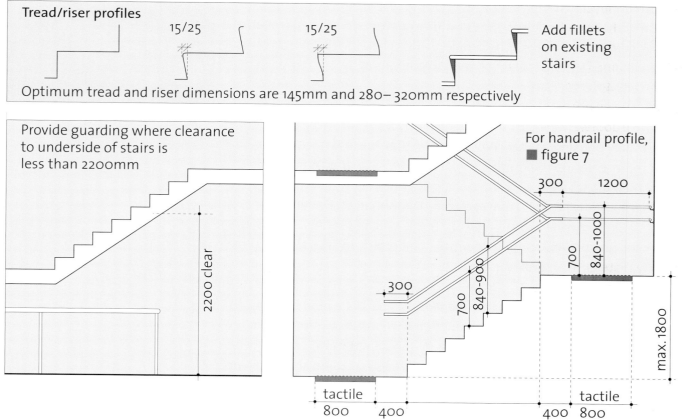

Provide guarding where clearance to underside of stairs is less than 2200mm

2200 clear

For handrail profile, ■ figure 7

300   1200

840-1000

700

max. 1800

300

700   840-900

tactile   tactile
800   400   400   800

figure 25 **Internal stairs**

handrail should be 840–900mm above the pitch line of the steps. A second handrail, 700mm above the pitch line of the steps, is desirable, ■ figure 7. The handrail should be 840–1000mm above any landing and should extend 300mm beyond the first and last step of a flight. Handrails should be continuous around half-landings, unless there are doors leading from them. This will assist someone with a visual impairment, as well as people with impaired mobility.

Access on existing stairs can be improved by fitting new or additional handrails, by providing contrasting adhesive or painted nosings, by fitting non-slip nosings and by the possible provision of additional space on landings by removing cupboards or ducts.

6.7.3   Internal ramps

Ramps can be an effective means of moving up and down within buildings. Ramps which travel from one storey to another are at present generally only found in large public buildings such as museums, airport terminals or shopping centres, as the space required is much greater than for stairs or lifts. Much more common are ramps which accommodate a change in level within a storey of existing buildings. Where either type of ramp is provided, it should only be in conjunction with a stairs as an alternative.

There are many advantages to ramps. A ramp will obviously benefit someone pushing a trolley or buggy or using a wheelchair. They are also effective in evacuating people, as people are less likely to trip than on stairs. Able-bodied people will feel much more confident assisting someone on a ramp than on a stairs.

There are also disadvantages. If the slope of a ramp is too steep, a person with a trolley or using a wheechair may find that the effort required to propel themselves up the ramp is too great. They also may not be able to control their rate of descent! People using crutches or even a walking stick may find themselves a lot less steady on a ramp than on flat ground or even a stairs. Someone using a walking frame will find ramps impossible to negotiate, especially coming down, as their own body weight tends to fall forward over the handles.

If a storey-to-storey ramp is to be considered as part of a new building, it should always be provided in conjunction with a stairway or lift as an alternative. Changes of level within a storey should not form part of a new building's design and therefore the question of a short ramp should never arise.

In an existing building, where there is already a change in level, a short ramp should be considered but, again, only in conjunction with a stairs as an alternative. Where there is insufficient space to provide a ramp, a platform lift may suffice, but only if kept for the exclusive use of people with impairments, ● section 6.7.5.

Ramps should have a maximum gradient of 1:20. Many wheelchair users have great difficulty in pushing themselves up, or controlling their descent, at a steeper gradient.

The clear width for an internal ramp should be 1200mm, minimum 1000mm. Ramps longer than 9.0m must have landings and no section of the ramp should be longer than 9.0m. Note that BS 8300:2001 limits these distances to 6.0m. The landing should be at least as long as the narrowest clear width of the ramp. If a doorway opens onto the landing, there must be at least 1300m between the end of the sloped section and the doorway, ■ figure 7. The top and bottom landings of any ramp, irrespective of its length, should be 1800 x 1800mm.

Passing bays will be required if a ramp is less than 1800mm wide and longer than 20.0m including the landings, just as if it were a corridor. Passing bays should be 1800 x 1800mm and should be located on the flat at intermediate landings. There should be no more than 20.0m between passing bays.

All ramps should have a raised kerb on any open side. Kerbs must be at least 75mm high above the ramp surface.

Handrails should be provided on both sides of the flights and landings. They should be 45–50mm in diameter, spaced 45mm from the wall, 840–900mm above the ramp surface and 840–1000mm above the landing surface. They should extend at least 300mm beyond the ramp onto the top and bottom landings and should be continuous on intermediate landings. Where a handrail terminates, it must have a closed end which turns back onto a supporting wall or, in the case of a handrail on an open side, turns down for 150mm, ■ figure 7. Advice on handrails on stairways also applies to ramps.

A tactile warning, in the form of a corduroy type material or rubberised tiles etc, should be provided in advance of any change in level. It should be the full width of the ramp and should occupy the space 400–1200mm from the ramp.

6.7.4   Passenger lifts

General
Most people find that, given acceptable waiting times, a conventional passenger lift is the most convenient method of travelling between storeys in a building. For people with impaired mobility, a lift might be the only means by which they can access vital facilities within a building.

It makes practical sense to install a passenger lift wherever possible, particularly if life-cycle costing is the criterion used. The lift chosen should serve the greatest number of users. A surprising number of people with mobility difficulties or poor stamina or balance will still choose to climb a stairs rather than enter a lift. For this reason, a lift should always be located adjacent to a stairs, so as to offer an alternative.

Glass-walled lifts can be a source of terror for people suffering from vertigo, who will not use them in any circumstance. A conventional lift should always be provided as an alternative to a glass-walled lift. Platform lifts and wheelchair stair lifts, occasionally installed into existing buildings, have limited use. Lack of familiarity with them, the necessity to get assistance and a wish not to be conspicuous make many people reluctant to use them.

Power failure normally results in lifts not being available for use. An alternative means of exiting, or escape in an emergency, must be provided.

Detail consideration
If a lift car has been correctly dimensioned, it will be much easier to incorporate other details which will improve usability for people with various impairments.

The dimensions of passenger lifts place them in one of four categories for a wheelchair user:
1   a car with sufficient space for a full turning circle
2   three point turn required to exit
3   enter forwards, reverse out
4   inaccessible.

Clearly, the bigger the lift the better, as it allows for flexibility of use, carrying more passengers and permitting independent access. The minimum 1100 x 1400mm lift required by current legislation is of the third type, requiring a wheelchair user to reverse out. A lift car of 1500 x 1500mm would at least allow a wheelchair user or someone pushing a baby buggy or trolley to do a three point turn while inside the lift. It will also leave more room for other passengers. Better still, an 1800 x 1800mm lift will allow full turning without the need for three point turns.

Full turning circle

1800

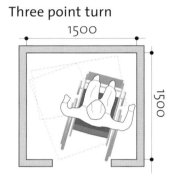

1800

Three point turn

1500

1500

Drive in / reverse out

1100

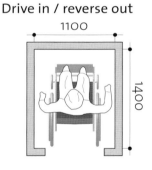

1400

Inaccessible

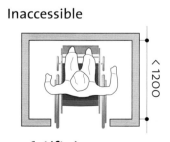

< 1200

figure 26   **Lift sizes**

Landings

Clear space to be minimum
1800 x 1800mm, with a suitable
tactile floor covering

Floor numbers to be indicated
visually and in a tactile manner

Lift car

Preferred car size – 1800 x 1800mm

Lift doors to have minimum 800mm
clear opening

Continuous handrail on 3 sides to
be 900mm over floor

Locate all controls minimum 500mm
from internal corners and
900–1200mm over floor level

Emergency telephone

Half-height mirror on rear wall

Visual and audible indication of floor

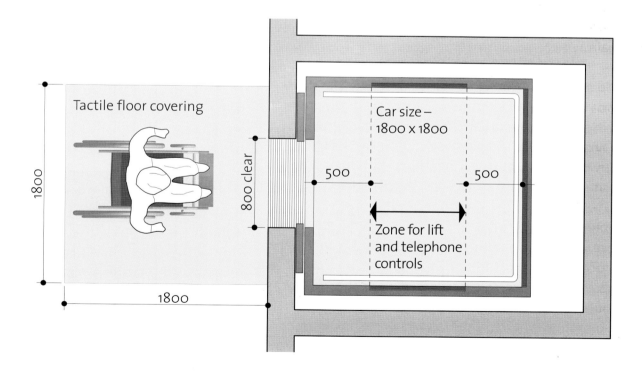

figure 27 **Lift detailing**

All lifts, of whichever category, require the installation of a **half-height mirror** on the wall opposite the door, to allow someone to see what is behind if they need to reverse out, ■ figure 27.

The **landing** and **car controls** should be **500mm**, from any adjacent wall or projecting surface, 900–1200mm from floor level and with minimum 900mm clear approach in front. Locate control buttons in a contrasting colour surround, well spaced and, ideally, facing upwards at a 45° angle. The numbers should be raised minimum 1.5mm from the button face and be minimum 15mm high.

On **landings**, there should be a clear space of 1800mm square, minimum 1500mm, outside the lift door. This should be marked with a tactile floor covering. Floor numbers should be indicated both visually and in a tactile manner. Large raised relief characters and Braille text is ideal. If it is not possible to use both, only raised relief characters should be provided, ● section 8.2.2. The lift signalling system should provide **both visual and audible confirmation** on each landing that the lift is answering a call, and that it has arrived. A gong on each landing will provide sufficient audible notice.

Inside the lift, an announcement on arrival should state the appropriate floor and that the doors are opening, and then repeat the floor of arrival. It should then state the next direction of travel and that the doors are about to close.

Handrails at 900mm above floor level should be provided on three sides, ■ figure 27, and should follow the advice on handrails generally, ● section 6.7.3.

Lift doors should have a minimum 800mm clear opening. Doors should stay open for a minimum of 8 seconds. Doors should stay open longer in lifts where a significant proportion of the people using them are elderly or have disabilities. Provide a 'rapid close' button and a 'hold open' button in the lift car. There should also be a 'hold open' button on landings which should hold the door open for 30 seconds. Doors requiring manual operation should be avoided.

Various door opening mechanisms are available which will re-open the door in the event of an obstruction. Curtain-type sensors on the leading edge of the door can be hazardous or frightening, as they require physical contact in order to be activated. An **array of photoelectric cells** over the full height of the door is much better, as it can detect the presence of an interruption without physical contact and can make the door stay open or re-open automatically. A single photoelectric cell is dangerous as it will detect obstruction only at one level. It has been known to happen

that someone entered a lift car and the doors closed, only to find that their child or dog on the end of the lead was still standing on the landing!

The **emergency telephone** is an important component of the lift car. The phone should be obvious and readily retrievable. It should be suitable for use by people with impaired hearing, ● section 8.3. Place the telephone so that the handset base is 900–1200mm over floor level, and positioned 500mm from corners. Mark the cabinet clearly and position the door so that it does not obstruct access to the telephone when open. Avoid sharp edges to the door and provide a handle which is operable by people with impaired grip. Provide a sign on the door with the words 'emergency telephone' in minimum 20mm high lettering, red upper and lower case on white background, with a minimum 100mm high telephone symbol. Instructions for use of the telephone should be in minimum 10mm high lettering, sited on the inside of the cabinet door or on the telephone itself.

Once lifted from the cradle, the telephone should indicate automatically which lift, if there is more than one, is the source of the call, and then allow two-way conversation. Avoid telephones which require dialling unless the building does not have a control room. Some emergency telephones will signal an alarm when the door of the cabinet is opened. If this is the case, provide a notice to that effect.

Checklist
Lifts
- If at all possible, lift cars to be 1800 x 1800mm.
- Landing and car controls to be 900–1200mm above floor level.
- Controls to be 500mm from internal corners, with visual and tactile indication.
- Car floor level indicators to be visual and audible.
- Controls to permit adequate time to enter and leave lift.
- Provide handrails in lift car.
- Lift telephone to have hard of hearing facility.
- Provide a half-height mirror on the car wall opposite the entry doors.

6.7.5   Platform lifts

Powered lifting platforms, commonly known as platform lifts, can be used in existing buildings where there is a need to accommodate an existing change of level within a storey. Their use should be restricted to people with disabilities. They should only ever be considered as a last resort where no other solution is possible, as their use inevitably attracts spectators, putting an uncomfortable spotlight on the person using them.

Platform lifts should not encroach on escape routes and should be installed with the agreement of the Fire Authority. Some types of platform lift have a standby power unit to permit use in the event of power failure or in an emergency evacuation. Assign trained personnel to operate the lift in an emergency and post a step-by-step notice of the procedure beside the lift.

Externally, platform lifts may be used to access basement areas or raised ground floor levels of existing buildings. They should never be used at entrances to new buildings in place of a ramp. When selecting a lift for external use, consider ease of use and maintenance and the risk of vandalism. Use of external lifts can be controlled by a lock or combination number, or from inside the building via an intercom, ● section 7.6.

For safety it is important to equip the platform lift with gates which lock automatically during transit. Platform lifts designed for transporting goods are not suitable for personal use.

BS 6440: 1983 limits the vertical travel distance of platform lifts without enclosing sides to 1980mm.

Checklist
Platform lifts
*   If a ramp is unfeasible, provide platform lift at a change of level within a storey in an existing building.
*   Ensure that fire safety is not compromised by any installation.
*   Provide an unobstructed space of at least 1800 x 1800mm at the landings.
*   Platform to be minimum 800 x 1100mm.
*   Controls at the landings and on the platform to be 900–1200mm above floor level and platform level, and 500mm, minimum 300mm, from any adjacent wall or obstruction.
*   Platform to return automatically to lower level and allow egress in event of power failure or emergency.
*   Provide stairs as alternative.
*   Check operation regularly.

6.7.6   Stair lifts

A **stair lift** is a motorised unit which travels along a track following the risers on a stairs. They are intended for use only in domestic situations. There are three main types of stair lift. Not all types will suit all users.

- Seated stair lifts, where the user sits on a seat while resting their feet on a footrest.
- Perching stair lifts, with a small platform on which the user stands, perhaps resting on a small, high ledge.
- Platform stair lifts, with a platform large enough to carry a wheelchair.

Seated and perching stair lifts cannot accommodate wheelchairs, and are therefore intended only for ambulant disabled people who have difficulty climbing stairs. They are never suitable for use by the general public, but might be appropriate in limited circumstances in an existing workplace to accommodate a particular member of staff.

Platform stair lifts (not to be confused with powered lifting platforms, ● section 6.7.5) will accommodate a wheelchair. They might be acceptable outside of domestic situations, but only in an existing building in which there are no other alternatives are possible, for example in an existing small two-storey shop, to provide access to the upper level for wheelchair users.

If any type of stair lift is installed in a building to which the public has access, the **effective clear width of the stairs must not be compromised by the stair lift or the track**. When the unit is folded, all parts must be recessed out of the circulation route, and any exposed edges padded, so that people are less likely to bump into the platform or catch their clothing on sharp edges. A powered lifting platform, ● section 6.7.5, is a preferable solution, as it is does not interfere with the stairs.

Checklist
Stair lifts
- Install stair lifts to travel between storeys in very limited circumstances where the installation of a passenger lift is impracticable.
- Platform to be 800 x 1100mm to accommodate a wheelchair.
- Platform to be powered so as to revert to its folded position when not in use.
- Platform to return automatically to lower landing in event of power failure or emergency.
- Fixed controls at both landings to be easily identifiable and positioned at 900–1200mm over floor level.
- Check operation regularly.

6.7.7   Escalators and travelators

Escalators make travel between storeys easy for many building users. However, they are not suitable for some people, such as people with buggies or wheelchair users, and they present difficulties for people with balance problems. Dogs, including guide dogs, are not permitted on escalators because of the danger of entrapment. Accordingly, an escalator is not suitable as a sole means of access to a storey and a stairs, ramp and/or a lift must also be provided.

Where an escalator is used as the principal means of access, signs should direct people to alternative means of access. Provide an 800mm long advance tactile warning at entry points similar to that on stairs, ● section 6.7.2. Handrail support is essential at entry and exit points, to finish 840–900mm over pitch line.

Travelators (powered moving pathways), frequently installed for general use where long internal horizontal distances are to be travelled, are hazardous for people who are unsteady on their feet. People using crutches cannot use travelators. Accordingly, always provide an alternative route in conjunction with a travelator. Provide advance tactile warning at entry and exit points and signs to direct clearly to alternatives. Handrail support is essential at entry and exit points, to finish 840–900mm over floor level. The maximum travelator gradient should be 12 degrees.

6.7.8   Through floor lifts

Through floor lifts are not suitable for use in public buildings and are restricted to domestic use, ● section 9.11.2.

6.8   Toilets

6.8.1   General

Toilet spaces are notorious for being poorly designed in terms of their dimensions, detail design and fittings. Toilets are often given the minimum space possible, so as to maximise other parts of a building. Many **designers are simply not aware** of the issues involved in providing adequate and usable toilet spaces. Great care needs to be given to toilet design so as to minimise the difficulties many people will have in using them.

Toilets at present generally fall into three categories, except in particular building types where specific provisions might be made. The first are the standard 'ladies and gents' toilet blocks, which comprise of rows of cubicles, wash hand basins and urinals as appropriate. The second is similar to the first but one or more of the cubicles will be designed for **ambulant disabled** people. The third is the **wheelchair accessible** toilet, which is

generally unisex and accessed separately from other sanitary accommodation. Do not assume that providing a wheelchair accessible toilet
allows all other toilets in the building to be minimum size and to be
shoehorned into the most awkward spaces

Plan all toilets to facilitate the needs of a full range of possible users. Take
into account people's varying levels of ability to manoeuvre. This ability
is affected by many things, including body weight, overall health, use of
a walking stick, poor vision, limited reach, arm strength, or whether
someone is simply carrying parcels or minding small children. Personal
preference and levels of ability will influence how individuals will access
a toilet. As such, layouts need to be flexible to accommodate different
use patterns. Many people will need more space than the bare
minimum, to allow them to get in with their shopping bags, briefcase etc,
and close the door behind them.

Sanitary fittings should be free of sharp edges and the background colour
should contrast with the fittings. For additional advice on sanitary fittings
in housing, ● section 9.11.2.

The Technical Guidance to the Building Regulations describes a wheelchair
accessible layout which is broadly acceptable but does not suit everybody.
Many wheelchair accessible toilets, while they might comply with the
required dimensions, fall seriously short in terms of setting out of fittings
within the cubicle. The most common fault, which is rarely rectifiable, is
that the door is put on the long side of the cubicle, and not the short side
as indicated in all guidance on the matter. This has a seriously limiting
effect on how a wheelchair user can use such a facility. Grabrails, wash
hand basins and hand dryers are commonly positioned wrongly, thereby
limiting the number of people who can actually use them. It costs nothing
to set these out correctly in the first place.

6.8.2   Provision and siting

Toilets should be located where they can be reached conveniently by both
wheelchair users and ambulant disabled people, with accessible toilets
being located in the same general area as other toilets. The shortest
accessible route should be clearly signposted. To facilitate people with
impaired mobility, the travel distance from anywhere within a building
to the nearest toilet should be no more than 40.0m. Lobbies should be
omitted, except where specifically required by the Building Regulations.

The number of WC cubicles required in a building will be dictated by the
nature and size of the building and the number of people to be accommodated. All buildings to which the public has access should have a
wheelchair accessible toilet on all floors. If this cannot be achieved,

wheelchair accessible toilets must be located so that they are never more than one floor away, with access to that floor available via an accessible lift. In existing buildings which have no lift to their upper floors, wheelchair accessible toilets and toilets for ambulant disabled people should be sited at entrance level. Where a building only requires one or two toilets, they should be unisex, with at least one of them being wheelchair accessible. Where occupancy demands more than two, there should be at least one unisex wheelchair accessible toilet, in association with the required number of ladies and gents toilets. Where occupancy exceeds 100 people, a second unisex wheelchair accessible toilet should be provided. Additional provision may be required depending on location or the nature of the building.

All buildings or parts of buildings open to the public must have at least one unisex wheelchair accessible toilet, approached separately from other sanitary accommodation.

6.8.3   Standard ladies and gents toilet blocks

A clear space of at least 1200 x 1200mm should be provided outside both the toilet lobby door, if any, and the cubicle door. Any lobby should conform to the guidelines in this book, ● section 6.3.

Cubicles should be sufficiently sized so as to allow someone to enter and close the door behind them with ease. It is not acceptable that they might have to squeeze in between the toilet and the cubicle wall, so as to clear a path for the door swing. Cubicle doors should have a lever door handle and a locking device which is easy to grasp. Doors should open inwards and should have a pivot hinge set and removable door stops. At least one in six cubicles should be suitable for ambulant disabled people, ● section 6.8.4.

Cubicle doors should not open outwards, as they may be a hazard to someone outside the door. In existing buildings where no other solution is available, an outward opening door may be unavoidable. If this is the case, hang the door to open against a perpendicular wall, to minimise risk of collision with those passing, ● section 6.6. If an outward opening door has to be fitted, provide an additional pull handle to enable it to be closed with ease, ● section 6.8.5.

The WC pan should finish 395–410mm over floor level, so as to be suitable for most users. In buildings with a high occupancy of small children, a lower height may be used. The flush control on the cistern should be a lever or spatula type.

Washbasins should finish 750–900mm over floor level. Where feasible, provide a choice of heights within this range, so as to accommodate children and people of different heights. Lever taps offer ease of use,

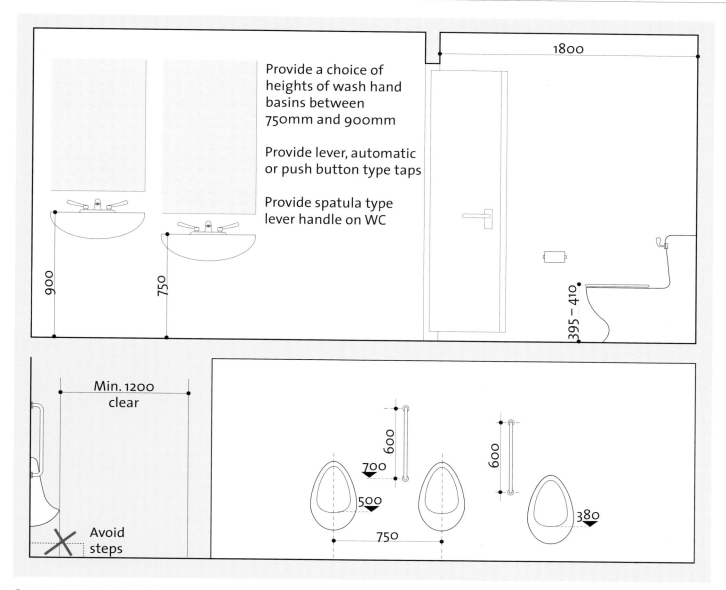

figure 28 **Standard ladies and gents**

especially for people with poor grip or arthritic hands. Push-button and automatic taps are also available.

Urinals should be stall type or wall-hung bowls, at minimum 750mm centres, with no step leading up to them. Urinal troughs should never be used, as visually impaired people often run their hands along walls to orient themselves and so may encounter the unprotected surface. In a row of urinals, place one in six at a lower height, 380mm over finished floor, instead of the standard 500mm. Provide grab rails located between pairs of urinals, to allow both left and right hand support. Provide minimum 750 x 1200mm clear space in front of urinals to permit a forward approach.

Earthing connections to pipework should not project so as to cause an obstruction or personal injury.

Checklist

Standard toilet blocks

- Clear space of 1200 x 1200mm outside all lobby and cubicle doors.
- One in six cubicles to be suitable for ambulant disabled people, ● section 6.8.4.
- Cubicle doors to open inwards.
- WC pan seat to be 395–410mm over floor.
- Washbasins to finish 750–900mm over floor.
- Taps to be lever type or automatic.
- Urinals to have 750 x 1200mm clear approach.
- One in six urinals to be 380mm over floor.

6.8.4   Accessible cubicles for ambulant disabled people

These toilets are suitable for people who are unsteady on their feet or who have difficulty with balance. They are generally located within the ladies and gents toilet blocks, and are essentially a larger than average cubicle with grab rails on the walls, essential for many ambulant disabled people.

Given the small additional space requirements of such a cubicle, serious consideration should be given to designing and fitting out all cubicles to this standard. If this is not possible, **at least one in six cubicles** should be suitable for ambulant disabled people.

The cubicle should be 900mm wide and 1800mm long, with an inward opening door, offering a clear opening of 800mm. The door itself should be fitted with lift-off hinges. If, in exceptional circumstances in existing buildings, there is insufficient space for an 1800mm long cubicle, a 1500mm cubicle may be used, but only if it can have an outward opening door. In such cases, the door must open against an adjacent wall, so as to prevent collision with people outside, ● section 6.6.

The **WC pan** should finish at 395–410mm over floor level. The cistern should be enclosed at either low or high level. WC flush handles should be spatula-shaped, requiring the minimum of pressure to operate. Automatic and push-button cisterns are also available.

Horizontal and vertical **grab rails**, 600mm long and 35mm in diameter, should be provided on both sides of the pan. The horizontal rail should be fixed 700mm over floor level and should start 200mm from the leading edge of the pan. The vertical rail should be at the end of the horizontal rails, ■ figure 29.

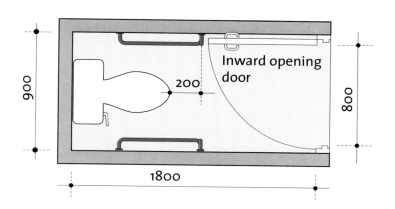
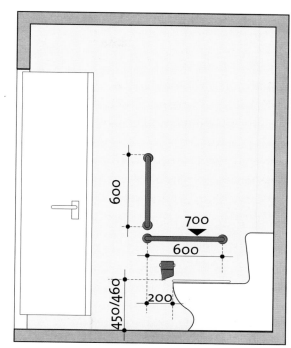

figure 29   **Toilet for ambulant disabled people**

Checklist
Toilets for ambulant disabled people

- 900mm wide and 1800mm long.
- Horizontal and vertical grab rails on both sides of pan.
- Standard pan – seat at 395–410mm over floor.

6.8.5   Wheelchair accessible toilets

General

These are toilets designed specifically for people who use wheelchairs. They are essentially large cubicles containing the full range of facilities found in any other toilet block, with some additional features such as grab rail support. The correct setting out of all the components of these toilets is crucial to ensure that everything is within reach from the seated position on the WC.

Wheelchair accessible toilets are often provided as unisex facilities, accessed independently of other sanitary accommodation. In such situations, an approach lobby should never be incorporated unless required by regulation for separation from areas where food is prepared or consumed. Unisex toilets should not be located where they are in view of the public, such as opposite a lift.

Wheelchair accessible toilets are used by ordinary people carrying out normal bodily functions. They do not need to look and feel clinical. They do not have to be white. Fixtures and fittings do not have to be metallic and shiny. Contrasting colours in finishes and components should be used to ensure that people with visual impairments will be able to locate all the facilities within the toilet.

Wheelchair users need space to approach, enter the toilet and close the door behind them. Inside the toilet, enough space is needed to manoeuvre the wheelchair to the selected position so as to transfer onto the toilet. The transfer method used may be lateral, frontal, oblique or pivotal, ■ figure 31. Many people do not need the help of another person in using the toilet and can transfer with the support of suitably positioned grab rails. The toilet should be adequately sized to accommodate both a wheelchair user and an assistant if necessary. 2700 x 1500mm is the preferred size indicated below, which is in excess of that often provided, ■ figure 30.

The cubicle door should have a horizontal pull handle, 400mm long and 35mm diameter, fixed 1000mm above floor level. This will assist closure of the door in the confined space.

In exceptional circumstances where space is limited in existing buildings, a sliding door may be used to maintain the recommended dimensions of an accessible WC facility. A single leaf straight sliding door should be used with a minimum clear opening width of 800mm. Projecting D handles should be fixed to both sides of the door. Tracks should be recessed into the floor.

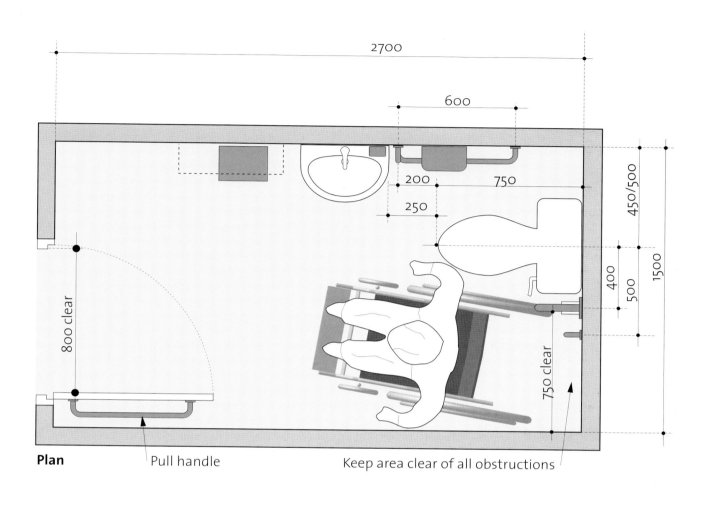

Plan

Pull handle

Keep area clear of all obstructions

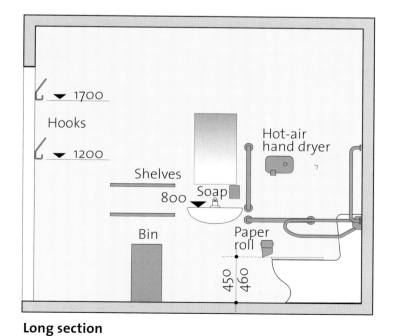

Long section

Hooks

Shelves

Soap

Bin

Paper roll

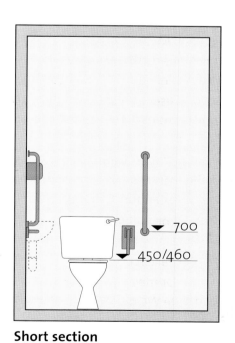

Short section

figure 30 **Wheelchair accessible toilet**

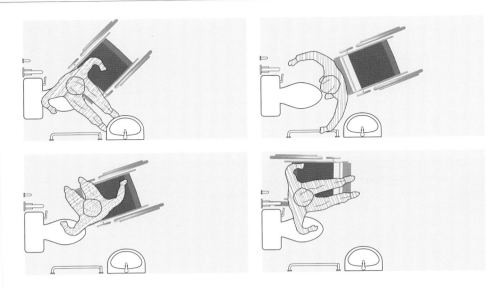

figure 31 **Transfer methods**

Each wheelchair accessible toilet should be indicated outside as such by a suitable sign, ● section 8.2.3.

Detail consideration
Where more than one unisex toilet is provided in the same building, hand the layouts to ensure that those who require a left-hand or right-hand transfer are facilitated.

A clear space of 750mm is required between the pan and the adjacent wall to position a wheelchair beside the WC. Ensure this dimension is not reduced by obstructions such as skirting boards, pipes or radiators. This dimension is of critical importance for transfer purposes and is frequently compromised in practice, rendering the cubicle unusable by the people it is intended to accommodate. Similarly, cisterns should never be boxed in, as this also reduces the transfer space significantly.

The front of the WC pan should be 750mm from the back wall to allow a wheelchair user to transfer from a position forward of the wheels. If the pan is not far enough forward from the wall, the transfer will have to be made over the wheel, with consequent risk of injury. It is vital that this dimension is not reduced by pipes or any other obstruction in front of or on the rear wall.

The pan itself should be wide enough to allow the user to wipe themselves while sitting on the bowl. It should be a robust floor-mounted pan rather than one fixed to the wall. The seat should be strong, fitted with effective stabilisers and fixed rigidly to the pan to cater for the variety of transfers.

The shape of the pan should allow toe space under the bowl to facilitate people effecting frontal transfer and male users.

Some trade literature indicates WC pans specially designed for disabled people, finishing at 510mm high overall. These pans are designed to facilitate specific groups, such as people with arthritis, and are not suitable for general use. The correct seat height for wheelchair accessible toilets is 450–460mm, and units of this dimension are available from most manufacturers. Alternatively, a standard pan may be used in conjunction with a plinth to finish 450–460mm high. Take care that the plinth is flush with the pan base and does not project beyond it.

The **centre line** of the pan should be 450–500mm from the side wall of the toilet. This permits use of the horizontal grab rail for lateral transfer and achieves the correct distance in relation to the washbasin, ■ figure 30.

Grab rails should be provided on the rear and side walls of the toilet. On the **rear wall**, provide a **folding horizontal grab rail** and a **vertical grab rail**, 400 and 500mm respectively from centreline of WC. Both should start 700mm over floor level. On the **side wall**, provide **two 600mm long grab rails**. One should be horizontal, 700mm over floor level, starting 200mm from the rear wall. The second should be vertical, starting 800mm above floor level, and 200mm from the leading edge of the WC pan. The combination of these grab rails will give support and stability to people transferring from a wheelchair to the WC and to those standing to dress themselves or use the basin. All grab rails should be 35mm diameter and extend 600mm. Secure fixings are essential to support the full body weight of a wheelchair user.

The **cistern lid** of low-level or close-coupled WCs should be securely fixed, as they are often used as a back support. Some types are easily displaced or broken during use of the toilet. High-level cisterns are best where assistance in toileting is required, ● section 6.8.6. Always provide a backrest where high-level or mid-level cisterns are used.

The **flush handle** should be spatula-shaped to facilitate people with impaired grip. It should be located on the transfer side, so as to be within reach once the person is back in the wheelchair.

Toilet paper dispensers should be within reach while sitting on the WC pan. The dispenser should be suitable for single-handed use and have a pull/lock mechanism to cut the roll at the required length. Large industrial dispensers are not satisfactory as the roll may get trapped inside the dispenser and be difficult to access. For this reason, individual toilet roll holders are preferable.

The **wash hand basin** should be 250mm from the leading edge of the WC. The tap should be on the side away from the WC or in the middle. This will ensure that the tap and sink are usable while sitting on the WC. Basin height should be 800mm from floor to rim. Basin dimension should be 450 x 300mm approximately. Care is needed in siting larger basins, as they may intrude on the circulation space around the WC pan. Provide a plug that is easy to use.

Provide a **single mixer tap** with lever operation for ease of use. Automatic infra-red and push-button taps may also be considered, although some confusion will be experienced until these are more commonly found.

Soap dispensers should have pull levers to dispense the soap, rather than push buttons.

Hand dryers, whether hand towels or hot air dryers, should be easy to use and reach while sitting on the WC pan. Site hand dryers with the underside 1100mm over floor level and 600mm from internal corners. To minimise obstruction, use a slim line type, to project maximum 130mm from the wall.

The **mirror** over the sink should start 900–1000mm above floor level and finish 1600–1800mm above floor level.

A **shelf** is useful. It should be 750–1000mm over floor level, sited clear of manoeuvring space, such as in the corner beside the door.

Provide a **sealed waste container** located at the side of the basin away from the WC.

Provide **coat hooks** at both 1200mm and 1700mm over floor level, so as to suit both ambulant people and wheelchair users.

Provide an **alarm** to summon help. Install the alarm so that it can be used in the area where transfer from wheelchair to toilet takes place. For details on alarm types, ● section 7.9.

The **floor** should be covered with slip-resistant material. A drainage gulley is desirable, with a slight fall on the floor towards the gulley.

A **baby-changing facility** is often incorporated in wheelchair accessible toilets. A pull-down changing unit ensures that the service does not impact on the accessibility of the toilet for people with disabilities. Where possible, provide separate accommodation.

In public buildings, where vandalism might be anticipated or where non-disabled people might use a wheelchair accessible toilet, management will need to exercise vigilance to ensure that toilets are available when required by disabled users. The practice of keeping wheelchair accessible toilets locked, with the key kept in another location, should be discouraged unless absolutely essential. Where unavoidable, the universal key system should be used, ● Appendix 1.

Checklist
Wheelchair accessible toilets
- Cubicle to be 1500mm wide and 2700mm long.
- Ensure all dimensions of space and positioning of fittings are strictly adhered to.
- Inward opening door on short side.
- WC seat height 450–460mm.
- Securely fix cistern lids to WCs.
- Provide backrest where high level cisterns are used.
- Use lever type flush handles.
- Avoid split toilet seats.
- Locate flush handle on transfer side in wheelchair accessible WC.
- Rinse basin to be 450mm x 300mm, and 800mm above floor.
- Use single mixer taps with lever or automatic operation.
- Mirrors and coat hooks to be universally accessible.
- Floor finish to be slip-resistant.
- Provide easy-to-use locks.
- Ensure sanitary fittings contrast in colour with the walls.
- Avoid fittings with sharp edges.

6.8.6   Toilets for people who need assistance
A peninsular type toilet is suitable for hospitals, nursing homes and other buildings with a significant occupancy of wheelchair users who need assistance to transfer. The minimum 750mm clear unobstructed width required in the wheelchair accessible toilet should be provided to both sides of the pan. Boxed-in cisterns should be avoided. This allows for either left- or right-handed lateral transfer and for space for an assistant at the same time. The provision of a peninsular type toilet does not preclude the need for the standard wheelchair accessible toilet. People who can use a wheelchair accessible toilet independently may not be able to use a peninsular type without assistance.

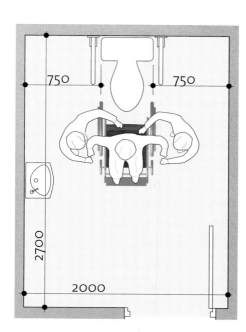

figure 32 **Toilet for people who need assistance**

6.9   Bathrooms and shower rooms

6.9.1   General

Bathing facilities are provided for public use in a range of building types, including guest accommodation, sports buildings, hospitals and some workplaces. Bathrooms can present a myriad of obstacles and hazards to all sorts of users, not least to those who have impairments. By carefully detailing bathroom layouts and correct specification of fittings, the potential difficulties and hazards can be significantly reduced.

In general, if correctly detailed, showers are more accessible and safer than baths. In guest accommodation, at least half of the en-suites in wheelchair accessible rooms should incorporate a level deck shower rather than a bath. In standard rooms, the majority of people use the bath as a shower, and not as a bath. Consideration should therefore be given to fitting a proportion of standard rooms with showers rather than baths, and offering guests a choice.

In bathrooms for general use, provide fittings which suit the broadest range of users. Provide a mirror over each washbasin, to extend from 900 to 1800mm over floor level. This will facilitate people standing or using a wheelchair.

Position towel rails etc at a height to provide access for all: maximum 1300mm over floor level, 1000mm for children. Shelves at different heights, in the range 450–1300mm over finished floor, will satisfy most users.

Switches and controls should be at a readily accessible height of 900–1200mm over finished floor. Hairdryers, shaving sockets and other fittings should also be reachable, with controls which are simple to operate.

Avoid loose mats as they can be a trip hazard.

To ensure that wheelchair users and others can open windows, site opening lights at accessible height. Provide winding or mechanical remote control gear only where this is not possible. Controls for ventilation equipment must also be accessible.

Make sure that all washing facilities in workplaces, including showers and drenches, are usable by people with physical and sensory impairments, at the least making provision to adapt the components as the need arises.

6.9.2   Wheelchair accessible bathrooms

The clear space required for a wheelchair user to transfer into a bath is minimum 1800mm long x 1200mm wide. The person transferring into the bath lowers themselves with the aid of a grab rail. A ledge or platform at the bath end, minimum 400mm long, will facilitate a wheelchair user to effect a two-stage transfer into the bath.

Bath profile should allow the user to slide down gently into the water. People have a tendency to slide down into a long bath until their feet meet the support provided by the bath end, so a 1600mm bath length is preferable to 1700mm. Rim height should be 450mm. Avoid bucket or steep end baths, as these are difficult to enter and exit. A slip-resistant base helps control movement and enhances safety. Built-in slip resistance is prefer-able to loose mats.

Grab rails will facilitate stability. Provide one 500mm long vertical grab rail and one 1200mm long horizontal grab rail, ■ figure 33. This will facil-itate sliding down into the bath from the ledge, as well as getting back up on it. Both grab rails should be 35mm diameter.

Bath taps should be lever type. Taps located centrally on the inner rim of the bath are generally preferred as they do not inhibit access or cause obstruction. If taps are positioned at the end of the bath, provide space there to allow a wheelchair user to get into a position to reach them.

Washbasins, as distinct from rinse basins used in lavatories, should be wider than conventional sizes (c. 500mm) to accommodate face and hair washing. The washbasin should finish 750–800mm over finished floor level, have 700mm knee space and should project 430–450mm from the wall. Adjustable washbasins, which can be varied in height from 750–900mm over finished floor level, suit different users and are ideal. Dimensions apply equally to standard washbasins, to vanity units and built-in basins.

The knee space under the unit should be free of obstructions and should not be boxed in. Pedestals inhibit manoeuvrability and should be avoided. Use brackets instead. Protect water supply pipes if they are exposed to leg or foot contact.

The washbasin should ideally be within reach of the WC. In this situation, take care to maintain adequate toilet transfer space, ● section 6.8.5. Other fittings should be positioned as described in ● section 6.9.1.

Accessible shower room

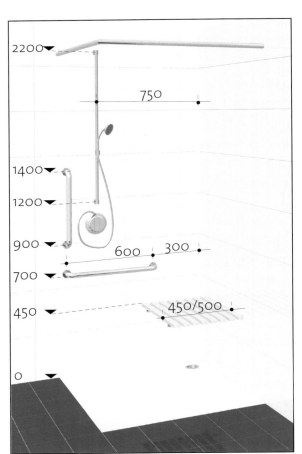

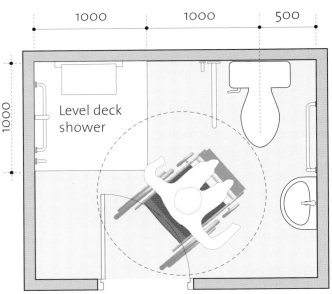

Level deck shower

Provide privacy by means of a curtain rather than rigid doors

All grab rails 35mm diameter

Shower tray to be 1000 x 1000mm and flush with shower room floor

Position lever type controls 900–1200mm above floor

Shower head to be height adjustable

Accessible bathroom

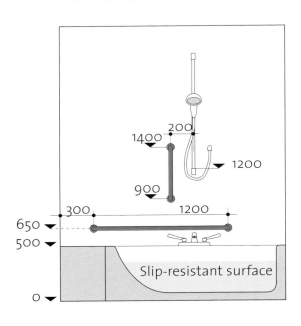

Slip-resistant surface

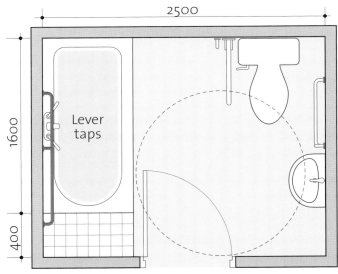

Lever taps

For setout of wash hand basin, toilet and associated grab rails, see figure 30.

figure 33 **Wheelchair accessible bathrooms**

Checklist

Bathrooms

- Provide minimum 400mm wide ledge or platform at the end of the bath.
- Bath to be 1600mm long, 500–550mm high (450mm in wheelchair accessible bathrooms), with built-in slip resistance, sloped end and lever type taps located on inner rim.
- Provide grabrails, ■ figure 33.
- Provide washbasin extending to 430–450mm out from wall, finishing 750–800mm over floor, fitted on brackets, within reach of WC.
- Provide accessible mirror and towel rails.
- Floor finish to be slip-resistant, avoid loose mats.
- Ensure ventilation controls are accessible.
- Provide a level deck shower in place of a bath in wheelchair accessible en-suites.

6.9.3   Wheelchair accessible shower rooms

If a shower or shower room is wheelchair accessible, it will be easier for everyone to use. The main requirement is that the tray should be flush with the floor. This can be achieved in a number of ways:

- full shower room with sloped floor
- level deck shower trays
- recessed shower trays
- shower cubicle with enclosing sides.

The entire shower room can act as the shower compartment, with a slightly sloped waterproof floor finish. A 1:40 slope to a screeded concrete floor runs to a drainage point. Either the entire floor or only the shower area may be sloped. The floor finish can be glazed or unglazed slip-resistant tiles or slip-resistant synthetic sheet.

Level shower trays, suitable for both concrete and timber floors, can be installed without the need for a depression to be formed in the floor slab. The requisite small sloping ridge can be negotiated in a wheelchair. The trays have an integral slope to drain water away. Alternatively, trays are available to be built into a floor recess and finish flush with the surrounding area. A folding shower door or long curtain will form a watertight seal around the tray. Level shower trays are easy to install and maintain and come in a variety of shapes and sizes, ● Appendix 1.

Recessed trays are also available. These are built into the floor, and a proprietary plastic-covered metal grille fits into the recess. The flat strips to the grille top, separated by narrow gaps, permit use with a wheelchair, ● Appendix 1.

A **shower cubicle** is essentially an accessible level tray complete with enclosing side walls and top. The tray, fitted to a level floor, has a low lip or small ramp for wheelchair access and can be fitted with integral corner seat and electric shower with, in many instances, a WC. As it is delivered to the site ready assembled, this type of cubicle is relatively simple to install, ● Appendix 1.

In all shower rooms, tiling or sheet flooring material should be detailed so as to contain the water and to avoid sharp edges or trims. Durability is important.

The shower tray should be **1000 x 1000mm** and, ideally, open on two adjoining sides. A clear transfer area, minimum dimension 1000 x 1400mm for side approach and 1000 x 1200mm for forward approach, is essential.   These transfer areas can be shared with those for a WC.

An unobstructed **turning circle of 1500mm diameter** inside the shower room will allow a three point turn. An 1800mm circle allows full turning.

A **flip-up seat** should be provided on the wall adjoining that with the shower controls. It should be 500mm wide, finishing 450mm over floor level, in a position suitable for easy wheelchair transfer.

Shower curtains are the most convenient method of providing privacy where required, as rigid doors demand space to swing and can be hazardous where people are manoeuvring.

Provide two 35mm diameter **grab rails**. One should be horizontal, 600mm long, sited 700mm over the finished floor level, and the other vertical, from 900–1400mm over finished floor level, ■ figure 33.

The **controls** for temperature and flow rate should be lever type and easy to use. The shower head should be adjustable from 1200–2200mm over floor level. All controls should be easy to read and use and should be positioned 900–1200mm over floor level, ● section 8.5. Thermostatic control is essential to avoid scalding.

A full-length warm air body dryer should be considered. This is a fan which distributes warm air through grilles in a vertical conduit and is particularly useful for people who have difficulty in drying themselves due to restricted movement. It can be located easily within a bathroom or shower room without intrusion on the overall floorspace.

Checklist

Shower rooms and compartments

- Provide clear approach to tray, sized as above.
- Shower trays to be level entry type, minimum 1000 x 1000mm.
- Fix 35mm diameter horizontal grab rails, ■ figure 33.
- Provide suitably adjustable shower head.
- Provide flip-up shower seat.
- Use fabric shower curtains rather than glass doors.
- Floor finish to be slip-resistant.

6.9.4   Improvements to existing showers and bathrooms

Improvements can be made within existing facilities, even where a fully accessible arrangement is impossible to provide. The following features are useful and easily achieved:

- fit grab rails and shower seat
- replace any fixed shower heads with a flexible hose
- replace existing shower trays with flush trays
- fit easily-operated lever taps
- fit easily-operated shower controls, with clearly legible indications of shower settings
- provide a large changing cubicle with wide door or curtain
- provide a full-length warm air body dryer.

Detail design

7

7.1 General

Detail design is a crucial part of good building design. Just as proper detailing will make a particular building feature easy to use, poor detailing can render it unusable. Detailing is a very broad term, covering everything from the selection of wall and floor finishes to the location of light switches. It encompasses window and door ironmongery, colours, signage, power outlets, furniture and machines, ventilation, lighting and communication systems. Without proper detailing, many buildings would simply fail to perform adequately.

Consistency of detail design throughout a building is essential. People should quickly develop a feel for where things are likely to be found. Light switches should always occupy the same position relative to a door frame. Colour and lighting schemes can be used to differentiate areas within a building. **Contrasting colours** of doors and light switches with the background wall will make them easy to find. Door furniture should contrast with the door itself. Signage should be consistent in both design and location throughout the building.

7.2 Floor finishes

The selection criteria for floor finishes include slip resistance, ease of movement, colour, acoustic qualities, durability and ease of maintenance.

Slip resistance is important to people who are unsteady on their feet, particularly those using crutches or walking sticks. Consider the slip resistance of any product under dry and wet conditions.

Movement is generally considered easier across a hard surface than a soft one. Anyone using crutches, or who has difficulty lifting their feet, will be much more likely to trip on a deep pile carpet than a more solid floor covering. Carpet pile should not exceed 12mm. Wheelchairs are often forced in the direction of the weave of deep pile coverings, requiring much greater physical effort on the part of the wheelchair user.

Contrasts in colour and texture of floor coverings can be used creatively to define different areas within a building. People with impaired vision will be **safer** if level changes, borders, doorways, junctions and other significant locations are easy to recognise. The **approach to a flight of stairs** or a ramp should be signalled by a tactile area, such as corduroy hazard warning or rubberised flooring. A **visually contrasting strip** should be provided on the first and last nosing in any flight of stairs, ● section 6.7.2. Corridors or storeys within a building can be differentiated by colour and pattern. Carpet borders and highlighted areas can define particular areas or room entrances. Large swirling patterns, like those found on contemporary rugs, may confuse people and should be avoided. Similarly, highly polished floors will reflect both natural and artificial light, which can be confusing for visually impaired people.

Many people with impaired sight orientate themselves using **audio clues**. Different floor finishes produce different sounds when walked upon. A hard surface set into a carpet could identify a circulation route through a hotel reception area or a strategic point along a corridor. The possibilities are endless and limited only by the designer's understanding and imagination.

Durability of floor coverings should be considered in light of the volume of traffic the area is likely to receive. Fraying edges, loose tiles or boards and poor quality mats will cause tripping and slipping. Floors need to be maintained in a safe condition and should be easily and quickly cleaned in the event of a spillage.

In addition, the effect a floor finish has on indoor air quality should be considered. Research is not at a stage where judgements can be made about the possible effects of synthetic finishes, particularly sheet finishes from a petrochemical base, on people with impaired breathing or allergies. Slip-resistant flooring made from natural materials may be best.

Small changes in level, no matter how insignificant to most ambulant people, should be avoided, as they cause tripping and impede the passage of wheelchairs. A wheelchair user will use momentum to glide over a small bump such as a saddleboard but, if not approached square on, the wheelchair can be jolted and the user tipped out. If, on the other hand, they have to stop first to open the door, the lack of momentum will mean that a much greater force is required to overcome the bump. Knuckles are also at risk if the clear space is confined.

Flush thresholds should be provided at all doors. Saddleboards should be avoided. If, in existing buildings, saddleboards are necessary, the maximum vertical lip should be 6mm, with the total height not exceeding 15mm. Bevel the edges to a maximum gradient of 1:6.

Damp proofing of flush external thresholds can be difficult to achieve. Recessed doorways, overhanging canopies and even external planting can significantly reduce the likelihood of driving rain crossing from outside to in. If the weatherproofing must project above the floor surface, square edges should have a maximum height of 10mm. Any bevelled edges must not exceed 15mm in height.

Mats should be set into a matwell so that the mat surface is flush with the adjoining floor. The mat pile should be maximum 12mm deep. Loose mats should be avoided, as they are notorious for curling at the edges, not lying completely flat and sliding around on certain floor surfaces. Visually impaired people will trip on them if this is the case and others will fall over if the mat slips from underneath them.

Checklist

Floor finishes

- Consider slip resistance, particularly if floor is likely to become wet.
- Consider ease of use for buggies and wheelchairs when selecting pile depth for carpeting; avoid deep pile carpets and coir mats.
- Consider the use of natural materials in relation to the needs of people with impaired breathing.
- Provide flush thresholds internally and externally.
- Detail matwells so that mat pile is maximum 12mm deep and finishes flush with floor generally.
- Avoid loose mats.
- Detail floor finish, colour and texture to highlight room entrances and other significant elements or components.
- Provide colour and texture signals at tops and bottoms of all ramps and flights of stairs.
- Select non-reflective floor finishes.

7.3   Wall and ceiling finishes

As with floor finishes, the wall finishes on similar corridors or storeys within a building can be differentiated by colour to help people to orient themselves. Avoid polished and reflective finishes which are likely to cause glare. Window walls should be pale coloured so as to minimise the glare of the bright window against the surrounding wall. Ceilings should be bright so that both artificial and natural light sources will be reflected and distributed more evenly, ● section 7.5.

Wheelchairs will knock against walls and doors occasionally, particularly in confined spaces. Shield walls from possible damage with wall protecting boards to 400mm above floor level and protect exposed corners where necessary. These measures are often seen in hospital buildings, where there is a high volume of wheelchair traffic.

7.4   Ventilation

Research on indoor air quality indicates that a relatively high air change rate is important for people with impaired breathing. This is particularly true in smoky environments and in spaces using many synthetic materials. Research is not at a stage where precise guidelines can be given. Provision of adequate ventilation can conflict with heat conservation and energy consumption requirements. A heat recovery system might be considered in these cases.

The most acceptable way of achieving ventilation is by provision of **adequate and easily accessible window openings**, positioned so as to avoid draughts. This gives the user complete control. Windows must not open into circulation spaces as they cause obstruction and reduce effective width. Provide ready access to opening lights.

Otherwise, buildings must have mechanical ventilation or air-conditioning. If this is the case, the system must be maintained so as to achieve acceptable standards of filtration and dust extraction. Fans are often used on a hot day but noise and air turbulence associated with them can be disturbing, particularly if dust maintenance is not to the highest standard. Localised air extract systems should be installed in any smoky environment, as many people find smoke-filled air unacceptable.

7.5   Lighting and power

7.5.1   Lighting
Light is essential in the perception of space and colour. Older people generally need more light than the young to distinguish shape, colour and texture. Good light facilitates lip-reading and can make the difference between independence and disability for some people with visual impairments. Colour contrast between surfaces can be enhanced or obliterated by light. In the wrong place, light can cause glare, washing the colour from surfaces, while inadequate light makes visual differentiation impossible.

Do not position sources of natural or artificial light at the ends of corridors or behind people at reception areas or counters. Such light sources place people in silhouette, which creates difficulties both for people who lip read and for visually impaired people who cannot identify the proximity of oncoming people or objects.

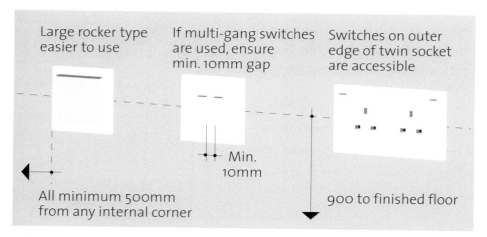

Large rocker type easier to use

If multi-gang switches are used, ensure min. 10mm gap

Switches on outer edge of twin socket are accessible

Min. 10mm

All minimum 500mm from any internal corner

900 to finished floor

figure 34 **Light switches and sockets**

Avoid design which causes excessive **shadows** on walls and floors, particularly if there is a change of level. Adequate artificial lighting should be provided at the top and bottom of each flight of stairs, so as to minimise the shadows cast on treads and risers. Shadows can be confusing and dangerous for people with impaired vision.

Position all light sources, including windows, roof lights and artificial lights, to **distribute light evenly** throughout rooms. White window frames and surrounds will assist in throwing light deeper into a room. Walls and roof light coffers near natural light sources should also be pale coloured, as dark surfaces adjacent to bright light sources can cause glare and eye fatigue. In **corridors**, comfortable lighting can be achieved by fixing light fittings in a line down the centre of the corridor. Fluorescent fittings fitted transversely across a corridor are not satisfactory.

Give careful consideration to the direction of natural and artificial light in **workspaces**, so as to avoid glare and silhouetting. People who work at computers often have this difficulty.

Many tasks have optimum **light levels**. Too much light can cause discomfort, while too little will be inadequate. Design which permits **flexibility and control of intensity is ideal**. The design of a lighting system will depend very much on the nature and use of a particular space. Natural light can be controlled using blinds or louvres. In **deep plan environments** where background lighting is provided by artificial means, provide local lighting and task lighting which can be controlled by individuals. This approach will be more energy efficient than simply providing a high degree of illumination over large areas. Dimmer switches might be appropriate in some locations. Passive infra-red sensors can be used to increase light levels automatically.

Lighting controls should be easy to operate. Wall-mounted switches should be fixed 900–1200mm over floor level, minimum 500mm from internal corners. The switch housing, wall and rocker should contrast with each other in colour. Large rocker-type light switches are the easiest to operate. Avoid multi-gang switches and switches which require twist operation. Consider passive infra-red light switching which obviates the need for manual dexterity.

Consistency in relationship between fixtures helps everybody. For example, light switches should be at a consistent height and proximity in relation to door handles.

In **accessible bedroom accommodation**, it is essential that users can control lights from the bed. This can be done by additional two- or three-way switching reachable from the bed, remote control operation or press-cable control switches. Pull-cord controls should be capable of operation without gripping or clasping. Avoid trailing cables and lamps with switches beside the bulbs.

The **colour temperature** of artificial lighting should match that of daylight where possible. The true reproduction of colour will assist people with impaired vision.

Do not use strobe lighting as this can induce seizures in some people with epilepsy.

Select light fittings for the particular function, with diffusers and shades as required. Fittings without diffusers can cause reflections more readily than those with diffusers. Some types of fluorescent lighting (but not high frequency lamps) interfere with hearing aids on the 'T' setting used in conjunction with induction loops.

External lighting at the approach to a building should define the entrance clearly. Reduce glare by concealing light fittings so that only the light, and not the light source, will be visible. The intensity of artificial lighting outside should be balanced with that inside, so that people experience a gradual change on entering or exiting a building. In addition, the output from light fittings should be appropriate so as to illuminate the way, rather than to dazzle people.

7.5.2   Power

Cables, such as incoming mains and parts of equipment emanating **electromagnetic fields**, can interfere with the use of hearing aids. They should be sited away from areas where hearing is important, such as telephones, reception areas, meeting and consulting rooms.

Locate all power outlets and other controls 900–1200mm over floor level, so as to be within reach of wheelchair users. Ideally, they should be 500mm from internal corners. They should always contrast in colour with the background wall on which they are mounted.

If **switched twin socket** outlets are installed, for ease of use ensure that the switches are on the outside of the unit, rather than between the two plug tops, ■ figure 34.

Checklist

Lighting and power

- Use light to express texture, colour and shape.
- Select appropriate light intensities for specific tasks.
- Position light sources to maximise distribution, minimise glare and avoid shadows.
- Plan stairwell and step lighting to avoid shadows.
- Avoid light sources which put building users in silhouette.
- Provide lighting controls to permit variation in light intensity.
- Provide blinds to permit control of natural light.
- Provide dimmer controls for artificial lighting.
- Controls should be easy to operate and located in accessible positions.

7.6   Communication

All buildings should be designed and equipped so as to facilitate adequate communication. Careful consideration should be given to every aspect of communication: the door intercom, the public address system, reception desk, meeting rooms etc.

Door intercoms should be at an appropriate level to accommodate people standing and people using wheelchairs. The controls should be in the range of 1000–1200mm over ground level. The microphone should be capable of picking up voices in the 900–1600mm range. A large, easily operated bell push facilitates those with poor hand function. The most suitable door bell is one which gives a visual indication of its operation, such as a light which flashes when the button is pressed. A video intercom will allow visual identification of a visitor, prior to opening the door. A deaf visitor will also benefit from such a system.

Public address should be made using a combined visual and audible system. The spoken message can be augmented by lighted numerals, LED messages or flashing lights, depending on the circumstances, to facilitate people with impaired hearing.

To facilitate most people with impaired hearing, a signal about 20dB louder than that received by other people is needed. This amplified sound level is achieved by using either an induction loop or an infra-red communication system. People with varying degrees of hearing impairment use hearing aids, lip-reading and sign language. Adequate detailing of a building, and the presence of staff with knowledge of sign language, is of great assistance to many.

Induction loop systems consist of a sound pick-up device, an amplifier and a loop. The loop is an insulated wire, disposed around an area, within which the signal can then be received by a personal hearing aid. The amplifier can be connected to a sound source such as a television, a radio or a microphone and the sound received is amplified and transmitted through the loop. When the hearing aid user is within or close to the loop area, the hearing aid picks up the transmitted signal and converts this into sound. This facilitates comfortable listening, ensuring that hearing aid users receive the desired sound clearly, without the amplification of background or incidental noise.

The area served by the loop may be a complete room, such as a boardroom, or part of an area, such as a particular range of seats in a cinema or theatre. Loops can be installed within the building structure, within the floor or on top of the floor surface. They should be protected by a non-metallic enclosure such as a PVC conduit. The loop should be sited very carefully, avoiding metal objects and anything which emits a magnetic field. Pay particular attention to reinforcing bars, metal-framed seating, computer monitors, digital cordless telephone systems, fluorescent lighting, lighting dimmers or electrical transformer equipment, all of which may affect the quality of the signal adversely .

Loop systems should be installed in all public buildings, especially where there are likely to be other conflicting noises nearby. Meeting rooms, areas of public performance, reception areas and many other busy areas will all be more usable if an induction loop is installed. Provide counter loops in ticket offices, customer service and information counters and also in confessionals and banks where privacy is required. A portable loop can be an acceptable alternative to a fixed induction loop in areas such as small meeting rooms.

Upon installation, loop systems should be commissioned with a number of people with impaired hearing so as to adjust to the optimum frequency. Places where induction loops have been installed should be indicated by appropriate signs, ● section 8.2.3.

Lip-reading and sign language are only feasible within a 15.0m range of the speaker and require particularly good lighting. To facilitate people who use both lip-reading and a communication aid, ensure that at least part of the loop system is located within 15.0m of the speaker.

Infra-red communication systems use a transmitter which relays signals capable of being received by headphones. They have the advantage of high quality sound reception and the avoidance of over-spill to adjacent spaces. The systems can be portable or fixed. Portable receivers resemble a small radio, with communication via headphones. Bench-fitted types require headphones to be plugged into a socket provided. They cannot, however, be used in conjunction with hearing aids unless an additional receiver is fitted. They are most commonly used where multi-lingual communication is required. They can be used in theatres and concert halls, where the headphones can be collected from and returned to a cloakroom attendant. Their disadvantage, in many circumstances, is that a sole user will be very conspicuous and people will often prefer to struggle to hear rather than choose to use the system.

Checklist

Communication systems

- Install induction and counter loops in all public buildings, especially in auditoria, meeting rooms, ticket offices, areas requiring confidentiality and where glazed screens affect communication.
- Provide appropriate signs to indicate installation of induction and counter loops.
- Make portable loops available for areas without permanent loop systems.
- Ensure that at least part of any loop system is located within 15.0m of the person speaking.
- Consider infra-red communication systems in theatres and concert halls.
- Locate doorbell controls 900–1200mm over finished ground level.
- Use large bell pushes, supplemented by light to indicate use.
- Use combined visual/audible public address and queueing systems.

7.7   Heating and hot water

7.7.1   Space heating

Optimum room temperature varies from one person to another. People who sit at desks will feel cold sooner than people who are moving around. People with impaired mobility may be particularly affected in this way. On the other hand, some people are susceptible to heat stress and care must be taken that room temperature is not set too high. As with ventilation and lighting, adequate control and flexibility should be provided to try to suit as many people as possible.

People with poor heat register can burn themselves without realising it. Low temperature radiators should be provided where the occupancy is likely to include older people and young children.

7.7.2 Hot water delivery

In public buildings, the temperature of hot water in washbasins should be restricted to no more than 43°C and should be thermostatically controlled in showers. People with poor heat register are likely to be scalded if water is too hot. The same is true for people with impaired movement, who may not be able to react quickly when scalding water issues from a tap or shower head.

Signs alerting people as to how to control water temperature properly are helpful, particularly in hotel bedrooms, sports centres and the like. Shower heads should be adjustable, to permit direction of the water away from the body in the event of a sudden change in water flow or temperature.

7.8 Automated teller machines and ticket dispensers

Machines for dispensing money, tickets or small goods should be accessible and, where possible, should be located on the same level as the adjacent floor or pavement.

The approach to dispensers should be clear and unobstructed, and at least 900mm wide. The clear area immediately in front of the machine should be at least 1800 x 1800mm, to allow a wheelchair user to approach the controls sideways, and to turn around after use. An area of this dimension also affords an element of privacy at ATMs if the queue starts outside the area.

A canopy, extending minimum 1200mm from the building face, should be fitted over any external machine, to offer some protection from the rain. The canopy should be fixed not less than 2200mm above ground, so as not to cause an overhead obstruction.

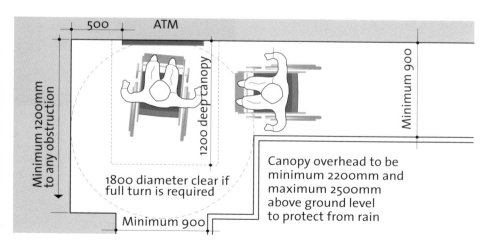

figure 35　**ATM**

Control pads should be located on the flat, but should be tilted up by 15 degrees and be not more than 150mm from the leading edge of the machine. They should be at a height of 780–1080mm above ground or floor level.

Keys on pads should be 15 x 15mm, and at 18.2mm centres. Numeric keypads should follow the same layout as a telephone rather than a calculator. Numerals should be 10mm high and contrast with the key. A raised pip on the '5' key assists orientation for people who are visually impaired. Keys should be matt finished, and lighting should be arranged so as to avoid any reflections.

Screens should be 750–1250mm above the ground, and tilted 55–70° from horizontal. Screens should be 230mm wide and 250mm high to accommodate 18 point text.

Instructions for use of machines should be clear and easily legible, minimum 18 point. Where machines involve reading screen text, the speed of text flow should be such as to allow time to pause and consider each instruction. There should be good contrast between text and screen backgrounds, and a logical sequence of commands. Screen software for ATMs can be designed so as to recognise individual users and to adjust the size and speed of screen information accordingly.

The way of inserting the card and the order or structure of commands should not be changed without warning, as this will confuse visually impaired customers who are accustomed to the machine.

Card readers should be at a height of 950–1000mm. There should an illuminated bar immediately above the slot, which should flash when a card is inserted or withdrawn. The mouth or lead-in for the card should be wide with a gradual reduction in area up to the intake. When a card is ejected, it should protrude at least 25mm to facilitate grasping.

Card swipes should be fitted so as to be used vertically. Proximity cards, which do not require contact with a card reader, are preferable to swipe cards.

7.9   Alarms

7.9.1   Emergency alarms

Fire detection and alarm systems should be of a type which people with disabilities can operate and which will alert all building occupants as speedily as possible in the event of an emergency. The alarm system should incorporate automatic fire detectors, as well as break glass units which can be operated manually.

The sound level of an alarm must be maintained throughout a building. Alarm signals louder than 120dB should not be used, as they can be painful and induce disorientation. A standard door will reduce sound level by 20–30dB, taking many sounds out of the range of someone with impaired hearing. Alarms often sound much lower in toilets and storage areas by virtue of the separating doors. Accordingly, a larger number of quiet alarms, rather than a few very loud ones, will achieve a more even distribution of the signal and will also make verbal communication easier for everyone during an emergency.

People with a moderate degree of hearing loss will be alerted by an alarm bell if it is within 1000mm range and is set at 65dB, or 75dB if they are asleep. People who are profoundly deaf, however, will not be alerted by such a bell. For them, a visual or tactile indicator, or an alert by personnel, will be required. High intensity beacons should be attached to the general fire alarm system in buildings to which the public have access. Vibrating pagers, activated by designated staff, can be provided to guests of hotels and other residential accommodation who have impaired hearing. These should be used only to supplement, rather than to replace, the visual system.

Careful consideration is needed when selecting alarm devices. Tests will often be necessary before a final decision is made. Very loud alarms can cause severe discomfort, obliterate other sounds used by blind people for orientation (eg. tapping of canes) and can make spoken communication very difficult. Certain flashing light frequencies can cause confusion or even epileptic fits. These problems will be more common where people are very old or confused, and designers and management need to be aware of the particular issues likely to affect them.

In buildings not normally open to the public, a two-stage alarm system might be considered. These have a separate evacuation signal and limited first stage evacuation, to give disabled people the chance to move before the congestion likely to arise in general evacuation. The case for a two-stage alarm, whether or not used in conjunction with phased evacuation, cannot be dictated solely by the needs of disabled people. The most important factor is whether it is safe for all the building occupants to have such a procedure. In practice, however, the structural arrangements recommended for the safety of disabled people are often the same as would support the adoption of two-stage fire alarms and phased evacuation as a matter of course. A fire alarm system to BS 5839: Part 1 will generally be suitable for people with disabilities, but in certain circumstances, additional provisions may be desirable.

Break glass units should be 900–1200mm above finished floor level, 500mm clear of room corners, and be positioned where the adjacent floor is unlikely to be obstructed. A minimum of 900mm wide clear space is necessary to allow a wheelchair user to approach and activate a unit.

Break glass units should be capable of being operated by simple hand, arm or general limb movement. Avoid systems which require the use of keys or dextrous hand movements. The units should be red, easily identifiable, contrasting with their background and located generally near exit points. Consideration should be given to how far people with mobility impairments must travel to reach one. No specific advice can be given in this regard, save to say that more, and not fewer, should be provided in any given building.

7.9.2   Other alarms

Wheelchair accessible toilets and bathrooms should be fitted with an alarm to be activated by the user in the event of emergency. Several types are available:
*   one which activates a light and sound outside the toilet area to attract the attention of passers-by
*   one wired from the toilet to a central control point
*   a radio transmitter type alarm to a central point.

The latter two may have a facility for two-way speech. The alarm should be operable by means of two distinctive push buttons, sited both at 900mm and at 200mm over floor level. A pull cord extending to the ground has been the conventional practice but it is not ideal as it often mistaken for a light switch.

> **Checklist**
> *Fire detection and alarm systems*
> *   In public buildings, supplement the audible alarm by visual indicators.
> *   Consider two-stage alarm system in buildings not normally open to the public.
> *   A larger number of relatively quiet alarms is preferable to a few extremely loud sounders.
> *   Alarms should be fitted in all accessible sanitary accommodation.
> *   Break glass units should be 900–1200mm above finished floor level.
> *   In hotels etc, provide people with impaired hearing with vibrating pagers.

Furniture and fittings 8

8.1 General

Design, selection and location of fittings, furniture and machinery should take account of the diversity of the people who will use them. Good design facilitates all. Whenever possible, select equipment capable of single-handed operation

Finishes should resist dust accumulation and be easily cleaned. Deep pile carpets, heavy curtains and soft furniture, often associated with comfort, can hold large volumes of dust, which can exacerbate breathing difficulties for many people. Particular attention should be given to specification of finishes in areas where people with breathing difficulties might have to sleep or spend long periods of time. Provide a **choice of accommodation** in hotels, with an appropriate proportion of dust-free, smoke-free and regular rooms.

Management of hotel and other accommodation should ensure regular cleaning of surfaces and mattresses, and the selection and replacement of pillows to reduce dust mites. This will facilitate people with asthma and other breathing difficulties and also make the accommodation more pleasant for other guests.

Furniture in public areas should be suitable for all and be free of sharp edges. Relatively high, stiff-backed chairs are easier to get in and out of and provide good back support. In reception areas, a proportion of seating should be upright, have arms and be moveable. Seats should ideally be minimum 455mm wide and finish no less than 450mm over floor level. Siting of loose furniture and fittings should not inhibit manoeuvring through the building.

Tables in restaurants and cafeterias should have legs recessed in from the edge to allow wheelchair users to approach, and should have a clear space of 700mm underneath.

Clothes racks and hanging facilities in shops, hotel bedrooms, theatre foyers and elsewhere should be accessible from a sitting as well as a standing position. Avoid pedestals and high hanging rails. To suit the broadest range of users, site hanging facilities in the range 1200–1700mm above floor level. Provide 900mm unobstructed space in front of racks to permit access for wheelchair users.

Wherever possible, **shelving** should be between 450 and 1300mm from the floor, so as to be within reach for the broad range of users, including wheelchair users.

First aid equipment and other safety provisions should be accessible to all.

Place **first aid fire fighting equipment** so as to be accessible and usable by everyone. The lifting handles of fire extinguishers should be 900–1200mm over finished floor. Provide adequate signage to indicate the location of fire fighting equipment, especially where sightlines are likely to be obstructed. Access to the extinguishers should be unobstructed. If sited on corridors, they should not intrude on the circulation space. Fire hose reels should be located so that they do not traverse and impede escape routes unnecessarily when in use. Avoid the use of heavy fire extinguishers, such as 9 litre water or 5kg CO_2 types.

All fittings, including door furniture, taps, light switches, power points etc, should be easily accessible and located so as to **avoid undue stretching or stooping** by wheelchair users and ambulant disabled people. Select fittings which require only **light pressure** to operate.

8.2   Signs

8.2.1   General

In an unfamiliar building, an adequate number of clearly legible, well-designed signs will help everyone to find their way around and are vital for people with speech or learning difficulties. Signs can indicate direction, alert to hazards or provide information. They can direct to the best and shortest route to a particular part of an environment or building and, on long routes, should also provide confirmation of direction.

Signs should be easily identifiable, clearly legible, distinguishable from their background and consistent in their design. Legibility is helped by using a combination of upper and lower case lettering. Signs with pictorial symbols are easier to understand, especially for people who cannot read or speak English.

Glossy or reflective surfaces can cause glare and confusion. Sign material and lighting should be selected so as not to cause mirroring or dazzling. Signs can be lit directly or from within.

All signs, whether temporary or permanent, should incorporate large letters and conventional symbols which contrast with their background. Signs should also be in Braille or raised lettering wherever possible, so that people with impaired vision can read them by touch. Sign surfaces should be smooth, with rounded edges.

Audio indication can complement signs in places such as shopping malls and supermarkets. Tourist venues, heritage centres and the like can use tape recordings to describe displays and presentations for visually impaired people.

In buildings such as museums, shopping centres, art galleries, hospitals, hotels etc, where visitors may be unfamiliar with their layout, a floorplan should be displayed. This should indicate key spaces, including information areas, sanitary facilities, circulation routes and any other relevant spaces particular to the building. If, however, the building is complex, a trained member of staff should also be available to provide such information.

The effectiveness of signage should be tested by travelling along all the possible routes, and back, while assuming a complete lack of familiarity with the building.

8.2.2   Detailing

Issues to be considered in sign design include:

- **location** for ease of reading or touch
- clarity and consistency of **colour** and **typeface**
- size of **characters**
- adequacy of **lighting**, whether internal or external to the sign
- clarity of **content** in text and symbol
- possibility of conveying information through **touch** as well as vision.

Locate signs where they are clearly visible, in advance of the area for which they inform. Signs indicating the direction to a room or facility should be repeated along the route to provide confirmation along the way. Signs which may require a significant period of time to read should be located where users will not obstruct the passage of others. On circulation routes, they should be in accessible locations, taking into consideration the angle of vision of people standing or using a wheelchair.

There is no 'perfect' dimension over floor level for the siting of signs inside a building. The best height for a wheelchair user may be too low for other people. For close viewing of signs, the optimum band is 1300–1600mm above floor level. Otherwise, signs may be viewed over head height. Those projecting from walls or ceilings should leave a clear height of minimum 2200mm to the floor.

Refuges should be clearly indicated for all building users, as well as for the emergency services. Misuse of refuges as storage areas can have fatal consequences. In this regard, a 'Refuge area – keep clear' sign should be incorporated 1200–1500mm above floor level at the designated space. Another sign should be positioned on the door leading to the refuge area.

Character height on internal signs should be at least 37mm for direction signs, and 25mm for information and identification signs. Characters of these dimensions are legible at up to 5.0m approximately. Externally, they should be 75mm high for direction signs, which will be legible from about 22.0m. If the available viewing distance is shorter, dimensions can be scaled down. **Floor storey numbers** in lift lobbies should be minimum 100mm high, sited 1600mm over floor level. **Pictograms** or logos should be minimum 150 x 150mm.

Direction signs frequently use a combination of arrows and text. On signs dealing with several directions, place text and arrows referring to 'straight ahead' at the top of the sign, with arrows on both sides. For right and left pointing arrows, justify text to the right and left respectively.

Emergency signs for fire escape should be sized to a degree larger than the minimum requirements, as they may need to be followed in smoky conditions or without good lighting.

Raised letters and numerals, and Braille, will facilitate many people with impaired vision. Characters should be raised by 1.5mm, and the stroke should be 1.5–2.0mm wide. Edges of raised characters should be slightly rounded but not half round in section. Engraving is not recommended as it is not legible by touch and can be hard to see.

It should be possible to approach and touch Braille or raised lettering on signs. Place wall-mounted signs to be read by touch at a height of 900–1500mm, maximum 1250mm for children. For clarity, provide only the necessary information on a tactile map or floorplan, omitting all extraneous advice. Represent walls by lines of a standard thickness and doors by gaps in walls.

Characters should be simple and sans serif type. Avoid elaborate typefaces, ● section 9.2.

Notices, whether temporary or permanent, should be in large print (minimum 18pt) and, where possible, also in Braille or raised lettering.

Conventions for colours and shapes of signs to communicate information effectively are as follows.

- Yellow triangles indicate the presence of a potential hazard. The triangle outlines black symbol or text.
- Green rectangular signs indicate safe condition, for example, 'Exit' or 'Push bar to open'. Text should be white on green background or green on white background.
- Red circles indicate prohibition. A red diagonal line through the symbol indicates the prohibition, for example, 'No smoking'.
- Blue circles indicate mandatory action to be taken, for example, 'Keep door shut'. The text of the symbol should be coloured white on the blue ground.

For information signs, pay particular attention to the colour contrast between the lettering, the signboard and the background to the sign. The following table offers guidelines in this regard.

Safety colours and contrasting colours

The meaning of Safety Colours, with some examples, is as follows:

Red — Prohibition

- stop signs
- emergency shutdown devices
- prohibition signs
- this colour is also used to identify fire-fighting equipment

Yellow — Caution

- identification of dangers (fire, explosion, possible danger, radiation, chemical hazard etc.)
- identification of steps, dangerous passages, obstacles

Green — No danger   First aid

- identification of emergency routes
- emergency exits
- safety showers
- first aid stations and rescue points

Blue — Mandatory signs

- obligation to wear individual safety equipment
- information
- location of telephone

Blue counts as a safety colour only when used in conjunction with a symbol or words on a mandatory sign or information sign bearing instructions relating to technical prevention.

Text and symbols should be in colours which contrast with the background safety colour.

Text Colour	Symbol Colour		
White	■	■	■
Black	■	■	■
White	□	□	□
White	□	□	□

Background	Sign board	Legend
Dark colour masonry	White	Black, dark green, dark blue
Vegetation	White	Black, dark green, dark blue
Light masonry/white wall	Black/dark	White/yellow

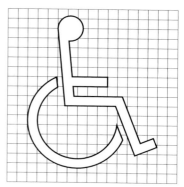

8.2.3 Symbols

Symbols should be of a type universally accepted and recognisable, clear and easily distinguishable. Avoid complex or personalised symbols, particularly when the information to be conveyed is of a functional nature, for example, location of toilets, lifts, exits. Pictorial symbols are readily understood.

Three internationally recognised disability symbols advertise the availability of facilities for different groups of people:

- accessibility
- access for people with hearing loss
- TDD symbol.

The international symbol of accessibility, used at a particular facility, for example, parking, indicates that the particular facility is for the exclusive use of people with disabilities. The symbol is also used to differentiate between facilities and services which are accessible to people with mobility disabilities and those which are not, for example, toilets.

The international symbol of access for hearing loss is used where systems are installed to facilitate people with impaired hearing, ● sections 2.2 and 7.6.

The international TDD symbol is used where text telephones are provided, ● section 8.3.

Checklist

Signs

- Signs to be legible by both sight and touch where appropriate.
- Site signs to avoid obstruction or reduced headroom.
- Position signs where the reader will not obstruct traffic flow.
- Use conventional sizes, colours and shapes.
- Position room numbers and names on the wall adjacent to the door handle.
- Provide for comfortable reading positions: tilt sign where necessary.
- Provide symbols to indicate services available for particular groups with disabilities.

8.3   Telephones

To facilitate as many people as possible, telephones should be 900–1200mm above finished floor level.

All telephones should have an induction coupler in the handset. It is essential that those for public use, and those used to summon help, such as in refuges or lift cars, have this facility. They are easily provided in new telephones and can be fitted retrospectively in existing telephones. The device permits people with hearing aids to use a telephone efficiently. The appropriate logo should be used to indicate availability, ● section 8.2.3.

Telephones should be readily detectable by use of contrasting colour. For particular requirements for telephones for emergency use, ● section 6.7.4.

Conventional push button telephones have a small raised dot on the 'five button' to facilitate use by people with impaired vision. To facilitate wheelchair users, coin or card slots should be between 900 and 1200mm off the ground. This can be increased to 1350mm for sideways reach. Coin and card slots should be funnel type, so as to facilitate people with impaired hand function, ● section 7.8.

Telephones which are laid on a table top or desk, rather than wall-mounted, should have sufficient cord to allow a wheelchair user to pick up the whole unit and see the digits.

Provide volume controls for people with impaired hearing, so they can adjust the sound to 12-18dB(A) above the standard levels. This facility should be provided on all public telephones, with its provision indicated by a suitable sign, ● section 8.2.3.

A telephone device for the deaf (TDD), also referred to as a text phone or a minicom, is a keyboard linked to a telephone. A message can be typed in and received by a similar device at the other end. The telephones of public service organisations, including hospitals, Garda stations, health centres, bus and train stations, hotels and road recovery services, should have TDDs. Private companies will also find them useful.

The device is inexpensive. To use a TDD on a telephone line shared with other devices (standard telephone or fax, for example) a network manager is available at low cost. Where a text phone is provided, staff should be trained in its use.

A seat beside a telephone will facilitate people wishing to sit during use. The seat can be a folding or flip-up type, so that it doesn't obstruct access.

Checklist

Telephones
- Ensure all telephones have a hard of hearing facility.
- Place telephones 900–1200mm above finished floor level.
- Ensure colour contrast with surroundings.
- Install TDDs in all public service buildings.

8.4   Door furniture

Careful selection of door furniture is important in ensuring accessibility for people with impaired grip or mobility. Door hardware which requires manual operation should be of a shape which does not require tight grasping or twisting of the wrist. Lever handles are much easier to use than circular knobs. Hardware should contrast in colour from the background. Keyholes should be located above the handle, rather than below, to facilitate people with impaired vision.

Automatic and power-assisted door opening devices are ideal, particularly when doors are heavy or difficult to open, ● section 6.6.2.

Hardware requiring operation should be 900–1100mm over floor level. In some cases where child safety is a concern, it may be acceptable to locate the handles higher, out of the reach of children. Vertical pull handles should be minimum 250mm long, with the lower end 900mm over floor level. Finger plates should extend 1000–1350mm over floor level.

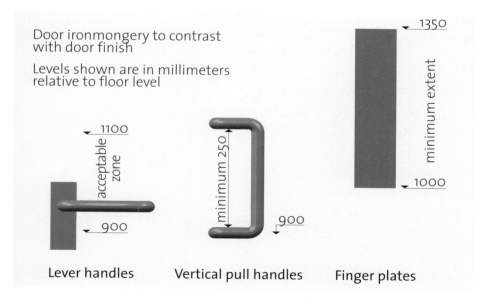

Door ironmongery to contrast with door finish

Levels shown are in millimeters relative to floor level

1100
acceptable zone
900

minimum 250
900

1350
minimum extent
1000

Lever handles   **Vertical pull handles**   **Finger plates**

figure 36   **Door furniture**

Hardware on emergency exit doors should be capable of easy operation for people with impaired grip. Mechanisms which demand a lifting/pushing motion are hard to use. Direct push operation is better.

Where kick plates are provided to protect against damage to door finishes (desirable where there is a significant occupancy of wheelchair users) these should extend to the full door width and 400mm up from the door base.

With respect to door closers, a door is considered 'heavy' if, when it is pushed by someone using a wheelchair, it resists opening, and the person in the wheelchair moves backwards. Where heavy doors are used, or where a self-closing device is fitted, resistance to opening should not exceed 12Nm pressure. Delayed-action door closers assist accessibility by making continued pressure against the door unnecessary as the person passes through.

Site letter boxes 900mm over ground level to facilitate use without bending, and provide a level approach minimum 900mm wide. For more discussion on doors at entrances, ● section 6.6.2.

Where an existing doorset is too narrow for wheelchair access, and where it is impossible to widen the opening, the clear ope width can sometimes be increased by fitting the door leaf with cranked hinges, to allow it stand open clear of the doorway.

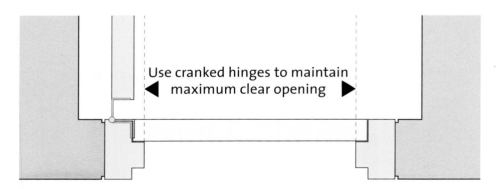

Use cranked hinges to maintain maximum clear opening

figure 37 **Cranked hinges**

Checklist

Door furniture

- Hardware which is to be operated should contrast in colour with door leaf.
- Site door controls at height for both seated and standing users.
- Locate letter boxes 900mm above ground level.
- If a door closer is necessary, ensure it is delayed-action or slow-action type, and operated at maximum 12Nm pressure.
- Use cranked hinges where necessary to achieve requisite opening widths.
- Kick plates, where provided, should be minimum 400mm high.
- Site and dimension pull handles to allow knuckles to clear adjacent frames or leaves.

8.5   Switches and controls

The advice in this book relates to the design of controls for general use, operated on a day-to-day basis by a broad range of people. Controls for specific use, operated by a limited number of people after special training, are outside the scope of this book.

Controls should be **obvious, easy to reach, simple to operate and consistent in design**. They should be easy to grip, turn or twist. Controls and switches should be adequate in size and contrast in colour with their background. When used for similar operations in the same location, control panels and switches should function in the same way or sequence.

Height of a control panel may vary, depending on the type of switch used and whether it is associated with a dial or other visual indicator. Switches on inclined surfaces are easier to operate than those on vertical surfaces. Controls on a vertical surface should be in the range of 900–1200mm above floor level. Controls on a flat surface should be tilted up by 15° and finish 780–1080mm above floor level. All switches and controls should be at least 500mm from any obstruction, such as internal corners. The approach should be at least 900mm wide.

When installing wall-mounted lighting switches in dwellings, provide 20mm deep switch housings in lieu of the usual 10mm, to facilitate possible future installation of remote control switches, ● section 9.11.2.

Colour can be used in many ways. Colour contrast between a switch and the wall can help people to locate the switch. Colour can also be used as a means of detecting the state or function of a single-function switch. For example, red indicates 'stop' or 'off', while green indicates 'go' or 'on'. Similarly, colour may be used on dials where, for example, 'full' may be indicated by the colour black and 'empty' by white. Where a switch is not available in a colour which contrasts with its surroundings, coloured margins, which are capable of providing the necessary contrast, are available for some of the more common switch types, such as lights or sockets.

Controls should generally be in reach of a wheelchair user, except where **interference by children** might be an issue. For discussion on light switches and power outlets, ● section 7.5.

Switches vary in type, depending on function. Many domestic appliances, such as cookers, microwave ovens and the like, are operated by small buttons which are difficult to see, twist or turn. The ESB and An Bord Gáis can advise on domestic appliances which are fitted with alternative control mechanisms and *Consumer Choice* magazine often evaluates accessible features in its surveys.

Switching by **sensors** is becoming widely used, particularly for lighting. Sensors can be activated through movement, temperature change, the sound of a voice, a break in electronic circuitry or infra-red beams. Such arrangements, used in automatic water taps, light switching and door opening gear, are ideal as they are independent of ability or disability. Where infra-red beams are used as a means of detection for automatic doors etc, ensure that people of small stature or in wheelchairs can be detected, ● section 6.7.4.

When arranging switches on control panels, place the most important switches in the most obvious locations. Priority displays should be sited within a cone vision of 30°. Controls or displays with similar functions should be grouped together. Position controls so that, when being used, the relevant displays are not obscured. Items should be capable of being located in a sequence, to enable progress from left to right and from top to bottom. Large buttons are easier to operate than those which require finger dexterity. For ease of operation the space between buttons should be at least 15mm clear in both directions. Where switches project, the distance from the face should be 5–12mm. It should not be necessary to press switches below the surrounding surface. On switched **twin socket outlets**, ensure that the switches are on the outer edges of the plate, rather than between the two plug tops, ■ figure 35.

For advice on ATMs and ticket machines, ● section 7.8.

Checklist

Switches and controls

- Switches and controls should be readily detectable and operable by light pressure and without undue stretching or stooping.
- Locate switches and controls 500mm, minimum 300mm, from internal corners.
- Optimum general operating zone is 900–1200mm.
- Switches should be large and easy to operate.
- Avoid the use of switches demanding finger dexterity.
- Make sets of controls consistent in design for easy use.
- Controls should be on inclined surfaces where possible.
- Use colour to locate controls and to distinguish between operations.
- Provide automatic or remote controls where possible.
- Arrange controls in a logical operating sequence.
- Any instructions should be easily readable and simply phrased.
- Wall-mounted lighting switches in dwellings should have 20mm deep switch housings.

Particular building types 9

9.1 General

This book so far has dealt with design issues affecting general access to buildings and external environments.

This chapter focuses on buildings with particular features which must be accessible and which are not dealt with in the earlier chapters. Specialised facilities, such as hospitals or jails, are beyond the scope of this book but, even so, the general advice given earlier still applies to all building types.

Some of the features relating to particular building types are common to more than one of the types discussed and, as such, are dealt with here.

Enquiry and booking facilities

Access to enquiry offices is particularly important for people with disabilities, as the advice they need may not be available elsewhere. Where enquiries are dealt with by telephone, a TDD, ● section 8.3, should be fitted to facilitate deaf people. At counters, install a counter loop and ensure full visual contact to enable lip reading, ● section 7.6. As with reception desks, a section of the counter, minimum 900mm long, should be 750mm above floor level to enable retrieval of tickets and written information while seated, ● section 6.4.

Ticket kiosks and booths should be accessible to everyone. An induction loop should be incorporated to facilitate people with hearing impairments. A section of the booking counter should be at 750mm above floor level to accommodate wheelchairs users and children. Where there are a number of kiosks, an appropriate proportion should be designed to incorporate the lower level counter. There should be a visual display of the price of tickets.

Ticket vending machines should be simple to operate and of an accessible design. They should not be the sole means of dispensing tickets and personal assistance should also be available, ● sections 7.8 and 8.5.

Waiting and queueing

Queueing for services is usually unavoidable. Queueing aisles should be minimum 1000mm wide, with a clear 1800 x 1800mm space at both ends of the queue to allow for turning around. Where possible, provide a ticket arrangement and seating to make queueing easier.

Waiting areas are an important feature in public offices and transport terminals, and common in hotels, restaurants, sports complexes and recreational buildings. They should be of sufficient capacity and provide an adequate number of seats. The seats should give good arm and back support, ● section 8.1. Within the seating areas, there should be spaces for wheelchair users, ● section 6.4. Announcements should be made visually and aurally. Convenient access to sanitary facilities from these areas is essential, ● section 6.4.

Signage

Signs, essential for everyone in many of the building types discussed in this chapter, should be adequate, well positioned and clear, ● section 8.2.

Dual heights

In buildings which accommodate children, additional handrails should be incorporated on stairs and ramps to finish 650–700mm above floor. An appropriate number of WCs and sinks should be 350mm high and 750mm high respectively, and urinals should finish 380mm above the floor. For dual height reception desks see previous page.

Other common facilities

Cash registers should provide visual display of prices, visible to the customer as well as the cashier. This facility is particularly welcomed by people with hearing impairments, and by tourists.

Refreshment facilities should be 900–1200mm over floor level so as to be universally accessible. Restaurants, cafes, canteens etc in all building types should follow the guidance in section 9.8.

9.2   Public offices

Public offices are buildings, offices or other facilities from which public bodies provide services and facilities which are available or accessible to the general public.

Public bodies include Departments of State, Local Authorities, Health Boards, any board or body established under statute and State and publicly owned companies. They also include museums, libraries, galleries, auditoria, post offices, social welfare offices, Garda stations and a wide range of buildings and environments.

A public body must ensure that its public buildings, environments, services and written or oral communications are available and accessible to all members of the public and its staff, including those with disabilities. It must ensure that the access for people with disabilities is fully integrated with that for non-disabled people. Where necessary, it must provide adequate support for people with disabilities in accessing services and, if appropriate, must also provide expertise and skills within the service in relation to access to it by people with disabilities.

Access to buildings

Designers should be mindful of the number of people likely to visit a public building, and that public buildings are likely to have employees and be visited by people with all forms of impairment. People with disabilities can perhaps choose which cinema, dry cleaner or newsagent they go to, but they may have no choice in which tax office, social welfare office or health department they attend. While all buildings should be designed and built to accommodate everyone, the onus on public bodies to achieve full accessibility is arguably greater.

The internal and external environments of public bodies should embody the same principles as all other places to which the public have access. In this regard, the advice given in Parts 2 and 3 of this book should be followed, with particular attention to building approaches, entrances, lobbies, reception areas and desks, circulation routes, information counters, signage and sanitary facilities.

The journey from the public road or footpath should be smooth and unhindered by obstacles, whether permanent or temporary.

Access to services

The full range of services which are available to the public generally must be available to people with disabilities. For the majority of services, this is easily achieved by following the advice in this book.

The point at which many services are provided is generally at a counter or desk. Once a person has got to that point, it is essential that they can avail of the services on offer. Counters must incorporate a low section, ● sections 6.4 and 9.1, to facilitate wheelchair users and people who may need to sit down. Any switches, keypads or card swipes must also be accessible, ● sections 7.8 and 8.5.

Designers need to be fully aware of the manner in which particular services are provided and ensure that details of furniture and fittings do not hinder the provision of services. The needs of people, both staff and visitors, must take precedence over design. As discussed earlier in this book, the detailing need not necessarily compromise the design, but the detailing certainly has the potential to compromise the provision of the service.

Access to communications

Communication and information are both vital to the proper provision of any service. Information can be made available in many ways, including printed material, signage and notice boards, by telephone, from staff and via the internet. Public bodies must ensure full access to all people with impairments, including those with sensory impairments and learning difficulties.

Printed information must be available in alternative formats (large print, audio tape, computer disk etc) to facilitate people with visual impairments and others. Signage, ● section 8.2, must be clear, simple, logical and adequately lit. Notice boards must be accessible, not obstructing any circulation routes, adequately lit and incorporate notices with large text, ● section 8.2. Where information is available by telephone, a TDD, ● section 8.3, must be fitted and staff must be adequately trained in its use. Where information is made available from staff, an induction loop, ● section 7.6, must be fitted to facilitate those using hearing aids, and lighting must facilitate lip-reading, ● section 7.5.1. Staff should be trained in sign language and also in facilitating people with learning difficulties and those who are easily confused. Simplified versions of printed information will assist those with literacy difficulties or for whom English is not their first language. When designing web sites, consult www.accessit.nda.ie for specific advice in relation to accessibility for the full range of users, including people with visual impairments.

Design for print

Good information design involves producing data in a form which can be easily understood, keeping distraction to a minimum. Avoid 'visual noise' by using as few colours, point-sizes and fonts as possible. The aim, above all, should be communication.

- Use unornamented, plain fonts – Gill Sans, Helvetica, etc.
- Avoid setting text too small. Letters such as the a, o and x should be no smaller than 2mm from top to base (a measurement known as the x height). Use fonts with a point-size of 12 or greater to be sure.
- Larger text is not necessarily clearer. Well-spaced small text is generally more readable than badly spaced large text (see next point)
- Lines of text too close together can be difficult to follow, so pay attention to the space between them, known as the leading or line-feed. A good rule of thumb is to ensure that the leading measurement is at least 3 points greater than the text size: 12 point text should have 15 point leading, 13 point text should have 16 point leading etc.
- Text should be set unjustified (also known as range left) in order to avoid large, distracting spaces between words.
- Avoid CONTINUOUS CAPITALS as people with visual impairments rely heavily on recognising word shapes.
- Do not condense or expand fonts as this impairs their readability.

Gill Sans   Helvetica

this type has an x-height of 2mm

the text in this book has leading
more than 3 points greater than
the text size

unjustified   justified
(range left)

9.3   Transport terminals

This building type includes bus and train stations, harbours and airport terminals. For taxi ranks, ● section 5.4.5.

Legislation governing transport terminals is constantly being updated in order to ensure full accessibility for everyone. New types of buses, trains and other modes of transport, more accessible than their predecessors, are being introduced. Access to public transport, however, starts not at the door of the bus but at the point where someone leaves their home or workplace to go somewhere else. The entire journey, from doorstep to bus stop, on the bus, into the train station, onto the train and off at the other end, needs to be a smooth and comfortable operation, irrespective of impairment. Chapter 5 deals with many issues relating to the terrain en-route to the transport terminal. This section deals with the terminals themselves.

Issues particular to the design and management of transport terminals include **layout**, 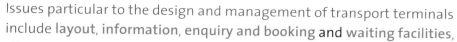 **information**, **enquiry and booking** and **waiting facilities**, ● sections 9.1 and 9.2. Parking, signage, ticket and reception areas and induction loop systems are also relevant to buildings of this type, ● sections 5.4, 6.4, 7.6 and 8.2.

For discussion of safety where large numbers of people gather, ● sections 7.9 and 10.1 .

Layout

A simple layout in large terminals, eg. airports, ferry terminals and main bus and train stations, benefits everyone. Movement through these buildings should happen in a logical sequence. All issues of entrances, circulation etc, discussed earlier in this book, are relevant, ● chapters 6–8. In addition, places where passage is restricted, such as passport control and security check points, should have wider passage-ways for wheelchair users immediately adjacent, ● section 9.1. Booths should also be fitted with induction loop systems to facilitate people with impaired hearing, ● section 7.6.

Information

Everyone using public transport needs sufficient information to allow them to plan their journey in advance. This is particularly important for people with disabilities. The required information includes timetables, journey times, pricing information, availability of particular facilities and last-minute updates. Such information should be provided in a number of alternative formats, including visually and aurally.

Timetables and journey times are published for most forms of transport. Information on stop-offs can also be crucial in planning a journey. The font size generally used on timetables is so small as to be illegible to many people, not just those with particular visual impairments. Printed timetables should be available in 12 point sans serif text, similar to the text on this page, and large print versions (18 point sans serif text) should also be available. Public timetables should be available inside the terminal at an accessible location and should follow the advice given for signage, ● section 8.2. The information presented on timetables can often be quite complex. The layout, therefore, should be as clear as possible in order to facilitate the broadest range of users, ● section 9.2.

For people who cannot read timetables, schedules should be available by telephone, including TDD, ● section 8.3. This is best done via an operator who can answer specific enquiries directly and should be available on a 24-hour basis, not just during office hours. The menu of talking timetables should be logical and should be considered carefully so as not to frustrate or confuse people using it. Talking timetables cannot be used by deaf people, and so should not be the sole source of this information.

Pricing information should also be available to allow people to budget their journey and to make the necessary arrangements for payment upon arrival at the terminal. Not everybody uses credit cards, and many people, including older people and those with disabilities, do not carry large amounts of cash for security reasons. At the terminal, prices should be clearly displayed, ● section 8.2, to facilitate tourists.

Particular facilities will be required along a journey by many people with impairments. Disabled travellers need information to allow them to plan a journey, to know where they might encounter difficulties and where facilities are available.

Last-minute updates must be available, both prior to leaving home and at the terminal itself. Delays in travel schedules are annoying for everyone but can cause difficulties for people with disabilities and people who may have a particular medical condition. Inside terminals, this type of information should be delivered aurally to all parts of the building, in addition to the visual displays in the main areas.

Where ticket bookings or enquiries are handled by telephone, a TDD is necessary, ● section 8.3.

Management should allocate adequate time when organising timetables so that people with mobility impairments are not put under pressure in transferring from one location to another. Buggy-type transport can be provided to assist people with mobility impairments where there are long travel distances.

Checklist

Transport terminals

- Layout should be simple and logical.
- Fit induction loops to all areas where communication is required and allow for full visual contact at counter screens.
- Timetables should be simple to read and should be available in 12pt sans serif font.
- Information, including last-minute updates, should be available in a number of alternative formats.
- Provide a telephone device for the deaf (TDD) to handle enquiries and ticket bookings.
- Provide a 750mm high section of booking counter.
- Supplement ticket vending machines with personal assistance or alternatives.
- Design all signage carefully to ensure clarity.
- In waiting areas, communicate information visually and audibly.
- Plan transfer timings to facilitate people with mobility impairments.

9.4   Workplaces

Working areas and workstations should be adaptable in order to suit as many employees as possible. Issues particular to the design and management of workplaces, include height of work surfaces, widths of circulation spaces, especially in open plan offices, ● section 6.5, quality of seating, indoor air quality, provision of individually controllable lighting and heating, ● sections 7.4–7.7, and access to storage. Where staff are dealing with the public, training in serving people with impairments is essential. Premises should also be considered in terms of access and use for visitors.

Good design maximises ease of use by everyone. There should be sufficient storage at the optimum height of 700–1300mm above floor level to accommodate the most commonly required items. The top drawer of a four-drawer filing cabinet, for example, is inaccessible to wheelchair users. Office furniture and fittings should be accessible to everyone, ● section 8.1, and adaptable where possible. While manufacturing or other facilities may not lend themselves to being accessible to everyone, good design can accommodate modifications of layout or the installation of specific equipment which may facilitate particular individuals.

Good quality seating, with a full range of adjustment, is important, especially where people are sitting for extended periods of time. Furniture and floor coverings which harbour dust should not be used, ● sections 7.2 and 8.1. Clear dimensions of circulation routes, which would allow a wheelchair user to get around, should not be compromised by the layout of work-stations, furniture or equipment. Clear space at the end of any 'dead end' passages should be provided to allow a wheelchair user, or people pushing trolleys, to turn around, ● section 6.5.3.

FÁS administers a **Workplace/Equipment Adaptation Grant Scheme** through which grants of up to €6500 are available towards the cost of adaptations to premises or equipment to benefit employees or self-employed people with disabilities. Further information is available from any FÁS Employment Office.

The **Employment Equality Act, 1998** outlaws discrimination against people with disabilities in the workplace. It is important that employers and employees ensure that they are promoting equal opportunities in their work practices and employment premises. It also makes sound commercial sense for companies and entities which have contact with the public to ensure that their staff, especially management and those who deal directly with the public, are trained in how best to serve and work with people with impairments.

FÁS operates a **Disability Awareness Training Support Scheme** that provides funding for private sector organisations to introduce disability awareness training for their staff. Organisations can be funded for 90% of the cost of this training up to a maximum of €20,000 in the first year of application or 80% (to a maximum of €20,000) in subsequent years. Further details and application forms are available from FÁS Services to Business offices. FÁS Services to Business staff can also put companies in touch with disability awareness trainers who can run awareness programmes tailored to individual client needs.

FÁS also has a **Positive to Disability** award scheme, which offers companies recognition for their demonstrated commitment to equal opportunities for people with disabilities. Further information is available from FÁS offices.

9.5   Retail outlets

Design issues particular to the design of retail outlets include the **width of aisles, design and layout of counters, widths of checkouts, display of goods** and **changing rooms**. Premises should be considered in terms of access and use for both staff and shoppers.

Design
An **aisle** is essentially a corridor and should therefore be at least 1800mm wide, which will allow two wheelchair users, or trolleys, to pass one

another, ● section 6.5.3. A smaller dimension of 1500mm might be acceptable on aisles less than 20.0m long, but only if there is a clear 1800mm turning space at both ends.

Free-standing displays within an aisle should be avoided, as they reduce the effective width of the aisle and are a hazard to visually impaired people. **Pyramids of goods** at the ends of supermarket aisles, stacked on top of each other rather than on shelves, are often unstable and so can be hazardous.

Counters should facilitate both people standing and those in wheelchairs. Conventional counters are 1050mm over floor and 900mm deep. A minimum 900mm long section of counter, 750mm over floor level, will facilitate wheelchair users and children.

In a row of **checkouts**, at least one in every six, located at ends of rows where they can be found easily, should be at least 800mm wide, to suit wheelchair users and people with buggies. If planned so as to be back-to-back, all aisles can be accessible without reducing the number of available checkouts.

Shelving should be solid and stable, without sharp edges, and should allow goods to be viewed and selected easily. Avoid oblique-angled shelves above 1000mm from the floor as wheelchair users cannot see items displayed at a 45° slope above this height. A **vertical stacking approach** for displayed goods will ensure maximum accessibility. In this arrangement, a proportion of every item for sale is placed on a number of shelves at different heights. The optimum shelf heights are 450–1300mm and 450–1060mm for people standing and wheelchair users respectively.

Wall fridges and freezers are more accessible than chest type units, as they do not require people to stretch out and down at the same time. The vertical stacking approach, mentioned above, should also be implemented in wall-mounted units. Doors on freezer units, wall and chest type, often have vacuum seals which are difficult to open. Sliding doors and lids provided with a D-shaped handle are easier to use.

Changing rooms should be adequately sized and fitted and should allow for privacy. Where curtains are fitted, **individual changing cubicles** require a minimum 900mm wide unobstructed approach. Treat the approch to cubicles with doors in the same way as the approach to doors from corridors, ● section 6.6.3. Avoid outward opening doors where possible. However, in existing buildings where space is at a premium, doors may open outwards, provided this is against an adjoining wall.

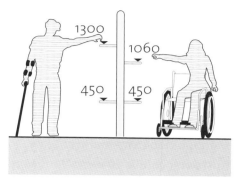

figure 38 **Retail shelving**

Inside a changing room, provide a **fixed seat** where sufficient space is available. Where space is at a premium, provide flip-up seats, 450–500mm deep, to finish 450–460mm above floor level. Position a grab rail, 35mm diameter, beside the seat. Provide a **full height mirror** from 450mm to 1800mm over floor level, ● section 9.10. **Hanging hooks or rails** should be in the range of 1200–1700mm over floor level. Those at the lower height will facilitate children and wheelchair users, while the higher ones will be accessible to ambulant adults.

Management and maintenance

Customer care is an important aspect of management in all retail outlets. The provision of appropriate shopping trolleys is one aspect of best practice in customer care. A variety of shopping trolleys should be available, including standard trolleys, trolleys to carry smaller baskets, trolleys suitable for wheelchair users and, in shopping centres, powered wheelchairs with integrated shopping baskets. The appropriate number of each type should be readily available when required. Trolleys, especially their wheels, must be maintained properly, as one stiff wheel which causes the trolley to pull to one side can be impossible to manage for someone with poor grip or who is using a walking stick.

Personal assistance can overcome the occasional shortcoming and should always be available if required. If, however, assistance is needed for every second item, the customer will no longer feel that they have independent access. Careful design and management can overcome the need for personal assistance.

Smaller shops, adjacent to supermarkets, often erect barriers to restrict access with trolleys. Such barriers deny access to wheelchair users as well and thus contravene equality legislation. Signage stating the necessary prohibition, together with vigilant management, is more appropriate.

Self-service weighing facilities should have scales which are easy to read, with ready access to the controls for printing out the labels. Key pads should use pictures of the products as well as text and should be in alphabetical order. Where possible, tactile indication on the key pads will assist further. A knee space under the scales, 750 high x 750 wide x 400mm deep, facilitates wheelchair users.

Background music, often relayed through public address sound systems, should be at a comfortable level for normal hearing. If it is louder, customers using hearing aids may experience considerable discomfort. To enable hearing aid users to communicate easily, provide adequate breaks in the music.

Alternative plans

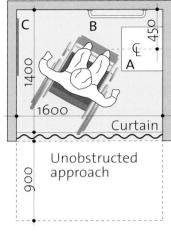

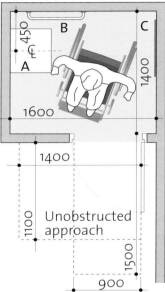

Section

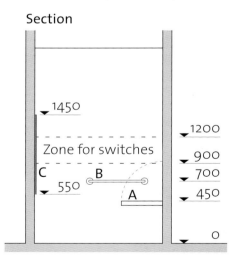

A   Flip up seat
B   600 long horizontal grab rail
C   Mirror

figure 39   **Changing rooms**

Signs providing information about special offers etc should be supplemented by audio announcements.

Checklist
Retail outlets

- Aisles should be 1800mm wide.
- Avoid the use of free-standing displays and of pyramids of goods at ends of aisles.
- Shelving to be solid and stable and free of sharp edges.
- Avoid oblique-angled shelves above 1000mm.
- Use a vertical stacking approach for the display of goods.
- Provide length of accessible counter, 750mm over floor level.
- Size one checkout in every six to be minimum 800mm wide.
- Cash registers should provide visual display of prices.
- Use wall freezers in preference to chest freezers.
- Freezer doors and lids should slide open horizontally.
- Provide shopping trolleys suitable for wheelchair users.
- Use visual symbols on self-service weighing facilities and provide knee space underneath.
- Provide periodic breaks in background music.
- Consider changing rooms in terms of customers with disabilities.
- Train staff to provide personal assistance when requested.

9.6   Museums and galleries

Significant issues particular to the design and management of museums and galleries include information, access to exhibits, legibility of signs and display legends and admission of guide dogs. In addition, the provision of books, video and audio recordings might allow people with impairments to experience displays in existing buildings which otherwise would not be available to them. General access should follow the advice in earlier parts of this book.

Information

Information should be available in advance of a visit so that people know what level of accessibility to expect. Where events and facilities are advertised, this information should be incorporated into all publicity material. Where information is available by telephone, a TDD, ● section 8.3, should be fitted.

Many museums involve long distances between exhibits. Near the entrance, provide information on distances in the venue so that mobility-impaired visitors can plan their visit, ● section 8.2. The provision of

wheelchairs on loan will help visitors with limited stamina to move around the venue in comfort. Provide seating at regular intervals along corridors and in galleries. Provide at least some of the seating with armrests, ● section 9.1.

Accessing exhibits

Where possible, objects should be mounted on an inclined surface, maximum 1000mm above ground, so as to facilitate those standing, children and wheelchair users. Ensure that glass used to protect exhibits is not of a reflecting type. Where low light levels are necessary for the conservation of exhibits, accompanying labels should be well-lit and carefully positioned, ● section 7.5.1. Lighting strips at ground level can mark a route in an area with low levels of lighting.

For legibility, labels should be in minimum 18 point type and in a sans serif font. Explanatory information and guidebooks should be printed in a 12pt sans serif font, with alternative formats available on request. Labels using raised lettering can be read by touch by somebody with impaired vision, ● sections 8.2 and 9.2. Plastic magnifying glasses, available on loan, can assist many visitors to examine exhibits and labels. Thermoforms of paintings and replicas of objects kept under glass can assist blind and visually-impaired visitors to enjoy collections and exhibitions, especially when used in conjunction with an audio guide.

Guide dogs should be admitted to all parts of the building, including restaurant facilities, ● section 9.8.

Videos, books of photographs and talk/slide shows should be provided for certain exhibits where it is completely impracticable to provide independent access for people with disabilities.

9.7   Hotels and guest accommodation

The building type includes hotels, motels, hostels, guest-houses, bed and breakfast accommodation and self-catering apartments. Significant issues particular to the design and management of these building types include **bedrooms**, **sanitary facilities**, fire alarms, **signage** and **self-catering facilities**. In addition, recreation and social facilities, such as swimming pools, leisure centres, restaurants, bars, crèches, meeting rooms, function rooms and stages must be considered in terms of use by people with disabilities, ● chapters 6–8 and sections 9.1 and 9.8–9.10. For facilities associated with caravans or other moveable accommodation, ● section 4.3.10.

9.7.1   Bedrooms
Availability and choice of rooms
Regulations at present require a minimum of one in twenty bedrooms to be accessible to wheelchair users. It is not logical to assume that out of one hundred bedrooms, ninety-five should be identical and suitable for anyone who is ambulant. Given a number of bedrooms, therefore, it should be practicable to fit out rooms in different ways so as to accommodate a wide range of users. Already 'no smoking' bedrooms are widely

Where more than one accessible ensuite is being provided, up to 50% of such rooms may incorporate a bath rather than a shower, ■ figure 33.

figure 40 **Hotel bedroom**

available in hotels. In a similar way, it should be possible to designate and detail some rooms as suitable for people with impaired mobility, breathing, vision or hearing. These rooms can still be allocated to the general user and many of the provisions involved are of a type which are imperceptible to all but those to whom they are essential.

Maximise choice and provide for all guests on an equal basis as regards location, view, convenience and safety. Avoid layouts which require management to make special arrangements for people with impairments. In small premises, where lifts are not available, it will be necessary to provide accessible bedrooms on the entrance level. Where lifts are available, it should be possible to integrate the accessible accommodation fully with the rest.

Location of bedrooms relative to sources of external noise such as traffic, or noise from adjacent facilities, lift motor rooms or air handling equipment etc, should always be given careful consideration. It is particularly important for people who use hearing aids.

Detail design

Bedrooms should be easy to locate and identify and as close to the main facilities as possible. Place room numbers or name plates on the wall nearest the door handle, 25mm from door frame, with the top of the sign 1600mm over floor level. The number should be in raised numerals, and in a contrasting colour to the background, ● section 8.2.2. The location of doors should also be identified in a tactile manner, by incorporating a piece of flooring material with a different finish to that of the general corridor floor, ● section 7.2.

Good natural lighting makes for a pleasant room and helps maintain visual contrast, ● section 7.5.1. Avoid table lamps which are easily knocked over or which have complex switch arrangements or trailing cables. Light fittings should have diffusers, to avoid casting potentially confusing shadows.

Controls for heating, ventilation, lighting, curtains, radio and TV should be reachable from a seated position, ● section 8.5. Lights should be controllable from the bed. Remote control units are ideal.

Beds should be 450mm high to provide for easy transfer, and should have firm edges on the outer rim. Ensure a minimum 1500 x 1500mm turning space and an 800mm zone around the bed to facilitate access and movement around the room. Plan so as to permit alternative bed positions, enabling both left- and right-hand transfer from wheelchair to bed.

Keys or cards can be used to operate bedroom door locks. The lock should be 900–1200mm over floor level. Ensure that keys are easy to clasp, demanding neither a steady hand nor a strong twisting motion. Avoid the use of entry systems which require the use of both hands simultaneously, ● sections 7.8 and 8.4–8.5. Card entry systems should have a funnelled entry to help direct the card into the slot. A flat card can be difficult to pick up from a flat surface, so something attached to the card to help retrieval is welcome. A visual indicator, which alerts the occupant visually when somebody knocks on the door, is also desirable, ● section 8.4.

TV sets should be able to carry teletext subtitles and a TV listening aid should be available on request. The **telephone** should have an induction coupler to assist people with impaired hearing, ● section 8.3.

Good **indoor air quality** is necessary for people with impaired breathing. Indoor air quality is significantly affected by dust concentrations in bedrooms, particularly in the bed itself and in surrounding areas. Avoid ledges or other areas which collect dust. Headboards should be of timber or other solid materials, not fabric finished. Use non-fabric type blinds instead of heavy curtains. Synthetic-filled duvets, quilts and pillows are preferable to those with feather or down.

9.7.2 Sanitary facilities

In all bedrooms, it is always preferable to provide en-suite accommodation. Such accommodation must be safe, independently accessible and usable. It must provide for people with impaired hearing or sight, as well as people with impaired mobility and/or grip.

Bathrooms are notorious for accidents. A **spacious layout**, with appropriate grab rails, ● section 6.9, will render any bathroom much safer, as well as making it more easily usable by a broad range of people. In most hotels, baths are provided in favour of showers. In reality, most people actually use the bath as a shower. Current legislation requires a level deck shower as distinct from a bath in at least half of the wheelchair accessible accommodation. Consideration should also be given to the provision of showers, rather than baths, in at least a proportion of general bedrooms. This will cater for older people and those with limited mobility who may be more prone to accidents, as well as those whose personal preference is for showers rather than baths.

In all wheelchair accessible bedrooms, an en-suite should be provided. Such bathrooms must be a minimum of 2000mm x 2500mm in dimension, ● section 6.9. At least half of these must incorporate a level deck shower, rather than a bath. Where a bath is provided, there must be appropriate grabrails and a 400mm ledge at the end, ■ figure 33.

Towel rails should be sited consistently to the right or left of washbasins, rather than remote from them, where a visually impaired person would have difficulty in finding them. A towel rail should never be positioned at high level over the end of the bath where it is hard to reach or may be an obstruction to someone trying to get into the bath. Avoid unusual design approaches in this regard.

For discussion on bathroom dimensions, layout and fittings, ● section 6.9.

9.7.3   Fire alarms and means of escape

For general discussion of fire alarms, ● section 7.9.1. In a small premises, complementary management procedures will help to ensure safety of guests. In larger premises, the alarm system itself should have a complementary method of alerting deaf people, ● section 10.1. Aids are available to alert deaf people, such as a vibrating pad placed under a pillow and connected to the alarm system, ● Appendix 1.

9.7.4   Signage

For general discussion on the detail design of signs, ● section 8.2.2. In many buildings, good signage can obviate the need to ask for directions. Locations of lifts, escape routes, sanitary facilities, dining rooms, leisure facilities, bedrooms etc should all be clearly signalled both en-route and upon arrival at the location. Signage should not be over-stylised so as to make it difficult to read. The effectiveness of signage should be tested by travelling along all the possible routes, and back, while assuming a complete lack of familiarity with the building.

9.7.5   Management and maintenance

To complement the combined audio-visual fire alarm system, ● section 9.7.3, a guest's particular needs should be discussed at time of registration, the appropriate room identified and staff designated to help if required, ● sections 7.9.1 and 10.1.

Good housekeeping, to keep corridors clear of linen bags, cleaning gear, trolleys and other obstructions, is important in the safe management of a hotel. Bed clothes should not be discarded onto floors, where people with visual impairments may trip over them, ● chapter 10.

9.7.6   Shared accommodation in hostels

Hostels provide shared sleeping accommodation, sanitary facilities and kitchens to their guests. The access issues for these facilities in a hostel are the same as if they were provided in a hotel. The detail design of bedrooms and bathrooms should follow the advice given above, ● sections 9.7.1–9.7.2; for kitchens, ● section 9.7.7 below.

9.7.7 Self-catering accommodation

Self-catering apartments, cottages and the like should provide for people with disabilities. Consider each individual apartment or cottage so that people with impairments can be accommodated both as visitors and as occupants. The provisions within the layout of this type of accommodation should be the same as those for housing in this regard, ● section 9.11. An appropriate number of units should incorporate wheelchair accessible bathrooms, ● section 6.9, and kitchens, see below. Such units should be fully integrated with the rest. On complexes which group separate cottages or houses, external spaces should incorporate the advice in Part 2.

In wheelchair accessible units, the layout of the bathroom should follow the same guidelines as that for accessible en-suites in hotels, incorporating a level deck shower tray rather than a bath, ● sections 9.7.2.

Kitchens

Kitchens should be flexible in their layout, so as to be suitable for a broad range of users. Locate dining areas to minimise the task of carrying food. An open plan arrangement is preferable.

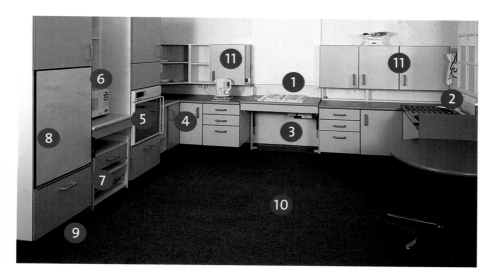

1   wall-mounted, height adjustable hob
2   wall-mounted, height adjustable sink unit with lever taps and swan neck
3   knee space under hob
4   carousel unit to facilitate easy access
5   oven with side hung door at accessible level
6   microwave oven with aural indication of settings
7   pull out unit on wheels to facilitate access to microwave oven above
8   fridge at accessible level
9   minimum 250mm high x 150mm wide toe recess
10 adequate turning space for ease of movement throughout kitchen
11 high level units within reach and only 200mm deep

Provide adequate floor space to facilitate wheelchair manoeuvring. In galley kitchens, a minimum clear space of 1500mm diameter between units is required to allow wheechair users to turn. Flooring should be slip-resistant.

A counter height of 900mm above floor is the standard for a standing adult, 750mm for wheelchair users. A height of 850mm may provide a workable compromise for wheelchair users. Adjustable height worktops are available and are very suitable, ● Appendix 1.

A toe recess, 250mm high x 150mm deep, allows wheelchair users to access counter units. In fitted kitchens omit one or two low level units, thus providing a knee space under counters and affording greater access while working at the counter or worktop. Where storage space is at a premium, such units may be fitted with castors, to allow them to be replaced when the knee space is not required. Such units may also be used as a low worktop. Fit carousel units under worktops in corners to afford greater accessibility.

The kitchen sink should be shallow to facilitate a wheelchair user reach-ing into it. The outlet and associated plumbing underneath the sink should be fixed as close to the wall as possible, to maximise the knee space underneath. Insulate hot water pipes if people are likely to brush against them, ● section 7.7.

The tap should be lever type, with a high swan-neck mixer type outlet. It should be positioned so that the swan neck can be twisted over the draining board to fill kettles and saucepans. This removes the need to hold the pot while filling with water. The cooker should be in the same row of units as the sink, so that kettles and pots can be slid along rather than lifted.

Hob and oven units should be separate, which will allow each of them to be placed at their optimum height. Install ceramic hobs which allow pots to be slid rather than lifted. Position ovens so that the lower rim is 450–600mm over floor level, 750–850mm in the case of microwave ovens. These dimensions will allow ease of access for a broad range of users. Oven doors should be side hung so as not to interfere with the approach space.

Controls should be readily detectable and easy to use, ● section 8.5. Hob controls should be along the front, rather than down the side, of the hob, as the risk of burning is greatly reduced. Select a microwave oven which has simple easy-to-operate controls.

Cooker hoods generally have fixed controls which are out of the reach of wheelchair users. Re-organisation of switches or a low-level pull cord is desirable.

Storage presses, fridges, freezers etc, should be located 450–1300mm above floor level and be fitted with large D-shaped handles.

A first aid cabinet, fire blanket and a multi-purpose hand-held type fire extinguisher should be provided at 450–1300mm above floor level and should be easily accessed.

Kitchen utensils and crockery, if provided, should contrast with the work-top colour, to assist people with impaired vision.

Checklist
Hotels and guest accommodation
General
- People with disabilities should be able to avail of the full range of accommodation and facilities.
- Avoid layouts which require management to make special arrangements for people with disabilities.
- Hotel reservation lines should have a TDD.
- Detail flooring, lighting, finishes and colours to facilitate access.
- In hostels, follow the advice for hotels in relation to bedrooms and sanitary facilities.
- In self-catering accommodation, follow the advice on housing generally.

Bedrooms
- Provide wheelchair accessible bedroom and sanitary accommodation in no less than one in twenty rooms.
- Designate and detail some rooms as suitable for people with impaired mobility, breathing, vision or hearing.
- Bedrooms should be easy to locate and identify.
- Avoid door hardware and locking mechanisms which must be operated by both hands.
- Bedroom heating, ventilation, lighting, curtains, radio and TV controls should be reachable from a seated position.
- TV sets should be able to carry teletext subtitles and a listening aid should be available.
- Room telephone should have an induction coupler.
- Beds should be 450mm high to provide easy transfer, with 800mm zone round the bed to allow for ease of movement around the bed and room.

Checklist (continued)

Kitchens in self-catering accommodation
- Plan flexibly, to allow for different users: sufficient space, simple layouts.
- Locate dining and cooking areas close to each other, preferably open plan.
- Ensure there is 1500mm diameter clear floor space between units in galley kitchens.
- Use slip-resistant floor finish.
- Counters to be 850mm high generally, part at 750mm; adjustable tops are ideal.
- Units to have 250mm high x 150mm deep toe recess and provide knee space in key areas.
- Use contrasting colours for work tops, utensils, crockery and appliance controls.
- Provide shallow sink, convenient to cooker, with swan-neck mixer lever tap.
- Separate oven and ceramic hob is best.
- Use D-shaped handles on fittings.
- Provide accessible first aid cabinet, fire blanket and fire extinguisher.
- The zone from 450 to 1300mm over finished floor level is the most accessible for everybody. Site all critical items in this zone.

Day-to-day management
- Keep circulation spaces free of obstruction.
- Emergency planning should take account of people with impairments.
- Provide vibrating alarm on request.
- Avoid strong-smelling detergents and air fresheners.

9.8   Restaurants and cafes

The building type includes cafes and restaurants, snack bars, canteens, public bars and lounges. Significant issues particular to the design and management of restaurants and cafeterias include **tables and chairs**, **bars and counters**, **access to equipment**, **menus**, **reservations**, **staff training**, **self-service facilities** and **access for guide dogs**.

Traditionally, **changes in level** were frequently incorporated as design features in such premises. In existing buildings, ensure that at least two-thirds of the total floor area is accessible to wheelchair users, involving access to the full range of services including food and service counters, bar areas and sanitary facilities. Where there are **different categories of seating**, such as self-service and waiter service, smoking and non-smoking, inside and outside, an adequate proportion of each category should be accessible.

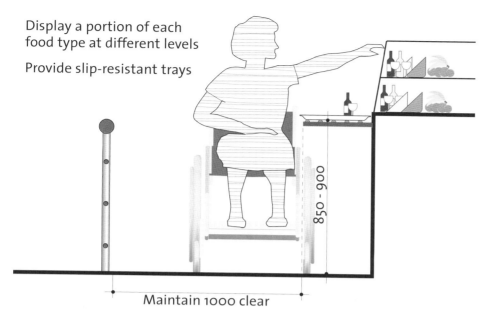

Display a portion of each food type at different levels

Provide slip-resistant trays

850 - 900

Maintain 1000 clear

figure 41 **Self-service facilities**

Tables and chairs should be laid out so as to provide adequate circulation areas between adjacent tables, ● section 6.5. Where fixed seating is provided, some tables should have at least some removable chairs, to allow space for a wheelchair user. The knee clearance under tables should be 700mm.

Where **bars and counters** are used for dining, the section at 750mm above floor level should be 1500mm long, to accommodate a wheelchair user and a companion, ● section 9.1.

Equipment such as vending machines, food storage and display units should be considered in terms of accessibility and ease of use, ● sections 7.8.8, 8.5 and 9.5.

Menus and other printed information should be available in 12pt sans serif text and in large print and other alternative formats, ● section 9.2.

Reservations are generally made by telephone, thus requiring the installation of a TDD, ● section 8.3.

Staff should be trained in dealing with people with disabilities, including giving assistance in emergencies. At least one member of staff should be able to use sign language, ● section 10.1–10.2.

For **self-service facilities** to be accessible to people with impaired mobility, the approach aisle should be 1000mm wide. Tray storage should be accessible and ideally at a height of 700–1200mm above floor level. Trays should be of a design which can be easily gripped and with a slip-resistant finish. The tray slide should be 850–900mm over floor level. Food displays

should be sited above the tray slide. Vertical stacking, ● section 9.5, will facilitate children, wheelchair users and people who have difficulty bending down to see into the back of a low shelf.

Guide dogs are exempt from standard health and hygiene regulations and thus are allowed into areas where food and drink are consumed, including carvery restaurants, even if food is stored and prepared there, ● section 2.3.

Checklist

Restaurants and cafes

- A minimum of two-thirds of total floor area, with a full range of facilities, should be wheelchair accessible.
- Allow for adequate circulation space, especially between tables.
- In self-service restaurants, approach aisle to be 1000mm wide.
- Tray sliding rail to be 850–900mm over floor.
- Trays to be easily gripped and with a slip-resistant finish.
- Provide vertical stacking of food displays.
- Provide section of bar and restaurant counters at heights accessible to wheelchair users.
- Consider vending machines, self-service cooking equipment, food storage and display units in terms of accessibility and ease of use.
- Provide knee clearance of 700mm at tables.
- At least some seating should be free-standing, so that it can be removed to enable a wheelchair user to sit with others.

9.9 Buildings with audience or spectator facilities

Audience and spectator facilities are incorporated into a wide range of building types, including theatres, cinemas, schools and colleges, churches, sports venues etc. The advice in this chapter generally relates only to the facilities for the audience and spectator in all such building types. Access for the performer should follow the general advice in this book. For specific advice on recreational facilities provided in sports halls and leisure complexes, ● section 9.10.

There are many significant issues particular to the design and management of buildings with audience or spectator facilities, whether newly constructed or refurbished. They include booking, availability of seating, the need for good sightlines, safe access and egress for all spectators, audience participation, communication facilities, circulation routes and management.

Booking

For general advice on booking, ● section 9.1. The requirement of advance booking notice for people with disabilities is unacceptable, especially in light of equality legislation. It should be possible to book accessible seats in the normal manner. An adequate number of suitable seat spaces should be permanently available, see below. This eliminates the delays and discomfort which may be caused by having to remove standard seats to make a suitable place available.

Seating

Numbers and proportions of wheelchair accessible seats depend on the capacity of a particular venue. In premises with less than 1000 seats, six wheelchair accessible seats, or 1/50th of the capacity, whichever is the greater, are required by regulation. For premises with capacities greater than 1000, at least 20 spaces, or 1/100th of the capacity, whichever is the greater, must be provided. Where there are a number of venues in a particular building, eg. a multi-screen cinema, the standards apply to each venue independently of the others. These are minimum standards, and careful consideration should be given to the likely numbers of disabled visitors to particular venues to ensure that an adequate number of spaces is provided. Among the general seating, consider the needs of people with other impairments. A person with a guide dog, for example, will need additional space beside the seat for the dog.

All wheelchair accessible spaces should be permanent. Regulations allow for the provision of accessible spaces by the temporary removal of a seat. This practice is not recommended, however, as it mitigates against equality by causing undue delay and discomfort for the person waiting for the space to be made available and relies too much on good management practice.

Wheelchair users must be able to get to their seats without assistance. Accessible seats should be dispersed throughout the entire venue and integrated fully with the other seating. This avoids the formation of 'wheelchair ghettoes' and allows wheelchair users and their companions to sit together and enjoy the same choice of locations within the venue as everyone else. The full range of public facilities within a premises, such as bars, toilets etc, must be accessible from all wheelchair accessible seats. Where seating is provided on different levels, ensure that some accessible seats are available on each level.

In existing premises, ambulant disabled people must be able to access all levels even where it is not possible to provide wheelchair accessible seating at every level. If this is case, ensure that the accessible seats provided are in locations which yield a good view. In outdoor venues such as sports stadia, most wheelchair users prefer a position under cover and above the level of the pitch.

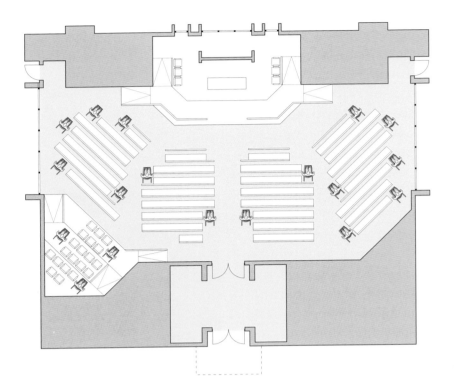

figure 42   **Dispersed seating**

The minimum dimension of a **wheelchair space** (900mm wide and 1400mm deep) is acceptable if the space is immediately adjacent to a standard seat, so that a wheelchair user can sit with a companion. If the space is not adjacent to a standard seat, the width of the space should be increased to 1400mm to allow for a companion.

Seats should give **adequate back support**. In rows of **fixed seating**, the seats should fold up automatically when not in use, so as to maximise the clear space between rows when people are taking up their seats or leaving.

Some people, including older people who use wheelchairs only some of the time, will want to **transfer** to a seat. It is a management issue that the wheelchair is kept nearby and delivered if required at an interval and at the end of a show.

In **places of worship**, the vertical supports at the ends of traditional pews can be an obstacle for many people. Consider the provision of pews in which the end seats are cantilevered, so that the first upright is always one seat in from the aisle. The **back of seats**, or the elbow rests of pews, should have edges which are easy to grip and which can also provide

support while standing. Vertical supports under the front edges of seats inhibit easy access, and should be avoided in favour of cantilevered seats. A loop should be fitted to confessionals to facilitate people using hearing aids, ● section 7.6.

Sightlines

Good sightlines are important for all spectators and congregants. A person using a wheelchair will, on average, be 40–60mm higher than someone sitting on a chair or an average seat. As such, it might be prudent to locate accessible spaces to the rear of a given seating area, so as not to reduce visibility for others. Principles of equality, though, suggest that not all such seats should be at the rear.

Safe access and egress

Places of assembly pose a particular fire hazard, in that they host a large number of people, probably unfamiliar with the building, in a space which may not be day-lit. Consider seating layout in terms of emergency evacuation. UK research on safety of people with disabilities in the event of a fire indicates that people with disabilities should not be confined to one single area. They should be located in a number of areas, close to exit routes or storey exits.

The design and safe management of exit routes to ensure that large numbers of people, disabled and able-bodied, can leave an event at the same time, or in an emergency, is crucial, ● sections 6.5–6.7 and 10.1. Safety procedures should ensure that there is no movement against the general flow in both normal and emergency egress.

Audience participation

There are times when members of an audience or congregation participate in an event or ceremony. Access to areas such as podiums, stages, altar areas and choir stalls requires careful consideration. Requiring assistance, whether from other people or from mechanical means such as a platform lift, while under the gaze of the public, can cause delay and embarrassment. Independent access to such areas should be available, preferably by ramp, ● section 6.7.3.

Communication

For general discussion on communication, ● section 7.6. In theatres etc, provide access for people with visual impairments to audio description via headphones. This requires the fitting of headphone sockets at an adequate number of designated seats, including some wheelchair spaces.

Management

A **refreshment order service** for disabled spectators or members of an audience is greatly welcomed and increases sales.

The Department of the Environment's *Code of Practice for Crowd Control* gives useful advice in regard to the **provision of emergency information** by way of electronic scoreboards.

The **evacuation plan** for the premises should incorporate measures to evacuate spectators with disabilities, ● sections 7.9 and 10.1.

Staff training in assisting people with disabilities, is essential, ● section 10.2.

Checklist
Buildings with audience or spectator facilities

- Provide access to the full range of viewing areas.
- Seats to be flip-up and have adequate back support.
- Disperse wheelchair accessible spaces throughout the auditorium or stadium to integrate disabled spectators into an audience.
- Locate wheelchair accessible spaces so that they do not block the sightlines of others.
- At sportsgrounds, provide wheelchair accessible seats among supporters of both home and away teams, preferably under cover.
- Undertake staff training and fire drills to incorporate the needs of spectators with disabilities.
- Consider the implications for accessibility of audience participation.

9.10   Buildings with recreational facilities

Many people with disabilities participate in a wide range of recreational and competitive sports. The notable successes of Irish athletes at the Paralympic Games and the staging of the Special Olympics in Ireland in 2003 are evidence of people's wish to avail of sporting facilities to the maximum extent.

Recreational buildings include sports halls, swimming pools, leisure centres and bowling alleys. As buildings which are open to public, all parts should be fully and independently accessible by everyone, including staff, spectators and players. The full range of facilities offered within the building should be available to everyone. Wheelchairs used for sports can be wider than standard ones, and this should be reflected in the size of doorways and so on. **Gymnasia** should have ample space between pieces of equipment, ● section 6.5. In general, a minimum of 1800mm will allow wheelchairs to pass unimpeded.

In **existing buildings**, where wheelchair access is restricted due to changes in level which cannot be overcome, a full range of facilities must be provided within the levels to which wheelchair users do have access.

In swimming pools, ensure that there is a **hoist** available to facilitate people with mobility impairments.

Many recreational buildings are noisy by virtue of the activities they house. In such circumstances, communication can be difficult for people using hearing aids. Careful consideration should be given to the use of **acoustic materials** which might improve the acoustic environment. This is particularly important at reception desks and ticket offices, where verbal communication is needed, and in areas used for classes and coaching, ● section 2.2 and 7.6.

For advice on buildings with audience or spectator facilities in general, ● section 9.9. For **outdoor sports facilities** such as running tracks, golf courses and playing fields, ● sections 4.3 and 4.4.

Checklist
Recreational buildings
- Ensure that all facilities are accessible.
- Provide sound absorbent material in spaces where verbal communication is important.
- Provide generous space between items of fixed equipment.
- Fix mats and timber decking securely, flush with the floor.

Changing rooms

In **sports centres**, where there are communal shower and changing areas, provide some separate facilities for people who require a greater degree of privacy. A straightforward way of achieving this is to provide a large cubicle fitted with curtains or a wide door. The **best solution** is the provision of a complete changing room, similar to an accessible en-suite bathroom, ● section 9.7.2, which incorporates the full range of sanitary facilities, including a level deck shower. Such a room can be provided within each of the ladies and gents changing areas. Alternatively, it can be unisex, with its own access to and from the reception and leisure areas. Unisex accessible changing cubicles will facilitate a person of one sex helping someone of the other, ● section 9.5.

As with accessible sanitary spaces, ● section 6.8, provide an **alarm** so that the user, who will frequently be alone, can summon assistance in an emergency, ● section 7.9.1.

Some **lockers** should be minimum 1200mm high to accommodate storage of crutches or artificial limbs. If a walking frame is to be stored, the locker should be 800 x 600mm on plan. Wheelchair manoeuvring requires a minimum 900 x 1200mm clear space in front of the locker.

Checklist
Changing rooms
- Provide some individual changing areas, perhaps within a group area, or as unisex units.
- Provide a clear unobstructed approach to cubicles.
- Provide an alarm so that the user can summon assistance in an emergency.

Maintenance and management
Keen management will ensure ensure that all **equipment** in gyms and other sports facilities is easy to operate and provides the maximum degree of access for everyone, including disabled people. Equipment which is simple to use benefits everyone, particularly people with learning disabilities, ● section 8.5.

Ensure that **mats** are maintained flush with floor finishes, so as not to be a tripping or slipping hazard, particularly to visually impaired people, or to reduce the mobility of wheelchair users, ● section 7.2.

9.11 Housing

9.11.1 General

The Building Regulations, 2000 introduced, for the first time in Ireland, a requirement that all new housing be socially accessible, ie. visitable by people with disabilities. Prior to the regulations, houses and apartments were becoming so compact that even fully ambulant residents had little or no space to spread out and move around in, never mind wheelchair users. The regulations were introduced to ensure that the young, the old and people with disabilities could not only visit houses and function there independently, but also have a choice of where to live.

Lifetime housing embodies all of what the regulations require, and then goes one step further by making provision for possible alterations at a later date to accommodate the changing needs of occupants which might be brought about by older age, ill health or accidents. Lifetime housing, which can be provided at marginal extra financial cost, permits people to spend longer in their own homes, is more adaptable for use by others and can be readily accessed and enjoyed by all visitors. Lifetime housing should properly be seen to be part of sustainable building.

■ Figures 44 and 45 show a typical, conventional semi-detached house layout and that layout adapted as required for lifetime housing, while figure 46 shows typical conventional and lifetime apartment layouts.

The advice in this section applies to all new housing and to housing refurbishment wherever practicable. The aim is to yield a more adaptable type of dwelling, which can be altered according to individual needs. The advice does not cover customising houses to accommodate specific individuals with particular disabilities.

9.11.2 Lifetime housing

The most significant issues determining accessible and lifetime housing include the approach to the house, a level main entrance, horizontal circulation, including the provision of a WC on the principal floor and an appropriate kitchen layout, and vertical circulation.

Approach

The approach to a dwelling should be accessible to all, and should be considered as the journey from the public footpath to the principal entrance. In some cases, where the distance involved is too great or site conditions will not allow a level, sloped or ramped approach from the public footpath, it may be acceptable to consider the approach as the journey from a parking space within the site to the principal entrance. The latter, however, mitigates against wheelchair users who are not arriving by car.

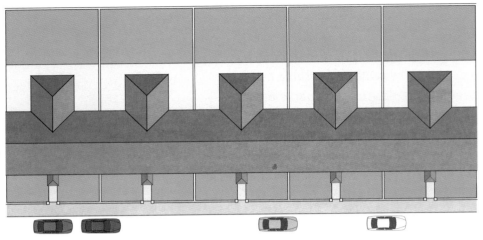

Terraces

Pedestrian gates from public footpath to have minimum clear opening of 800mm

Paths to be level or gently sloping and minimum 900mm wide

Provide 1200mm deep canopy at entrances

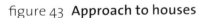

Semi-detached houses

Point of entry from public footpath to be minimum 800mm wide, but can be combined with a driveway

Route to be level or gently sloping

3.0m wide driveway allows 900mm clear space adjacent to parked car

Provide 1200mm deep canopy at entrances

Detached houses

Ensure that route from public footpath and parked car to door is always minimum 900mm clear of obstructions

Paths to be level or gently sloping

Provide 1200mm deep canopy at entrances

figure 43 **Approach to houses**

The point of entry from public footpath to the site must have a clear opening of at least 800mm, but could form part of a vehicle gateway. The route between the opening and the principal entrance must be at least 900mm wide but could be combined with a driveway, providing such a driveway is at least 3.0m wide, ■ figure 43.

The route should be **as flat as possible** or gently sloping, and where the adjacent ground is not graded to the approach, it should incorporate a 75mm raised kerb. The route should have a firm surface which is suitable for wheelchair use and minimises slipping, ● section 5.1, and should incorporate adequate lighting which does not cause glare, ● section 7.5.1.

Where an approach is sloped, it should be considered as a ramp, and should follow the advice in ● section 5.2.2. If a slope is such that the ramp exceeds 1:12, a stepped path might be considered. Provide handrails as if it were a ramp, ● section 5.2.2. Where site conditions will not permit the incorporation of ramps or stepped paths, and a stepped approach is the only solution, follow the advice in section 5.2.2.

Entrance

Every entrance should have a canopy which projects at least 1200mm to protect people from the rain. The door should have a clear opening of 800mm and a flush threshold. Doorbells, letterboxes etc should be at a height of 900–1200mm above ground level, ● sections 6.2, 6.6 and 8.4.

Horizontal circulation

Areas normally used by visitors, such as the hall, living room and the WC, should be accessible to people with disabilities, including wheelchair users and elderly visitors. This requires:

- turning spaces of minimum 1500mm diameter
- adequate width, in general minimum 1200mm, of the circulation spaces on the principal storey, ● section 6.5
- minimum 800mm clear ope width of internal doorsets, ● section 6.6
- door opes which do not incorporate door saddles
- clear space of 500mm, minimum 300mm, at leading edges of doors
- door furniture which is easy to see and to operate, ● section 8.4
- provision of a toilet of adequate size, to contain WC and hand rinse basin, see below and ■ figure 47, convenient to the living spaces.

Room size should not hinder movement. Very small kitchens or bedrooms are not usable by many people who use a walking frame or a wheelchair. The order of priority for the allocation of additional space to rooms is as follows:

- bathroom
- bedroom
- kitchen
- storage
- living room.

Bathrooms should be 2000 x 2500mm to allow enough space for a wheelchair to turn, ● section 6.9. Ground floor WCs should be at least 1500mm wide x 1400mm deep, and the door should be modifiable so as to open out against an adjacent wall if necessary, ● sections 6.6 and 6.8. Use lever type taps in washbasins, sinks and baths. Door handles should be lever type and not circular, ● section 8.4.

In bedrooms, a wheelchair user needs a 1500 x 1500mm turning space. Otherwise, an 800mm zone around the bed will afford greater accessibility. Plan so as to permit alternative bed positions, enabling both left-hand and right-hand transfer from a wheelchair to the bed, ● section 9.7.1.

figure 44 **Current inadequate practice: semi-detached house identifying shortcomings in typical details commonly in use**

Hallway and landing

1. stairs cranked and too narrow for future addition of a handrail
2. door handle too close to adjacent wall to allow access, saddleboard impedes easy access
3. hotpress difficult to access
4. less than 1500mm restricts turning

Living room

1. door handle too close to adjacent wall to allow access, saddleboard impedes easy access
2. transom level interferes with sightlines from seated position
3. clear opening of door leaves frequently less than 800mm each

Kitchen

1. window not accessible for opening and closing
2. door handle too close to adjacent wall to allow access, saddleboard impedes easy access

Bathrooms

1. room too small to allow full access
2. door too narrow

Dining room

1. raised track for sliding door impedes movement
2. door handle too close to adjacent wall to allow access, saddleboard impedes easy access
3. clear opening of door leaves frequently less than 800mm each

Bedrooms

1. door handle too close to adjacent wall to allow access, saddleboard impedes easy access

Outside

1. no canopy for protection from rain
2. doorbell out of reach
3. step at door impedes easy access
4. letterbox too low down

figure 45 **Preferred practice: semi-detached house showing alternative detailing to yield a lifetime house**

General Notes

■ indicates a clear 300mm at leading edge of door to facilitate access to door handle

- hang doors to open into the room so as to facilitate access
- doorways without saddleboards
- doors and taps to have lever type handles
- top-hung windows are preferable as handle and lock are easier to reach
- plan rooms to allow for alternative layouts of furniture
- use rocker type switches, 900–1200mm above FFL, and 300mm from internal corners
- use 20mm deep light switch housing which will allow future installation of a remote control switch
- provide 900mm width for stairs which will accommodate a second handrail without reducing the effective width below 800mm
- if space permits, a landing half way up the stairs provides a welcome rest

Bedroom accommodation

- provide possibility of accessible first floor via through floor lift – best option
- provide for the possibility of a future ground floor bedroom extension – next best
- incorporate a wide enough stairs to accommodate a possible stair lift – least acceptable as a wheelchair cannot be carried on it
- consider evacuation in an emergency

Hallway and landing

1 handrail to project 300mm beyond last step
2 1500mm turning circle
3 possible future extra handrail
4 cupboard base flush with floor, as in continental practice

Living room

1 no transoms between 1000mm and 1400mm above FFL
2 trim timber floor above, size 1200 x 800mm, to facilitate possible future installation of a through floor lift

Kitchen

1 sockets on side walls instead of at back of counter to facilitate easy reach
2 swan-neck tap allows filling of kettle and pans on the drainer. They can then be pushed along the counter to the socket or cooker
3 carousel unit facilitates better access to corners
4 access to window not to be restricted by built-in furniture

Bathrooms and toilets

1 for full notes for bathroom, shower and toilets, ■ figure 47

Dining room

1 head built into partition to enable later wall removal to improve circulation
2 track for sliding doors to finish flush with floor surface

Bedrooms

1 plan to allow alternative bed positions to facilitate left- or right-hand transfer from a wheelchair
2 trim timber floor, size 1200 x 800mm, to facilitate possible future installation of a through floor lift
3 no transoms between 1000mm and 1400mm above FFL

Outside

1 make door entry, number, name etc clearly visible from the street
2 provide porch light
3 level entry
4 doorbell and letterbox 900–1200mm from FFL
5 ramp if necessary at max gradient of 1:15
6 canopy to project 1200mm to protect from weather when waiting at door
7 for approach to houses, ■ figure 43.

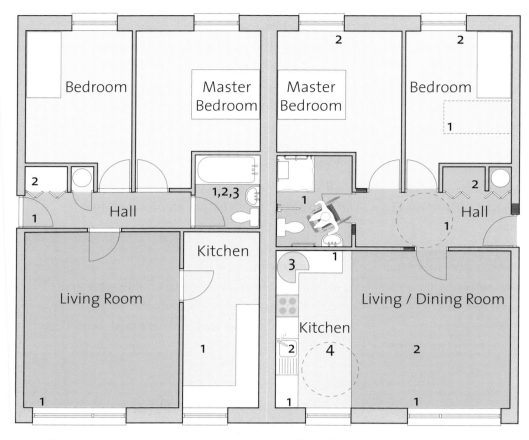

Inadequate

Preferred practice

figure 46 **Apartments**

Inadequate

Generally

- leading edge of doors too close to adjacent walls to allow access, saddleboard impedes easy access
- confined spaces restrict movement severely
- saddleboards restrict access

Hallway / circulation

1 inadequately sized lobby with no turning space
2 cupboard has raised floor which restricts access

Living / dining room

1 transom level interferes with sightlines from seated position

Kitchen

1 kitchen too small for turning circle and full accessibility

Bathroom

1 poorly planned with inadequate turning space and restricted access to facilities
2 WC has no space on either side for transfer
3 bath has no ledge for transfer

Preferred Practice

General notes

- ▰ indicates a clear 300mm at leading edge of door to facilitate access to door handle
- hang doors to open into the room so as to facilitate access
- doorways without saddleboards
- doors and taps to have lever type handles
- top-hung windows are preferable as handle and lock are easier to reach
- plan rooms to allow for alternative layouts of furniture
- use rocker type switches, 900–1200mm above FFL, and 300mm from internal corners
- use 20mm deep light switch housing which will allow future installation of a remote control switch

Hallway / circulation

1 minimum 1500mm turning circle
2 cupboard base flush with floor

Living / dining room

1 no transoms between 1000mm and 1400mm above FFL
2 open plan facilitates ease of movement

Kitchen

1 sockets on side walls instead of at back of counter to facilitate easy reach
2 swan-neck tap allows filling of kettle and pans on the drainer. They can then be pushed along the counter to the socket or the cooker
3 carousel unit facilitates better access to corners
4 minimum 1500mm turning circle

Bathrooms and toilets

1 for full notes for bathroom, shower room and toilets, ■ figure 47

Bedrooms

1 plan to allow alternative bed positions to facilitate left- or right-hand transfer from a wheelchair
2 no transoms between 1000mm and 1400mm above FFL

Domestic bathroom –
window opposite entrance

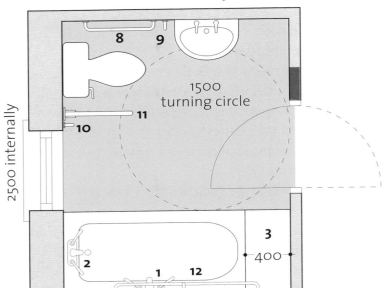

Domestic WC

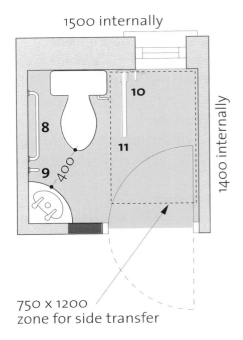

Domestic bathroom –
window at right angles to entrance

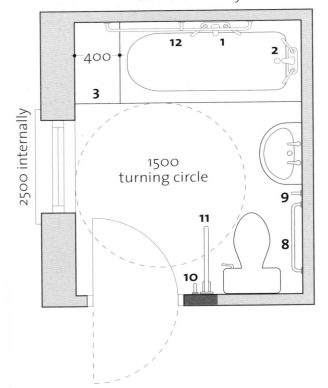

Domestic shower room

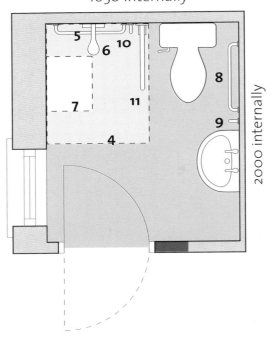

figure 47 **Suitable bathroom and shower room arrangements
for lifetime dwellings**

Bath and shower rooms

Doors

- 800mm clear opening width
- lever type handles with easy-to-use lock
- door frame to facilitate future reversal of swing – use pivot hinges and removable door stops; consider implications on space outside
- door to have fixing blocks 1000mm above FFL for a future 400mm long pull handle

WC pan

- seat to finish 450–460mm over FFL
- securely fix cistern lid
- flush handle to be position on transfer side of pan – see drawings opposite

Wash hand basin

- full size wall-mounted wash hand basin to finish 750–900mm over FFL
- use lever taps
- allow 700mm clear knee space underneath
- within reach of WC – for set out dimensions, ■ figure 30
- mirror 900–1800mm over FFL
- if basin is to be used for hair washing, provide one which extends 450mm from wall – ensure it does not hinder use of WC

Bath

- 1600mm long bath, 450mm rim height
- avoid bucket or steep end baths
- use lever taps
- bath to have built in slip resistance
1 ideal position of taps
2 acceptable position of taps
3 400mm deep ledge

Shower

4 either lay entire floor to fall, or use a proprietary flush finish shower tray surrounded by fabric shower curtain
5 lever controls for temperature and flow at 900–1200mm above tray
6 shower head adjustable within range of 1200–2200mm above tray
7 flip-up seat, 450–500mm wide, to finish 450mm above tray

Grab rails

- generally provide only fixing blocks for future installation of 35mm diameter grab rails as follows:
8 horizontal grab rail 600mm long, 700mm above FFL, and 200mm from internal corner
9 vertical grab rail, 600mm long, 200mm from tap centreline, starting 700mm above FFL
10 vertical grab rail, 600mm long, 500mm from WC centreline, starting 700mm above FFL
11 fold-up grab rail 400mm from WC centreline, 700mm from FFL
12 1200mm long horizontal grab rail in conjunction with 600mm long vertical grab rail, ■ figure 33

Floor

- slip-resistant material. Drainage gulley is desirable with floor finish falling towards gulley; site gulley where it will not cause an obstruction

Window

- provide direct access so as to open window and control ventilator fans

Kitchens should have a continuous counter and sequence of units. This will allow users to slide objects along, rather than constantly lift them from one place to another, ● section 9.7.7. Counter height should be 850mm generally, possibly with a low section at 750mm. There should be a toe recess of 250mm high x 150mm deep at all counters. Provide a minimum 1500 x 1500mm turning circle to allow the wheelchair user to manoeuvre. Install a shallow sink, convenient to the cooker, with lever-operated swan-neck mixer taps. Fit carousel units under worktops in corners for greater accessibility.

The floor of **storage closets** should be flush with the adjoining finished floor level to ensure full access for wheelchair users.

Vertical circulation

Most domestic accidents happen on stairs. Lifetime housing should ideally incorporate two short flights of stairs, in preference to one long one, each with a maximum rise of 1800m and landings which are at least 900mm long. This will not only make for a safer stairs, but will make it more manageable as the occupants grow old. Achieving this involves challenges to the conventional design of dwellings, and can require some additional floor space. The opportunities for doing so are greater in one-off housing than in the standard house type.

All stairs in housing should have a clear unobstructed width of 800mm, which will permit the incorporation of a folding stairlift without compromising usability by ambulant people. Each step should have a maximum rise of 175mm and a minimum going of 280mm. There should be a continuous handrail on each side of the flight and landings, ● section 6.7.

Lifetime housing should also provide for the fitting of a through floor lift. This is easily done by trimming the first floor joists to allow a section of floor, 800 x 1200mm, to be removed with ease at a later date, ● section 6.7.8.

Proper selection and detailing of fixtures and fittings can assist usability significantly. Locate **socket outlets** 900–1200mm above floor level and use rocker-type light switches, ● sections 7.5 and 8.5. Switch housings should be 20mm deep to permit the fitting of dimmer switches and remote control switching at a later date.

Checklist
Housing
■ figures 45-47 for typical lifetime semi-detached house, apartment, bathroom and shower room layouts.

Building approach
- Provide easy access to parking space.
- Approach should be as flat as possible with a firm surface.
- Provide handrails on any inclined approach.
- Provide adequate lighting which does not cause glare.
- Door entry, number and dwelling name (if any) should be clearly visible from street.

Entrance
- Thresholds at front and back entrances should be level.
- Protect entrances with canopies, minimum 1200mm deep, recesses and landscaping.

Internal planning generally
- Plan flexibly, to allow for different users: enough space, straightforward layouts.
- Locate dining and cooking areas close to each other, preferably open plan.
- Use slip-resistant floor finishes.
- Locate window opening lights for easy access. Top-hung casements may be particularly suitable.
- Allow for the possible inclusion of a through floor lift or a ground floor bedroom extension at a later date.

Internal circulation
- 1500mm diameter turning circle at critical positions ensures universal access.
- Doorsets to have minimum 800mm clear ope width.
- Provide 500mm, minimum 300mm, clear space at door leading edges.
- Use lever handle door ironmongery.
- Corridors to be ideally 1200mm wide.
- Doorways internally with level thresholds – avoid door saddles.
- Stairway to be two flights where possible, with 900mm long landings.

Sanitary accommodation
- Provide an accessible toilet and rinse basin downstairs.
- Bathroom to be minimum 2000 x 2500mm, ■ figure 47.

Checklist (continued)

Kitchen

- Counters should be continuous and 850mm high generally, part at 750mm; adjustable height counters are ideal.
- Provide 1500 x 1500mm turning circle.
- Units should have a toe recess 250 high x 150mm deep, with knee space in key areas.
- Carousel corner units under worktops provide the most accessible layout.
- Use contrasting colours to distinguish kitchen elements.
- Provide shallow sink, convenient to cooker, with swan-neck mixer lever tap.
- Split oven and ceramic hob is best.
- The zone 450–1300mm over finished floor level is the most accessible for everybody. Site all critical items in this zone.

Bedrooms

- 800mm clear zone around beds facilitates access.
- Plan bedrooms to allow both left- and right-hand transfer from wheelchair to bed.

Services

- Use rocker-type light switches in 20mm deep switch housings.
- Locate switches and socket outlets, TV and telephone points so they are accessible without undue stretching or stooping, 900–1200mm above floor level, and 500mm, minimum 300mm, from internal corners.

Part four

The building in use

Day-to-day management of buildings

10

10.1　Management

Good management can improve the accessibility of even a badly-designed building. By contrast, poor management will compromise the most accessible venue. For example, a badly fitting door, which catches on the floor finish, presents an obstacle to many people with disabilities. Management must ensure that accessibility is not inhibited by poor maintenance or by the actions of employees, customers or visitors.

In order to maximise accessibility for all, management must ensure that:
- circulation routes and spaces are kept free of obstruction
- facilities are kept clean and function properly
- light levels are adequate
- spaces primarily intended for people with disabilities, including refuges and wheelchair accessible toilets, are properly maintained and not used as storage spaces
- equipment such as platform lifts and induction loops are maintained in good working order
- safety and orientation features to assist people with disabilities, eg. colour contrasting door furniture, tactiling on floors and colour contrasting strips, are present and renewed when necessary
- signage is clear and legible, is consistent throughout the building and is revised after any modification to building use or layout
- staff are aware of how best to facilitate disabled users of the building
- carpets and soft furnishings are kept free of dust
- filters are replaced in mechanical ventilation systems
- smoking restrictions are enforced.

An **access handbook** is a simple way of listing and explaining the features and facilities of a building which must be maintained in order to ensure proper access for everyone. It should include a set of plans of the building, indicating all the locations where clear dimensions must be maintained for access and safety. It should also include commentary on all the access features of the building in the form of a simple specification of how they should be. Details such as the types of lightbulb for a particular fitting, colour contrasting arrangements, size and colouring of lettering for signage etc, should all be clearly set out in the book. The access handbook should be kept in the safety file and also made available to all staff.

Safety

Management must also consider **access and safety in emergency situations**. In an emergency, it cannot be assumed that the only people with disabilities are those who were identified before the emergency and that everyone else is physically fit and alert. Fatigue, medication or even alcohol can mean that some people will not respond at an optimum level. Others may have hidden disabilities such as epilepsy or being prone to panic attacks.

- Encourage people with disabilities to make themselves known, if their impairment is one which would compromise their response to a fire alarm.
- In a public building, an **emergency egress plan** should be drawn up for all people with disabilities, formed on the basis of the general need associated with a broad range of impairments. There should be a written and practised procedure on how to locate and assist people with disabilities. Appoint **fire wardens** to find people who may not be alerted by an alarm and to check out toilets, stores and other areas where there may not be any visual alarms.
- A **personal emergency egress plan** should be established for any members of staff with disabilities. This should be more specific than the general plan and can include the appointment of a specific staff member to ensure that people with disabilities are aware of the emergency and to assist them out of the building if necessary.
- Include all emergency egress plans in the general building **safety statement**.
- **Fire drills** should be practised regularly and should include people with disabilities.
- Ensure that fire alarms are **combined audio and visual two-stage systems**, and that visual alarms are free of obstruction.
- Staff must be trained in the safe transportation of people in wheelchairs in an emergency.
- Ask people with disabilities for their guidance on how best to assist them.

Checklist
Management and safety
- Management and maintenance manuals should be made available to all staff.
- There should be a systematic procedure for building maintenance.
- The emergency egress plan should include for both staff and visitors with disabilities.
- Personal emergency egress plans should be established for regular users of the building.
- All such procedures should be included in the general building safety statement.
- Safety procedures should be reviewed and revised regularly.
- Safety audits should take the needs of people with disabilities into consideration, ● section 10.4.
- Fire drills should be carried out regularly and include all people with disabilities.

10.2   Staff training and awareness

Disability equality training should be delivered to all staff, irrespective of sector or role, so that they gain a clear understanding of the issues which affect disabled users of buildings and environments. Staff need to be fully aware of all the access features of buildings and environments, and also of the manner in which people with disabilities are likely to use them. Without such awareness, proper service and maintenance is impossible.

Where particular facilities are installed, such as TDDs, platform lifts, stair lifts etc, staff must be fully trained in their use.

A short course delivered within the context of quality customer service to staff dealing with the public, either directly or by telephone, will increase their awareness of the needs of people with disabilities. Training packages for management are also available, ● section 9.4.

Training in lifting and carrying techniques is essential for staff members designated to help evacuate people in an emergency. Collapsible emergency type chairs should be used only by people who are properly trained. Most wheelchair users prefer to be carried in their own wheelchairs.

The building's access handbook should be available to all staff members, ● section 10.1.

10.3   Commissioning a premises

Every premises, whether a new development, an extension, a refurbishment or simply a fit-out, is handed over by the contractor to the client upon completion. The client body then undertakes the task of commissioning the building and making it ready for use.

Shortly before hand over, and as an integral part of the commissioning process, it is useful to examine the building so that any shortcomings can be identified and rectified. Emerging issues might include detail such as the re-direction of lighting or changes in light fittings to avoid glare, detailing to avoid hazards not visible on drawings or adjustments in positioning or sizing of fittings such as grab rails or handrails.

This examination should be separate from the normal 'snagging' of a building and should be in the form of a live audit, led by the people who will use the building, including people with disabilities. It should be comprehensive, including everything from the building approach, through the entrance areas, into all rooms, along all circulation areas, up and down the lifts and stairs, etc. It should also examine furniture, signage, fittings and the facilities of a building, including any fire safety equipment,
● section 11.2.

Such an audit, carried out by building users, rather than designers and builders, is likely to identify problems which will not have previously been considered. Such problems can be rectified prior to the actual hand over, thus minimising the potential disruption after occupancy.

10.4   Access and safety

If a building is fully accessible to disabled people, including wheelchair users, it is likely to be a safer building than one which is not. This will be true in day-to-day use of the building, as well as in an emergency. Many issues, such as ensuring the proper functioning of facilities and the vigilant maintenance of safety features of the building, have a direct bearing on the fulfilment of the Universal Right of Access.

The following list is a maintenance audit which identifies items which management must ensure are maintained. It is not an exhaustive list and will vary depending on the nature and size of the building.

Maintenance audit

Externally

Check that:

- designated parking bays are reserved for the use of disabled drivers
- ramps and circulation routes are free from parked bicycles and other obstructions
- circulation routes and escape routes from buildings to places of safety are on safe surfaces, free of obstruction and well lit
- areas being serviced or repaired are adequately protected and alternative routes are provided as necessary and clearly marked
- route surfaces are well maintained, clean, free of gravel, grit, mud, ice, snow and moss
- battery supplies to platform lifts are permanently charged
- aids to evacuation are in place.

Entrances

Check that:

- turning space at the top of ramps is kept free of obstruction
- approach to bells, letterboxes, door handles etc is free of obstruction
- doors are easy to open and closing devices are set at the minimum force needed to shut the door
- entrance lobbies are free of obstruction, both permanent and temporary, eg. delivered goods.

Horizontal circulation within the building

Check that:

- door mats are recessed and, along with rugs, are securely fixed so as not to cause tripping
- slip resistance of floor finishes is maintained, spillages cleaned up promptly and appropriate cleaning agents and polishes used
- worn floor finishes are replaced
- artificial lighting is at adequate levels
- doors are easy to open and door closers are set at the minimum force needed to shut the door
- doors are kept closed when not in use
- wheelchair spaces in waiting rooms and elsewhere are kept free of obstruction
- circulation routes are free of obstruction, both temporary and permanent, eg. toolboxes, boxes of files, vending machines, photocopiers
- refuges are kept free of obstructions
- adequate headroom is maintained throughout the building, with no trailing cables on floors or at heights below 2200mm
- approach to and egress from all lifts and stairs are kept free of obstruction

- high temperature surfaces (eg. open fires, radiators, portable heaters, hot plates, cookers etc) are protected
- both visual and audio fire alarms are operative and visual alarm indicators are unobstructed
- hazardous areas, such as plant and machine rooms, are kept locked.

Vertical circulation

Check that:

- stairs and ramps are free of obstruction, whether permanent or temporary, particularly on landings and at the tops and bottoms of ramps
- stairway finishes are maintained clean and slip-resistant and are replaced when frayed or worn
- stairway handrails are securely fixed
- visual strips on stairs nosings are clearly distinguishable from adjacent surfaces
- tactile areas at stairs and the colour contrasting strips of the first and last steps are maintained
- stairways are adequately lit, without confusing shadows adjacent to or on the stairs
- lifts are serviced and lift car floors align with finished floor levels
- lift controls are free of obstruction.

Signage

Check that:

- signage is clear and legible, and revised on foot of any alterations to building layout
- signs are replaced after redecoration
- bulbs in illuminated signs are replaced when performance is reduced, rather than when they fail
- access to tactile signs is maintained.

Sanitary facilities

Check that:

- toilet transfer areas are kept free of obstruction
- alarm facilities are maintained and any pull cords extend to within 100mm of the floor
- toilets used by people with disabilities are kept particularly clean, as these users depend on the WC surfaces for support
- sanitary disposal bins are provided, emptied regularly and positioned within reach of the toilet.

Furniture

Check that:

- loose furniture and fittings are placed so as not to obstruct circulation routes
- refuges and emergency escape routes are free of obstacles
- seats have good back and arm support
- storage units are accessible and securely fixed
- items in storage or on furniture are not at risk of being easily knocked over, and heavy items are stored at lower levels.

Communication devices

Check that:

- induction and counter loop systems are kept in good working order and their locations indicated
- communications systems (eg. queueing systems and alarms) are both audio and visual, and in full working order.

Cleaning and maintenance work

Check that:

- cleaning and maintenance work are carried out during off-peak periods or while the building is closed
- wet floors and similar hazards are cordoned off and/or indicated by warning signs
- equipment, trailing cables etc do not cause obstruction or hazard during cleaning operations
- polish applied to floor surfaces does not reduce slip resistance
- polishing of surfaces does not present glare and reduce contrast
- windows, lamps and lighting diffusers are cleaned regularly
- cleaning agents and applications are non-toxic and air fresheners are not of a type that aggravate respiratory difficulties
- mattresses and pillows are cleaned to inhibit dust mites and are replaced regularly.

Staff training

Check that:

- everyone understands their role in ensuring that the building operates efficiently, both on a day-to-day basis and in an emergency
- appropriate skills and disability equality training are included in staff induction training
- training is updated routinely
- contract workers are appraised of their safety duties and responsibilities in advance of commencing any work.

Retro-fitting and refurbishment

11

11.1 General

The principle of the Universal Right of Access applies equally to existing buildings and environments as to new ones. Traditionally, legislation in Ireland has rarely acted to impose change to existing buildings. Current legislation, however, such as the Equal Status Act, 2000, the Employment Equality Act, 1998 and the Health and Safety Act, 1993 require duties of care from building owners and employers which may indirectly imply the necessity to effect change in buildings and environments. Such changes may not be spelt out in other legislation and regulations such as the Planning and Development Act, 2000 or the Building Regulations, 2000.

The term 'existing buildings' includes everything from a 1980s office block to a protected structure of international significance. While it may be true that existing buildings don't always apparently lend themselves to the incorporation of new technology or new features, it does not mean that the challenge should be ignored.

Many of the problems associated with existing buildings, such as steep steps, narrow doors, cramped lavatories and socket outlets located on skirting boards, can be overcome with relatively minor intervention. The physical difficulties of creating wheelchair accessibility, particularly in some protected structures, should not preclude improvements for people with other impairments such as impaired vision or hearing. Every improvement, no matter how small, is still an improvement and must be worthwhile if it facilitates even one extra person.

11.2 Access auditing

Prior to the commencement of any design work on the project, an **access audit** should be carried out on the existing building or environment.

An access audit rates an existing building against given criteria for usability and accessibility. It involves not only the issue of ready movement to and around the building but also the use by people with sensory or intellectual impairments of the services which the building provides.

How an audit is carried out is as important as what it is looking for. Any professional or design audit must involve people with disabilities examining the building or environment with the designer, manager etc, in order to identify problems and suggest solutions. Consultants experienced in adaptive work may be of assistance.

Many access audits concentrate only on facilities for wheelchair users and are therefore only of partial value. More than 10% of the Irish population has a long-term impairment of some kind. This figure does not include those who are temporarily disabled (eg. by a broken leg, pregnancy, medication etc). Building access and use for all such people should be within the terms of reference of an access audit.

An all-inclusive audit involves examining staff attitudes and training and printed and personal information services as well as the building itself. Many of the items listed in the maintenance audit, ● section 10.4, should also be considered and an appropriate combination of all issues compiled.

A measured survey identifies areas of inaccessibility from which recommendations for improvement can be made. A good audit will go on to prioritise the findings, make detailed recommendations and consider timescale and cost, so as to arrive at an overall plan for improvement.

The following suggested general access audit outlines some common issues. Audits should be customised for particular types of buildings or environments. Measure the results of an audit against the advice in this book to highlight any shortcomings.

The audit should:
- examine the access features and requirements for all users, including visitors
- identify existing physical and communication barriers to access
- develop appropriate solutions so as to reconcile access needs with any requirements for building and site conservation.

The solutions form the **access plan**. Once implemented they should be recorded in the access handbook, ● section 10.1.

Access audit

Exterior: routes, parking, building approach and entrances

- parking facilities and signage
- vehicle access control measures
- route through the environs: pedestrian entrances, grounds, car parks, building entrance etc
- adequacy of main and secondary entrances
- entrance detailing: access control, thresholds, lighting, gradients, highlighting.

Interior generally

- doorways: control, dimensions, highlighting, door furniture, vision panels.

Circulation spaces

- corridors: dimensions, lighting, colours, floor finishes
- stairways: dimensions, handrails, tread and riser dimensions, finishes, tactiling at the top and bottom.

Particular rooms

- room-by-room evaluation, having regard to particular attributes detailed in this book.

Toilets

- locations on each floor, adequacy of provision
- dimensions, fittings (types, colour contrast, location and maintenance), taps, water temperature, lighting levels.

Showers

- dimensions, types, layout, controls, temperature, drainage.

Building services and finishes

- lifts: lobby size, dimensions, detailing, signs
- telephones: position, hard-of-hearing facility, provision of TDDs
- communications systems: induction loops
- fire detection and alarm systems: audio and visual alarm, alarm procedures
- security systems:
  – is their operation difficult for people with different impairments?
  – will building modifications require security system modifications?
- lighting adequacy: type of fittings to avoid glare etc, visibility of controls, accessibility of socket outlets
- colour contrasting finishes at doorways, skirtings, room entrances.

Furniture and fittings
- sign provision: quantity, location
- sign design: dimensions, colour contrast, typeface, positioning, lighting
- floor finishes: colour coding, slip resistance, ease of movement of wheelchairs and buggies
- loose furniture: avoiding obstruction; stiff, high-backed seating with arms.

Printed publicity and other material
- availability of information in alternative formats.

Staff training and awareness
- are staff who deal with the public trained in disability awareness?
- are individual staff members designated to help visitors with impairments?

Management procedures
- do emergency procedures incorporate planning for building users with impairments?

The **outcome** of the access audit should be in report form, including written text, drawings and commentary, photographs and a record of discussions. The audit should form the basis of an **access plan**, which should inform the design process for the retro-fitting or repair work under consideration. The audit should be kept in the safety file for the building, so that it can be referred to at a later date if further works are under consideration.

11.3   Refurbishment process

When contemplating improvements in access and use in refurbishment projects, the consultation and decision-making process should be similar to that for new buildings. It should start with an access audit and consultation with actual and potential users.

Audit for access and use
Examine the building's current use to see whether people have difficulty using it, by consulting present users and by inviting comment from local people with disabilities. Live auditing, ● section 10.3, and 11.2, along with a 'mystery shopping' exercise, will yield the most comprehensive results.

Assess the building in terms of current levels of access and use based on initial investigations. The access audit might use the form in ● section 11.2 as a starting point, with the addition of particular issues related to the building type.

Identify possibilities for better access and use through both building design and staff training measures by discussing these with actual and potential users.

Prioritise improvement measures on the basis of a cost-benefit analysis. Consider how the various measures might be implemented.

Consider both piecemeal and radical approaches to change before settling on a firm list of priorities. It might be that in the long term small-scale alterations would be less useful than more radical change to the way a building is organised.

Prepare detailed drawings and specifications for building work and organise any staff training programmes before proceeding to implement the changes.

The challenge of 'invisibility' referred to in chapter 1 may be greater in a refurbishment project than with a new building. The same universal access principles apply:
*   gently sloping access to a generously sized front door
*   few internal doors and lobbies
*   well-sized, well-lit corridors without changes in level
*   storeys connected by a well-sized lift
*   well-sized internal doors with vision panels and lever handle locksets – or no locking devices where practicable
*   all spaces roomy enough for everybody to use and move around in – particularly important in toilets, lobbies and other areas which are traditionally tight for space
*   switches, taps and handles which can be readily distinguished against their background and which are easily grasped or used
*   seats, desks and workstations which don't confine people unduly
*   natural materials which create a pleasing atmosphere.

An integrated approach to refurbishment
Consideration of accessibility and usability should be integrated with all other considerations from the outset. This will ensure that they are dealt with in a holistic manner, not in an 'add-on' way.

Priorities and strategies for refurbishment and upgrading
A set of priorities when implementing improvements in any existing building is essential where planning or budgetary constraints exist. For a given project, develop the priorities through consultation with building users, local people with disabilities and other interested parties.

As a general rule, the most frequently used services, along with those parts of the building most often visited by the public, should have maximum accessibility, both by way of building layout and facilities.

The fundamental **order of priority** is:
- getting into the building from the outside, and out again
- access and use of principal services
- use of sanitary facilities
- use of other facilities.

The potential of an ongoing strategy

Opportunities to make improvements occur regularly during the life of any building. Building services are renewed regularly, on a 15–25 year cycle. Lighting, light switching, access to power outlets, sanitary ware, sanitary fittings etc, are all renewed within this timescale. Renovations offer an opportunity to make good many of the shortcomings of a building. Decoration work is carried out as often as every five years or less, and offers a similar opportunity. Re-painting and installing new floor finishes can result in improved colour contrast throughout the building, and is achievable at no extra cost, save that of some forethought. The installation of a new signage or new partitions offers the chance to improve legibility, accessibility and ease of manoeuvre in the overall building.

Historic buildings and universal access

The number of people visiting national monuments and other historic buildings has grown rapidly in recent years. Conflicts can arise between the need to conserve the building and the need to improve access. In the UK, various guidelines on improving access to historic buildings and monuments have been published, and relevant references are given in Appendix 2.

Proper conservation may not preclude the incorporation of a platform lift at a small flight of steps, especially if it can be done in such a manner as not to damage or remove any of the original building fabric. Other interventions such as lighting, communication systems, signage and information boards etc may be incorporated readily and will greatly improve accessibility. Where physical solutions are impossible, a greater effort will be needed to find management solutions, which may include staff training.

Financial incentives

Local Authority funding is available for most residential conversions to suit people with disabilities. Some State aid (hotel refurbishment, for example) is predicated on improvements in access and use for people with disabilities. FÁS provides financial assistance for some adaptations to benefit disabled employees. There is, however, no financial incentive to improve buildings on a broad scale.

Appendix 1   Components

The following is a list of types and suppliers of equipment in the Republic of Ireland. It is not exhaustive and is for guidance only. Other makes and types of components are available from the UK and elsewhere.

Contents

1 ALARMS

Suppliers of alarm systems and components incorporating flashing lights and other facilities to alert people with disabilities.

Allied Security Products
8 The Mall, Donnybrook, Dublin 4
TEL: (01) 269 8899   FAX: (01) 269 7361

Carephone Direct
19 Ashgrove Avenue, Naas, Co. Kildare
TEL: (045) 875554   FAX: (045) 881189
LO-CALL: 1890 456 999

Connaught Electronics Ltd
IDA Industrial Estate, Dunmore Road, Tuam, Co. Galway
TEL: (093) 25128   FAX: (093) 25133

Eircom Phonewatch Medi-System
Unit 4, Sandyford Industrial Estate, Dublin 18
TEL: 1850 442 700
EMAIL: sales@phonewatch.ie

Emergency Response
Newtownbarry House, Bunclody, Co. Wexford
TEL: 1850 232 324

Gardiner Security (IE) Ltd.
Unit 5 Ballymount Business Park, Ballymount Road, Walkinstown, Dublin 12
TEL: (01) 450 1366

Legrand
Holly Avenue, Stillorgan Industrial Park, Stillorgan, Co. Dublin
TEL: (01) 295 4465   FAX: (01) 295 4671

M & J Electronics Security
6C Station Road Business Park, Clondalkin, Dublin 22
TEL: (01) 457 4444

Napier Alarms
Unit E7 Centrepoint Business Park, Oak Road, Dublin 12
TEL: (01) 456 4388   FAX: (01) 456 4334

Sun Security
Cornamagh, Athlone, Co. Westmeath
TEL: (0902) 72855   FAX: (0902) 76948

Task Community Care
Guardian House, Portrane, Co. Dublin
TEL: (01) 843 5889   FAX: (01) 843 5897

2 BATHS: ADJUSTABLE HEIGHT

J.B. Agencies
'Bromley', Putland Road, Bray , Co. Wicklow
TEL/FAX: (01) 286 2726

Liberty Lifts
11 Ballymount Court, Ballymount Road, Walkinstown, Dublin 12
TEL: (01) 450 7971   FAX: (01) 450 7978

M.I.M Ltd
2 St. Agnes Road, Crumlin, Dublin 12
TEL: (01) 455 1163   FAX: (01) 450 5497

3 BATH LIFTS: POWERED

Accel Mobility Ltd
5 Crannagh Grove, Rathfarnham, Dublin 14
TEL: (01) 490 4347   FAX: (01) 490 4320
EMAIL: info@accel.ie

Bishopsgate Homecare Ltd
Windermere House, Boley Hill, Ballycanew, Gorey, Co. Wexford
TEL/FAX: (055) 27948
EMAIL: bishopsgate@unison.ie

J.S. Dobbs & Co
Unit 84, Baldoyle Industrial Estate, Dublin 13
TEL: (01)839 1071   FAX: (01) 839 1049

Fannin Healthcare
14-16 Redmonds Hill, Dublin 2
TEL: (01) 478 2211   FAX: (01) 478 2895

Fannin Healthcare
15/16 Washington Street, Cork
TEL: (021) 427 4011   FAX: (021) 4277266

Health & Mobility Ltd
Unit 5, Old Sawmills Industrial Estate, Lower Ballymount Road, Walkinstown, Dublin 12
TEL: (01) 409 7706   FAX: (01) 409 7708
EMAIL: consolid@iol.ie

Irish Stairways Ltd
Unit 17, Thompson Enterprise Centre, Clane Industrial Estate, Clane, Co. Kildare
TEL: (045) 892 696   FAX: (045) 892 711

Lenken Healthcare Ltd
B6, Calmount Park, Ballymount, Dublin 12, Dublin 12
TEL: (01) 456 5565   FAX: (01) 456 5575

Liberty Lifts
11 Ballymount Court, Ballymount Road, Walkinstown, Dublin 12
TEL: (01) 450 7971   FAX: (01) 450 7978

Lifestyle Mobility
54 Rossvale, Portlaoise, Co. Laois
TEL: (0502) 44793   FAX: (0502) 44794
EMAIL: ianfarnan@eircom.net

Murray's Medical Equipment
20/21 Talbot Street, Dublin 1
TEL: (01) 855 5735   FAX: (01) 855 5880

Ortho-Kinetics
Unit 3, Ballymount Business Park, Walkinstown, Dublin 12
TEL: (01) 456 0088   FAX: (01) 450 3588

Premier Home Care
Unit 39, Southern Cross Business Park, Bray, Co. Wicklow
TEL: (01) 204 1924   FAX: (01) 204 1923
EMAIL: bac@indigo.ie

Smith & Nephew Ltd
Carrick Court, Georges Ave, Blackrock, Co. Dublin
TEL: (01) 285 2222   FAX: (01) 285 2516

4   GRAB RAILS

Architectural Hardware
Unit 6C, Citylink Business Park, Old Naas Road, Dublin 12
TEL: (01) 453 6044

J.B. Agencies
'Bromley', Putland Road, Bray , Co. Wicklow
TEL/FAX: (01) 286 2726

J.S Dobbs
Unit 84 Baldoyle Industrial Estate, Dublin 13
TEL: (01) 839 1071   FAX: (01) 839 1049

Evans Medical Ltd
12 Berkley Road, Dublin 7
TEL: (01) 830 7366   FAX: (01) 830 7862

Excel Industries
Coolmine Industrial Estate, Clonsilla Road, Dublin 15
TEL: (01) 820 7900   FAX: (01) 820 4797

Fannin Healthcare
14-16 Redmonds Hill, Dublin 2
TEL: (01) 478 2211   FAX: (01) 478 2895

Fannin Healthcare
15/16 Washington Street, Cork
TEL: (021) 427 4011   FAX: (021) 4277266

Irish Stairways Ltd
Unit 17, Thompson Enterprise Centre, Clane Industrial Estate, Clane, Co. Kildare
TEL: (045) 892 696   FAX: (045) 892 711

James Healy Founders Ltd
51A-54 Pearse Street, Dublin 2
TEL: (01) 677 2238   FAX: (01) 679 6808

KCC
Unit S4 Ballymount Industrial Estate, Ballymount Road, Dublin 12
TEL: (01) 455 2421   FAX: (01) 456 7409

Modern Plant Ltd
Otter House, Naas Road, Clondalkin, Dublin 22
TEL: (01) 459 1344   FAX: (01) 459 2329

MMS Medical
Forge Hill Cross, Kinsale Road, Cork
TEL: (021) 431 4111   FAX: (021) 496 2792
LO-CALL: 1850 774477

Murray's Medical Equipment
20/21 Talbot Street, Dublin 1
TEL: (01) 855 5735   FAX: (01) 855 5880

MSL Ltd
Unit 23A Moyle Road, Dublin Industrial Estate, Dublin 9
TEL: (01) 830 8266   FAX: (01) 830 8129

Necoflex Ltd
Unit 5, Kilcoole Industrial Estate, Kilcoole, Co. Wicklow
TEL: (01) 287 6111   FAX: (01) 287 6614

Nursing Needs Ltd
13 Gladstone Street, Waterford
TEL/FAX: (051) 874 622

Shires (Ire) Ltd
Broomhill Road, Tallaght, Dublin 24
TEL: (01) 451 5877   FAX: (01) 451 5534

John Usher Ltd
Unit 4A Goldenbridge Industrial Estate, Inchicore, Dublin 8
TEL: (01) 416 6350   FAX: (01) 416 6315

5   KITCHEN FITTINGS

Ashgrove Panelling Centre
Unit 3/4, Ashgrove Industrial Estate, Kill Avenue,
Dun Laoghaire, Co. Dublin
TEL: (01) 284 5088   FAX: (01) 284 3735

Hafele Ireland Ltd
Kilcoole Industrial Estate, Kilcoole, Co. Wicklow
TEL: (01) 287 3488   FAX: (01) 287 3563

McMally Kitchens Ltd
Ballyhea, Loughshinny, Skerries, Co. Dublin
TEL: (01) 849 1670   FAX: (01) 849 2783

George Tully & Sons
1-7 Haymarket, Smithfield, Dublin 7
TEL: (01) 872 5144   FAX: (01) 872 1187
EMAIL: sales@tullystiles.com

6   LEVER TAPS

Excel Industries
Coolmine Industrial Estate, Clonsilla Road, Dublin 15
TEL: (01) 820 7900   FAX: (01) 820 4797

Murray's Medical Equipment
20/21 Talbot Street, Dublin 1
TEL: (01) 855 5735   FAX: (01) 855 5880

George Tully & Sons
1-7 Haymarket, Smithfield, Dublin 7
TEL: (01) 872 5144   FAX: (01) 872 1187
EMAIL: sales@tullystiles.com

7   LOCKS

J. Williams
(for universal key system: Abloy 2590DP)
12 Bow Lane East, Mercer Street, Dublin 2
TEL: (01) 475 6307   FAX: (01) 478 4890

8   LIFTS: SHORT RISE

Suppliers of lifts which enable a wheelchair user to
move between levels, either indoors or outdoors,
where the installation of a ramp is not practicable.

BBS Elevator Co. Ltd
2 Shanliss Way, Santry, Dublin 9
TEL: (01) 842 3925   FAX: (01) 842 4394

Liberty Lifts
11 Ballymount Court, Lwr Ballymount Road,
Walkinstown, Dublin 12
TEL: (01) 450 7971   FAX: (01) 450 7978

MMS Medical
Forge Hill Cross, Kinsale Road, Cork
TEL: (021) 431 4111   FAX: (021) 496 2792
LO-CALL: 1850 774477

9   LIFTS: STAIRLIFTS

Accel Mobility Ltd
5 Crannagh Grove, Rathfarnham, Dublin 14
TEL: (01) 490 4347   FAX: (01) 490 4320
EMAIL: info@accel.ie

Barron Lifts Ireland Ltd
1st Floor, 48 South Street, New Ross, Co. Wexford
TEL: (051) 420575   FAX: (051) 420 520

Dolphin Stairlifts
67 Lower Dorset Street, Dublin 1
TEL/FAX: (01) 830 8310

Fannin Healthcare
14-16 Redmonds Hill, Dublin 2
TEL: (01) 478 2211   FAX: (01) 478 2895

Fannin Healthcare
15/16 Washington Street, Cork
TEL: (021) 427 4011   FAX: (021) 427 7266

Homecare Medical Supplies Ltd
Knock Road, Kiltimagh, Co. Mayo
TEL: (094) 81361   FAX: (094) 81370

Irish Stairways Ltd
Unit 17, Thompson Enterprise Centre,
Clane Industrial Estate, Clane, Co. Kildare
TEL: (045) 892696   FAX: (045) 892711

Liberty Lifts
11 Ballymount Court, Lwr Ballymount Road,
Walkinstown, Dublin 12
TEL: (01) 450 7971   FAX: (01) 450 7978

J.B. Agencies
'Bromley', Putland Road, Bray, Co. Wicklow
TEL/FAX: (01) 286 2726

MMS Medical
Forge Hill Cross, Kinsale Road, Cork
TEL: (021) 431 4111   FAX: (021) 496 2792
LO-CALL: 1850 774477

Premier Home Care
Unit 39, Southern Cross Business Park, Bray,
Co. Wicklow
TEL: (01) 204 1924   FAX: (01) 204 1923
EMAIL: bac@indigo.ie

10   LIFTS: THROUGH-FLOOR

For domestic use only.

Accel Mobility Limited
5 Crannagh Grove, Rathfarnham, Dublin 14
TEL: (01) 490 4347   FAX: (01) 490 4320
EMAIL: info@accel.ie

Barron Lifts Ireland Ltd
1st Floor, 48 South Street, New Ross, Co. Wexford
TEL: (051) 420575   FAX: (051) 420 520

Irish Stairways Ltd
Unit 17, Thompson Enterprise Centre,
Clane Industrial Estate, Clane, Co. Kildare
TEL: (045) 892696   FAX: (045) 892711

Liberty Lifts
11 Ballymount Court, Lwr Ballymount Road,
Walkinstown, Dublin 12
TEL: (01) 450 7971   FAX: (01) 450 7978

MMS Medical
Forge Hill Cross, Kinsale Road, Cork
TEL: (021) 431 4111   FAX: (021) 496 2792
LO-CALL: 1850 774477

Premier Home Care
Unit 39, Southern Cross Business Park, Bray, Co.
Wicklow
TEL: (01) 204 1924   FAX: (01) 204 1923
EMAIL: bac@indigo.ie

George Tully & Sons
1-7 Haymarket, Smithfield, Dublin 7
TEL: (01) 872 5144   FAX: (01) 872 1187
EMAIL: sales@tullystiles.com

11   PLAY EQUIPMENT

The Children's Playground Co Ltd
2 The Oaks, Clane, Co Kildare
TEL: (045) 893108

Seesaw Design Ltd
Unit 1a, Southern Cross Business Park, Bray, Co Wicklow
TEL: (01) 286 4995   FAX: (01) 286 4997

12   PLAY SURFACES

M & G Ltd
36 Cookstown Industrial Estate, Tallaght, Dublin 24
TEL: (01) 451 1144   FAX: (01) 451 1376

13   PORTABLE ACCESSIBLE PUBLIC TOILETS

Extraloo
Clondalkin Industrial Estate, Clondalkin, Dublin 22
TEL: (01) 450 1334   FAX: (01) 450 325

Hire-a-loo
Parkmore, Ballybrit, Galway
TEL: (091) 771177   FAX: (091) 796007

Tufloo
Unit 9, Goldenbridge Industrial Estate, Inchicore,
Dublin 8
TEL: 1800 762 762   FAX: (01) 473 1242

14   SHOWER STRETCHERS

Irish Stairways Ltd
Unit 17, Thompson Enterprise Centre,
Clane Industrial Estate, Clane, Co. Kildare
TEL: (045) 892696   FAX: (045) 892711

J.B. Agencies
'Bromley', Putland Road, Bray, Co. Wicklow
TEL/FAX: (01) 286 2726

Liberty Lifts
11 Ballymount Court, Lwr Ballymount Road,
Walkinstown, Dublin 12
TEL: (01) 450 7971   FAX: (01) 450 7978

Modern Plant Ltd
Otter House, Naas Road, Clondalkin, Dublin 22
TEL: (01) 459 1344   FAX: (01) 459 2329

MMS Medical
Forge Hill Cross, Kinsale Road, Cork
TEL: (021) 431 4111   FAX: (021) 496 2792
LO-CALL: 1850 774477

Shires (Ire) Ltd
Broomhill Road, Tallaght, Dublin 24
TEL: (01) 451 5877   FAX: (01) 451 5534

George Tully & Sons
1-7 Haymarket, Smithfield, Dublin 7
TEL: (01) 872 5144   FAX: (01) 872 1187
EMAIL: sales@tullystiles.com

15 SHOWERS

All in a Days Work
1 Templemanor Avenue, Greenhills, Dublin 12
TEL: (01) 450 1571   FAX: (01) 409 7862

Classic Bathrooms
Longmile Centre, Longmile Road, Walkinstown, Dublin 12
TEL: (01) 450 5411   FAX: (01) 456 8252

Excel Industries
Coolmine Industrial Estate, Clonsilla Road, Dublin 15
TEL: (01) 820 7900   FAX: (01) 820 4797

Irish Stairways Ltd
Unit 17, Thompson Enterprise Centre,
Clane Industrial Estate, Clane, Co. Kildare
TEL: (045) 892696   FAX: (045) 892711

J.B. Agencies
'Bromley', Putland Road, Bray , Co. Wicklow
TEL/FAX: (01) 286 2726

JCL International Sales Ltd
Coolmine Industrial Estate, Clonsilla, Dublin 15
TEL: (01) 820 8493   FAX: (01) 820 2349

Liberty Lifts
11 Ballymount Court, Lwr Ballymount Road,
Walkinstown, Dublin 12
TEL: (01) 450 7971   FAX: (01) 450 7978

MMS Medical
Forge Hill Cross, Kinsale Road, Cork
TEL: (021) 431 4111   FAX: (021) 496 2792
LO-CALL: 1850 774477

Modern Plant Ltd
Otter House, Naas Road, Clondalkin, Dublin 22
TEL: (01) 459 1344   FAX: (01) 459 2329

Necoflex Ltd
Unit 5, Kilcoole Industrial Estate, Kilcoole, Co. Wicklow
TEL: (01) 287 6111   FAX: (01) 287 6614

Original Bathrooms and Tiles
OB Heating, South City Link Road, Cork
TEL: (021) 431 0000   FAX: (021) 431 0003

Simply Bathrooms
Cromwellsfort Road, Dublin 12
TEL: (01) 450 8728

George Tully & Sons
1-7 Haymarket, Smithfield, Dublin 7
TEL: (01) 872 5144   FAX: (01) 872 1187
EMAIL: sales@tullystiles.com

16 SHOWER ACCESSORIES

Suppliers of grab rails, shower doors and screens,
shower seats etc.

Arthritis Foundation of Ireland
1 Clanwilliam Square, Grand Canal Quay, Dublin 2
TEL: (01) 661 8188   FAX: (01) 661 8261

Beechfield Healthcare
Unit 13, Deansgrange Industrial Estate, Deansgrange,
Co. Dublin
TEL: (01) 289 9742   FAX: (01) 289 9746

Classic Bathrooms
Longmile Centre, Longmile Road, Walkinstown, Dublin 12
TEL: (01) 450 5411   FAX: (01) 456 8252

Fannin Healthcare
14-16 Redmonds Hill, Dublin 2
TEL: (01) 478 2211   FAX: (01) 478 2895

Fannin Healthcare
15/16 Washington Street, Cork
TEL: (021) 427 4011   FAX: (021) 4277266

Galway Homecare
Terryland Retail Park, Headford Road, Galway
TEL: (091) 567812   LO-CALL: 1890 390590

Homecare Medical Supplies Ltd
Knock Road, Kiltimagh, Co. Mayo
TEL: (094) 81361   FAX: (094) 81370

Irish Stairways Ltd
Unit 17, Thompson Enterprise Centre, Clane Industrial
Estate, Clane, Co. Kildare
TEL: (045) 892 696   FAX: (045) 892 711

Irish Wheelchair Association
Blackheath Drive, Clontarf, Dublin 3
TEL: (01) 833 8241   FAX: (01) 833 3873

J.B. Agencies
'Bromley', Putland Road, Bray, Co. Wicklow
TEL/FAX: (01) 286 2726

J.S Dobbs
Unit 84 Baldoyle Industrial Estate, Dublin 13
TEL: (01) 839 1071   FAX: (01) 839 1049

Lifestyle Mobility
54 Rossvale , Portlaoise, Co. Laois
TEL: (0502) 44793   FAX: (0502) 44794

Limerick Homecare
4 Parnell Street, Limerick
TEL: 061 416671   FAX: 061 416671

MMS Medical
Forge Hill Cross, Kinsale Road, Cork
TEL: (021) 431 4111   FAX: (021) 496 2792
LO-CALL: 1850 774477

Modern Plant Ltd
Otter House, Naas Road, Clondalkin, Dublin 22
TEL: (01) 459 1344   FAX: (01) 459 2329

Murray's Medical Equipment
20/21 Talbot Street, Dublin 1
TEL: (01) 855 5735   FAX: (01) 855 5880

Murray Surgical Ltd
Unit 23A, Moyle Road, Dublin Industrial Estate,
Glasnevin, Dublin 11
TEL: (01) 830 8266   FAX: (01) 830 8129

Necoflex Ltd
Unit 5, Kilcoole Industrial Estate, Kilcoole, Co. Wicklow
TEL: (01) 287 6111   FAX: (01) 287 6614

Nursing Needs Ltd
13 Gladstone Street, Waterford
TEL/FAX: (051) 874 622

O'Beirns Pharmacy
11 Henry Street, Galway
TEL: (091) 582 479

Original Bathrooms and Tiles
OB Heating, South City Link Road, Cork
TEL: (021) 431 0000   FAX: (021) 431 0003

Shires (Ire) Ltd
Broomhill Road, Tallaght, Dublin 24
TEL: (01) 451 5877   FAX: (01) 451 5534

Simply Bathrooms
Cromwellsfort Road, Dublin 12
TEL: (01) 450 8728

George Tully & Sons
1-7 Haymarket, Smithfield, Dublin 7
TEL: (01) 872 5144   FAX: (01) 872 1187
EMAIL: sales@tullystiles.com

17   TABLES: ADJUSTABLE

SKM Products
Furze Road, Sandyford Industrial Estate, Foxrock,
Dublin 18
TEL: (01) 295 2676   FAX: (01) 295 5854

18   TACTILE PAVING

Roadstone
Fortunestown, Dublin 24
TEL: (01) 404 1200

Tobermore Concrete Products Ltd
Blakes Cross, Lusk, County Dublin
tel: 01 843 7443   fax: 01 843 7750

19   TACTILE SIGNS

Éolas
Unit 2A Merrywell Business Park, Drumree Park,
Co. Meath
TEL: (01) 825 8128   FAX: (01) 825 8129

Management Graphics
Wayfinder House, Baldoyle Industrial Estate, Dublin 13
TEL: (01) 832 6966   FAX: (01) 832 6970

Nameplate and Sign Services
Jamestown Road, Inchicore, Dublin 8
TEL: (01) 453 2659   FAX: (01) 453 1154

20   TEMPORARY OUTDOOR SURFACES

Erin Design
Llewellyn House, New Brighton Terrace, Bray, Co
Wicklow
TEL: (01) 286 4995

PVC
Burden House, Cloverhill Industrial Estate, Clondalkin,
Dublin 22
TEL: (01) 457 3900   FAX: (01) 457 3863

Appendix II   Further reading

Many of the items listed in this appendix are available at:
The NDA Library
25 Clyde Road, Dublin 4
TEL: (01) 608 0433
FAX: (01) 660 9935
EMAIL: library@nda.ie

ACTS, STATUTORY INSTRUMENTS AND OFFICIAL PUBLICATIONS

Ireland

Building Control Act, 1990

Building Control Regulations, 1997, S.I. 496 of 1997

Building Regulations (Amendment) Regulations, 2000, S.I.179 of 2000

Code of Practice for the Management of Fire Safety in Places of Assembly, 1989

Employment Equality Act, 1998

Equal Status Act, 2000

Fire Services Act, 1981

National Development Plan, 1999

Safety, Health and Welfare at Work Act, 1989

Safety, Health and Welfare at Work (Signs) Regulations, 1995, S.I.132 of 1995

Technical Guidance Documents to the Building Regulations, 2000, especially those to Part K, Stairways, ramps and guards, and Part M, Access and facilities for disabled persons.

European Union

COM(2000) 284 final, May 2000: Communication from the Commission to the Council, the European Parliament, the Economic and Social Committee and the Commission of the Regions: Towards a barrier-free Europe for people with disabilities

Council decision (2000/750/EC), November 2000: Council decision establishing a Community action programme to combat discrimination (2001-2006).

STANDARDS AND CODES OF PRACTICE

BS 4467: 1991: Anthropometric and ergonomic recommendations for dimensions in designing for the elderly

BS 5378: Part 1: 1980: Safety signs and colours: Part 1: Specification for colour and design

BS 5499: 1990: Fire safety signs, notices and graphic symbols

BS 5588: Part 8: 1999: Fire precautions in the design and construction of buildings: means of escape for disabled people

BS 5655: 1986: Lifts and service lifts

BS 5776: 1996: Specification for powered stair lifts

BS 5810: 1979: Code of practice for access for the disabled to buildings

BS 5839: Part 1: 1988: Code of practice for system design, installation and servicing

BS 5887: 1980: Specification for mobile, manually operated patient lifting devices

BS 5900: 1991: Specification for powered domestic home lifts

BS 6034: 1990: Specification for public information symbols

BS 6083: Part 4: 1981: Specification for magnetic field strength in audio-frequency induction loops for hearing aid purposes

BS 6130: 1993: Code of practice for powered lifting platforms for use by people with disabilities

BS 6206: 1981: Specification for impact performance requirements for flat safety glass and safety plastics for use in buildings

BS 6259: 1982: Code of practice for planning and installation of sound systems

BS 6262: 1982: Code of practice for glazing for buildings

BS 6418: 1989: Specification for cordless audio transmission devices using infra-red radiation

BS 6440: 1983: Code of practice for powered lifting platforms for use by disabled persons

BS 7036: Code of practice for safety at powered doors for pedestrian use

BS 7443: 1991: Specification for sound systems for emergency purposes

BS 7594: 1993: Code of practice for audible frequency induction loop systems

BS 8300: 2001: Design of buildings to meet the needs of disabled people

PERIODICALS

Access by Design – *Quarterly*
Centre for Accessible Environments, Nutmeg House, 60 Gainsford Street,
London SEI 2NY, England. Fax: 0044 207 357 8183, email: info@cae.org.uk

Crisp and Clear – European Magazine on Design for All – *Irregular*
Danish Centre for Accessibility, Graham Bells Vej 1A, DK-8200 Aarhus N,
Denmark. Fax 00 45 86 78 37 30

Design Insight – Journal of the JMU Access Partnership – *Quarterly*
JMU, 105 Judd Street, London WC1 9NE, England.
Fax: 00 44 207 387 7109, email: publications@jmuaccess.org.uk

European Institute for Design and Disability Journal – *Quarterly*
Institut TLP, Post Box 1186, 56831 Traben-Trarbach, Germany.
Fax: 00 49 6541 9237

OTHER PUBLICATIONS

A Guide to Easy Access: a national gazeteer,
Forestry Commission, Edinburgh, 1998

Access to ATMs: UK design guidelines,
Centre for Accessible Environments, London, 1999

Access to the Historic Environment: meeting the needs of disabled people,
Lisa Foster, UK, 1997, ISBN 1 873394 18 7

Access to Museums and Galleries for People with Disabilities,
Museums and Galleries Commission, London, 1997

Accessibility and Usability for e-Government: a primer for public sector officials,
Frontend, Dublin, 2000

Accessible thresholds in new housing: guidance for house builders and designers,
Department of the Environment, Transport and the Regions, London, 1999,
ISBN 0 11 702333 7

Advisory Notes on Access to Premises,
Human Rights and Equal Opportunity Commission, Sydney, 1997

Arts and Disability Handbook,
Arts Council, Arts Council of Northern Ireland, Dublin, 1999

Barrier-Free Design: a manual for building designers and managers,
James Holmes-Siedle, Butterworth Architecture, London, 1996,
ISBN 0 7506 1636 9

Building Code of Australia Access Provisions Review,
Australian Building Codes Board, Australia, 1996

Buildings for All to Use,
Sylvester Bone, CIRIA, London, 1996, ISBN 0 86017 448 4

Building Sight: a handbook of building and interior design solutions to include the needs of visually impaired people,
Peter Barker, Jon Barrick, Rod Wilson, HMSO in association with RNIB, 1997, ISBN 185878 074 8

Breaking the Silence: a study of services provided by restaurants and hotels in Northern Ireland to people who are deaf of hard of hearing,
RNID, Belfast, 1998

BT Countryside for All: a good practice guide to disabled people's access in the countryside,
Fieldfare Trust, Sheffield, 1997

A Cost-Benefit Analysis of Lifetime Homes,
Christopher Cobbold, Joseph Rowntree Foundation, York, 1997, ISBN 1 899987 40 1

Costing Lifetime Homes,
Kim Sangster, Joseph Rowntree Foundation, York, 1997, ISBN 1 85935 024 0

Creating and Managing Woodlands Around Towns, Forestry Commission Handbook 11,
Simon J. Hodge, UK, 1995, ISBN 011 710328 4

Designing Housing for Successive Generations,
Access Committee for England, 1996

Designing for the Disabled: a new paradigm,
Selwyn Goldsmith, London, 1997, ISBN 0 7506 3442 1

Designing Lifetime Homes,
Ed. Julie Brewerton and David Darton, Joseph Rowntree Foundation, York, 1997, ISBN 1 85035 025 9

Designing for Spectators with Disabilities,
Football Stadia Advisory Design Council, London, 1992, ISBN 1873831 30 7

Disability Resource Directory for Museums,
Museums and Galleries Commission, London, 1994

Disability and the City: International Perspectives,
Rob Imrie, UK, 1996, ISBN 1 85396 273 2

Dust in the Home,
Asthma Society of Ireland, Dublin, 1994 with 1995 supplement

Easy Access to Historic Properties,
English Heritage, London, 1999

Elimination of Architectural Barriers: Accessibility in Public Buildings,
Ivor Ambrose, Danish Building Research Institute, Denmark, 1996

Escape of Disabled People from Fire: a measurement and classification
capability for assessing fire risk, BR301,
TJShields, KE Dunlop, GWH Silcock, BRE, London, 1996, ISBN 1 86081 0675

Evaluation of Environmental Designations in Ireland,
David Hickie, Heritage Council, 1997, ISBN 1 901137 01 5

Fire and Disabled People in Buildings: Building Research Establishment
Report, BR 231,
TJ Shields, BRE, Watford, 1993, ISBN 0 85125 5469

Fit for the Job: Health, Safety and Disability at Work,
Peter McGeer, Howard Fidderman, Eclipse Group, London, 2000

Forestry and the Natural Heritage,
Heritage Council, 1999, ISBN 1 901137 08 2

Geographies of Disability,
Brendan Gleeson, Routledge, 1999, ISBN 0 415 17909 2

Heritage Awareness in Ireland,
Heritage Council, 2000, ISBN 1 901137 22 8

Housing for Varying Needs: a design guide - Part M: houses and flats,
Judith Pickles; David Taylor, HMSO, London, 1999

Inclusive Design: designing and developing accessible environments
Rob Imrie and Peter Hall, London, 2001, ISBN 0 419 25620 2

It's My Church Too: the inclusion of people with disability in the life of
the church,
Dublin Diocesan Jubilee Committee, Dublin, 2000

Landscape Design for Elderly and Disabled People,
Jane Stoneham and Peter Thoday, UK, 1996, ISBN 1 870673 20 4

Making Workplaces Accessible: a guide to integration,
*Office for Official Publications of the European Communities, Luxembourg
1999*

Meeting Part M and Designing Lifetime Homes,
*Catriona Carroll, Julie Cowans, David Darton, Joseph Rowntree
Foundation, York, 1999*

New European Standards on Man-Machine Interface for Card Systems,
RNIB, London, 1999

Personal Emergency Egress Plans,
Northern Officer Group, UK, 1993

Safety at Street Works and Roads Works,
HMSO, London, 1997

Submission to the Department of the Environment and Local
Government on its consultation document,
*Revision of Part M: Building Regulations Proposals for making new dwellings
visitable by people with disabilities,*
NRB, unpublished paper, Dublin, 1999

Sign Design Guide – a guide to inclusive signage,
Peter Barker and June Fraser, JMU and the Sign Design Society, London, 2001,
ISBN 185878 412 3

Tiresias – a family of typefaces designed for legibility on screens, signs
and labels,
RNIB Scientific Research Unit, London, 2000

Train and Station Services for Disabled Passengers,
Office of the Rail Regulator, London, 2000

Universal Design,
Selwyn Goldsmith, UK, 2000, ISBN 0 7506 4785 X

Which Button?: designing user interfaces for people with visual impairments,
John Gill, RNIB, UK, 2000, ISBN 1 86048 0231

Widening the Eye of the Needle: access to church buildings for people
with disabilities,
John Penton, London, 2001, ISBN 0 7151 7587 4

The following are all published by:
Centre for Accessible Environments, Nutmeg House, 60 Gainsford Street,
London SEI 2NY, England. Fax 00 44 207 357 8183, email: info@cae.org.uk

Access Audits: a guide and checklists for appraising the accessibility of
buildings for disabled users,
Denis Fearns, 1999, ISBN 0 903976 25 0

Designing for Accessibility: an introductory guide,
Tessa Palfreyman, 1994, ISBN 0 903976 23 4

Good Loo Design Guide: advice on WC provision for disabled people in
public buildings,
Stephen Thorpe, 1998, ISBN 0 903976 20 X

House Adaptations,
Stephen Thorpe, 1995

Reading and Using Plans,
Stephen Thorpe, 1994

Specifiers' Handbooks:
1.   Electrical Controls
2.   Wheelchair Stair Lifts and Platform Lifts
3.   Automatic Door Controls
4.   Internal Floor Finishes: improving access for all.

Index

W